John McCarthy

THE NEW MILLENNIUM GUIDE TO MANAGING YOUR MONEY

JOHN T. McCARTHY, CFP

MAGGIE PUBLISHING CO.

WAUWATOSA, WI

NOTE: This publication is designed to provide accurate and authoritative information in regard to the subject matter covered. It is published with the understanding that the publisher and author are not engaged in rendering legal, accounting, or other professional service. If legal advice or other professional advice, including financial, is required, the services of a competent professional person should be sought.

The case histories included in this book derive from the author's personal files. Names and details have been changed.

THE NEW MILLENNIUM GUIDE
TO MANAGING YOUR MONEY

© 1998 by John T. McCarthy

All rights reserved. No part of this book may be reproduced or used in any form or by any means—graphic, electronic, or mechanical, including photocopying, recording, taping, or information storage and retrieval—without the written permission of the publisher.

Address inquiries to:
John McCarthy
c/o Maggie Publishing
8207 Brookside Place
Wauwatosa, WI   53213

Phone: 414-475-1369
E-mail: mcfinmgt@execpc.com

Edited by Chris Roerden
Graphics by Susan Goulet

ISBN 0-9660577-0-8

Printed in the United States of America
First edition May 1998
10 9 8 7 6 5 4 3 2 1

DEDICATION

To My Father
Jack McCarthy
March 16, 1925 - June 21, 1996

May I grow and learn to be half the man he was.

CONTENTS

CHAPTER

1. FINANCIAL PLANNING: THE GOAL 1
2. SECRETS TO BECOMING A MILLIONAIRE 28
3. COMMON SENSE INVESTMENT PRINCIPLES 56
4. PATHWAY TO FINANCIAL SUCCESS 79
5. REDUCING YOUR TAX BITE:
   TAX PLANNING STRATEGIES 102
6. MANAGING YOUR NEST EGG: PORTFOLIO
   MANAGEMENT & ASSET ALLOCATION 134
7. THE IMPORTANCE OF PLANNING YOUR ESTATE 151
8. MUTUAL FUNDS: TOOLS FOR
   YOUR FINANCIAL PLANNING 174
9. INVESTING IN STOCKS FOR GROWTH 198
10. PRERETIREMENT PLANNING: THE CLIMB
    TO FINANCIAL INDEPENDENCE 213
11. INVESTING IN BONDS FOR INCOME 240
12. POSTRETIREMENT PLANNING:
    SECURING THE GOLDEN YEARS 257

EPILOGUE 274
RECOMMENDED READING 276
INDEX 277

ACKNOWLEDGMENTS

Retired journalist Dorothy Austin told me that the most important aspect of writing a book is to have something worthwhile to say. In this respect, I am most grateful to my clients for the privilege of listening to and learning from them these past 15 years while I developed the perspective and insight to address a wide range of personal finance concerns.

I am a financial planning practitioner, not a journalist, technician, or professor. I believe this gives me a distinct advantage in delivering my message. However, I did need considerable help in putting my thoughts into comprehensible text. I am fortunate that those who have helped me are also friends.

Special credit goes to Jan Lennon. Without her cheerleading, enthusiasm, direction, and extensive editing, it is probable that this book might never have been completed.

Her energy and generosity as a dedicated community volunteer and activist serve as the inspiration for the charitable and planned giving themes found in these pages.

A debt of gratitude is due my able administrative assistant, Avis Haasch. She good-naturedly spent countless hours inputting, typing, revising, and reviewing numerous drafts of the manuscript. Her positive attitude and encouragement are invaluable to me, and she has become a cherished friend of mine and my family's.

Among the friends and colleagues who added their expert review are Attorney Andy Willms for the estate planning chapter, and Tom Fredricks and Dennis Pelzek, CPAs and accounting instructors, on the tax planning chapter. Investment professional and neighbor Tony Leszczynski graciously read the entire rough draft.

Many thanks to my talented editor and publishing consultant, Chris Roerden, who patiently guided me through the process of putting this book together. She exhibited professionalism and an insistence on quality at every step of the project.

The same can be said of my graphics and cover designer, Susan Goulet.

Finally, I wish to express my sincere thanks to my wife and partner in life, Cathy, for all her love and support. Writing a book is a time-consuming, expensive, and at times frustrating undertaking. I pledge to make it up to my wife and our three wonderful children, Maggie, Martha, and Jack. Win, lose, or draw, we're off to Orlando and Disney World soon.

My sincere wish is that this book illuminates the way for readers to reach their goals and find satisfaction and financial security in the new millennium.

John T. McCarthy

CHAPTER 1

FINANCIAL PLANNING: THE GOAL

Financial planning is a simple process. You identify where you are, decide where you want to be, and determine the most expedient way to get there. Why then are so few individuals confident financial managers? Too often the rudiments of a plan are lacking. To produce success, we need a destination, a defined objective, a goal, a financial game plan, and a strategy.

> "If you don't know where you are going,
> every road will get you nowhere."
> —Henry Kissinger

We stand at the threshold of a new millennium, flanked by both excitement and anxiety about the future. We feel fortunate to live in this dynamic age, but we sense that planning is required to adapt to the monumental social, economic, and technological changes that lie ahead.

Consider the perspective historian Stephen E. Ambrose gives us on how far we've advanced. The early 19th century was no different than the first century, when nothing moved faster than the speed of a man on horseback. If the Lewis and Clark expedition to search for an all-water route to the Pacific Northwest had been put together during the tenure of President Abraham Lincoln rather than that of President Thomas Jefferson, the explorers would have had the benefit of the steamship, railroad, and telegraph. The years between 1803 and 1860 brought massive change.

The transcontinental railroad was completed in 1869, four years after Lincoln's death. Exactly 100 years later, following through on the mandate of President John F. Kennedy, the U.S. space program successfully landed a man on the moon.

Now, at the end of the 20th century, we look forward to sending a manned mission to Mars and exploring Jupiter and beyond. Because visionary leaders embraced the future, dared to dream, and implemented plans to reach lofty goals, the sky has become our highway to the stars.

Historians have observed that the ends of centuries seem to energize Americans' penchant for change. Even a visionary and genius of the stature of Jefferson would be awed at what has transpired over the last two centuries. Yet, if Jefferson were alive today, I feel he would embrace the future—daring to dream and willing to prepare, plan, and act to fulfill identified goals.

The lesson for each of us is that planning our financial future will be more necessary than ever before so we can recognize opportunities in the 21st century. It is valuable to gain an appreciation for both the accelerating pace of change and the major forces that will affect your financial future. The implications of these forces need to be examined and a route mapped, so we can navigate successfully new frontiers of promise and challenge.

THE AVERAGE BABY BOOMER WILL TURN 50

As the huge demographic bubble of 77 million babies born between 1946 and 1964 passes through each financial milestone, the effects are sure to reverberate throughout the economy. It is said that every eight seconds a boomer turns 50. The increased strain on the Social Security system could prove disastrous for those without plans for alternative retirement income. The reality will hit home for each person funding his or her retirement, fostering an urgency to increase the rate of personal savings, which might have a beneficial effect on financial markets.

A portion of this group is known as a "sandwich generation," squeezed between assisting elderly parents and educating children—while also struggling to build a retirement nest egg.

THE DOW JONES AVERAGE WILL REACH 15,000

Stock values do not rise in a straight line, contrary to the euphoric belief resulting from the long-term bull market that started in 1982. The stock market will continue to move in a tug-of-war between a bull and a bear market. Remember that the Dow, as a stock market barometer, first reached the 1000 point milestone on November 14, 1974; yet it wallowed for a decade before resurfacing at this same level in 1982.

Since 1982, the Dow has been on quite a ride, rocketing to 2000 in 1987, spiraling down abruptly to close at 1765 in the October 19, 1987, crash, continuing a trajectory to 3000 in 1991, 4000 in 1995, 5000 a short nine months later, and, in overdrive, racing to 7000 on February 13, 1997, and 8000 on July 16, 1997.

CHINA WILL BE AN ECONOMIC POWERHOUSE

The cover story in the June 1996 issue of *Forbes* magazine asked, "Is the 21st the Asian Century?" The emerging Asian region, China specifically, is on the brink of explosive growth, a situation similarly experienced in Japan in 1955. According to Bank of America CEO David Coulter: "The greatest capital market we'll see over the rest of my working lifetime is the Pacific rim. I think we're going to see growth that's nothing short of miraculous."

I recently heard management maven and author Tom Peters speak at a seminar. He advised those of us in attendance that we should be looking east and to China in particular for the real action in the next century.

Forbes magazine in a February 1997 special article expressed the same thought. "More wealth will be created on the Pacific rim during the next decade than in any other place at any other time in history. For investors and business people, East Asia presents a tremendous opportunity." As of this writing, Asia is suffering through wrenching economic turmoil. The question becomes, is this just a temporary setback?

One thing is certain: the world economy will become fully interdependent, with new global markets, leaders, and opportunities.

MORE OF US WILL SAY WE PAID MORE FOR OUR LAST CAR THAN FOR OUR FIRST HOUSE

In the same vein, an exasperated mother remarks that her child's preschool costs more than her college education did. The two major financial planning goals—a secure retirement and education funding—are hostage to escalating costs and inflation. Having been a bat boy for the

Chicago White Sox in 1967, I can recall that the average major leaguer made some $19,000 annually. Today, even a journeyman player can bring home well over a million dollars a year. But costs and values are relative. Find me a 75-year-old with a million-dollar net worth in the year 2000, and I will show you a child of the Depression Era who never dreamed of reaching the status of a millionaire.

THE TAX CODE IS GUARANTEED TO UNDERGO CONTINUOUS TINKERING

To the certainty of death and taxes, we must add changes in tax laws, with tax rates increasing, decreasing, and flattening. We will continue to witness a Ping-Pong–type game of reforms, adjustments, surcharges, new taxes, and other ways to generate revenues at all levels of government.

All financial decisions should be analyzed from a tax planning standpoint, a daunting challenge because we are dealing with a moving target. Currently, we need to adjust our finances to adapt to changes brought by the Taxpayer Relief Act of 1997.

THE FASTEST GROWING SEGMENT OF THE POPULATION WILL BE CENTENARIANS

According to the *1995 U.S. Census Statistical Bulletin,* since 1900 medical science has extended the average life span by 31 years. In the new millennium more of us can look forward to joining the once-exclusive club of centenarians.

An 84-year-old client of mine expressed concern as to how long I plan to work with her. She volunteered that she is healthier than her mother was at the same age, and her mother lived to 104. As the aging population increases, challenges related to long-term geriatric care surely will heighten.

TRILLIONS OF DOLLARS WILL PASS TO THE NEXT GENERATION

Some estimates claim $8 trillion to $10 trillion will be transferred to the next generation over the next 30 years. This impact spells a need for advanced estateplanning to minimize transfer taxation, formulate charitable and lifetime gifting strategies, and provide a framework for the responsible management of inherited sums by heirs.

THE COMING AGE OF PROSPERITY?

Many observers believe we are entering a period of unparalleled economic growth and opportunity. While I would like to accept this scenario, I am forced to be guarded, because the threats of recessions, depressions, wars, and social upheavals still are factors in economic cycles.

A case can be made that we already have enjoyed a period of prosperity because of a sustained bull market that started in August 1982. The lesson learned from history, however, is that to participate in such upside potential, you have to have capital deployed and be willing to accept the downside risk of financial markets.

THE FEDERAL DEFICIT WILL CONTINUE TO BURDEN THE ECONOMY

As a nation in the 21st century, we will continue to labor under a mountain of accumulated debt in excess of $5.4 trillion. According to the Concord Coalition, a nonprofit organization dedicated to fiscal responsibility and a balanced budget, the U.S. deficit in 1997 amounted to approximately $25,000 for every citizen. The deficit will drive tax policy, constrain government spending, and directly influence interest rate volatility and the financial markets. This burden is particularly troubling for our children and grandchildren. It must be addressed and mitigated if future generations are to have economic viability and security.

TECHNOLOGY WILL AFFECT EVERY ASPECT OF OUR LIVES IN WAYS WE CANNOT NOW IMAGINE

Breakthroughs from new drugs, therapies, and treatments hold the promise of longer, healthier lives. This is cause for hope and excitement to those living with diseases such as multiple sclerosis, diabetes, cancer, arthritis, heart disease, digestive disease, and AIDS. It is significant to note that *Time* magazine's 1996 Man of the Year was an AIDS researcher.

My own dream is that the scourge of cancer will be eliminated, for it is the culprit that prematurely took the lives of my parents, brother-in-law, father-in-law, and the loved ones of millions of other people.

We will witness massive changes in the nature of our employment. For example, I am self-employed, maintain an office in my home, and practice a profession that was virtually unknown until the 1980s. Recently I joined the on-line revolution to access cyberspace information and global communication instantly.

The pace of technological advances is staggering. Here's just one startling example from Intel Chairman Gordon Moore, who compares the auto industry of the 60s with the semiconductor industry of the 90s:

"If the auto industry advanced as rapidly as the semiconductor industry, a Rolls Royce would get half a million miles per gallon, and it would be cheaper to throw it away than to park it."

New industries will emerge, offering investors and entrepreneurs unlimited opportunities. Think of the prospects for global prosperity if cold fusion or a related technological breakthrough were to occur. How exciting it would be to benefit from an unlimited supply of a cheap, safe, clean, renewable energy source. The hot new growth stocks for the year 2005 might not even exist today.

The waves of technology are being harnessed by money managers. For instance, the T. Rowe Price family of no-load mutual funds has pioneered the development of funds that seek to benefit from trends that hold the promise of growth opportunities as we cross into the new millennium.

One such sector fund is the hot-performing T. Rowe Price Science and Technology fund. A new offering, the Health Sciences fund, seeks to benefit from favorable demographic trends and breakthrough medical advances. Both of these niche offerings are aggressive, long-term plays; nevertheless, such investments in future trends deserve consideration.

SOCIAL INSECURITY — THE AGING OF AMERICA WILL DWARF ALL OTHER NATIONAL ISSUES

As a baby boomer, I view with alarm projections that the Social Security system is due to run dry between 2015 and 2020, precisely my time to go to the well. Peter G. Peterson, author of *Will America Grow Up Before It Grows Old?*, says Social Security is a "Ponzi scheme," and the trust fund more accurately is a "distrust fund" filled with IOUs for our children. He labels Social Security and Medicare, respectively, as a "generational chain letter" and the "mother of all unfunded mandates." The possible solutions to avoid their collapse will inevitably affect future recipients.

EMPLOYMENT INCOME SECURITY IS A RELIC OF THE PAST

If you had taken a survey in my community of Milwaukee in 1986 to identify the most stable employment opportunities, heading the list would have been employers such as Miller Brewing, Milwaukee County Hospital, IBM, Wisconsin Electric, Wisconsin Bell, Sears, Marquette University, the *Milwaukee Sentinel,* and First Wisconsin National Bank.

One decade later, many of these institutions have been altered by mergers, new identities, and retrenchment. Thousands of once-secure employees at these and other large companies have been victims of a national workforce trend of downsizing, rightsizing, and outsizing that capsized their financial lives. Left with pink slips and retirement plan payouts, anxious employees have been forced to reorder their financial lives. Job changes, self-employment, and entrepreneurship will continue to flourish out of necessity. The challenge for the newly self-employed will be to construct an equivalent benefit package for health, life, and disability protection, and a retirement plan to survive in an altered working environment.

THE REVOLUTION IN DELIVERING FINANCIAL SERVICES WILL INTENSIFY

When I graduated from college in 1973, the financial services industry, if indeed it qualified as an industry, looked altogether different than it does today. There were no CFPs, IRAs, 401(k)s, PELs, LTC policies, GNMAs, ATM terminals, SEPs, ARMs, or HMOs; all in all, there were a whole lot fewer acronyms. The money market fund was a new innovation, and the mutual fund industry was in its infancy.

The next quarter of a century promises an even more dynamic change. A leading-edge example is the emergence of the Internet. Just point and click to handle banking chores and brokerage transactions, monitor personal finances, and track your investment portfolio. Access a wealth of instantaneous investment information, financial planning modeling, and charting; instantly reposition your retirement plan. Banking, mutual funds, asset management, and risk management will undergo further consolidation, innovation, and transformation on a grand scale. Your need to be a knowledgeable financial services consumer will be more urgent than ever before.

A COMMON SENSE APPROACH

> "Common sense is genius dressed in its working clothes."
> —Ralph Waldo Emerson

In the fall of 1986 I had an opportunity to hear Sir John Templeton speak to a group of financial planners. Templeton had gained respect and fame as a master of international investing. He founded Templeton Mutual Funds, now merged with Franklin Funds.

That Saturday afternoon in Chicago, all of us were intent on gleaning useful investment management tips to take back to our clients. But at the conclusion of his characteristically upbeat talk, this distinguished gentleman with a 1912 birthdate offered but a handful of points.

His first and major message covered an approach to personal finance. Its simplicity may have disappointed many in the audience, but in retrospect and after 15 years in the financial services industry, I believe Templeton was right on target. His advice was to employ a heavy dose of common sense.

Many fans of public television's *Wall Street Week* program will remember Templeton as the hastily summoned expert who appeared on the show after the October 1987 crash. His cautiously optimistic message reassured millions of viewers. Templeton and Peter Lynch, former star mutual fund manager of Fidelity Magellan, were voted among the most popular of *Wall Street Week* guests, probably because of their easy-to-understand, common sense messages on investing.

Templeton was not alone in advocating common sense in matters of personal finance. With *The Wealthy Barber,* author David Chilton created a best seller that is loud on common sense. His fictional barber, Roy, is mentor and financial role model to three impressionable young people. Scissors in hand, he schools them from his barber shop in the basics of personal finance and sound financial planning.

Warren Buffett, one of the wealthiest men in America, credits his phenomenal financial success to common sense. Unfortunately, as sales and motivation guru Zig Ziglar puts it, "Common sense is not always common practice."

I believe common sense is called for now more than ever. And this precept is as true in investing as it is in personal financial planning.

Common sense is a very democratic quality. It requires no large sums of money, no prerequisite knowledge, and no physical prowess. It has nothing to do with gender, age, social position, education, or the commitment of an inordinate amount of time. In short, common sense is available to everyone.

IF YOU DON'T HAVE A PLAN, YOU'RE PLANNING TO END UP DISAPPOINTED

Why don't more individuals undertake common sense financial planning? The answer is difficult to pinpoint, but I believe it flows from our basic human nature. Some contributing factors are these:

- Procrastination and inertia, the two biggest obstacles to financial success.
- Ignorance of the tremendous value of effective financial planning through investment management, tax minimization, professional guidance, goal identification, and action plans.
- Failure to appreciate the monumental difference that time-value-of-money principles make in planning efforts, including: starting early, letting money grow with regular additions and dividend reinvestment, and maximizing investment performance.

Success in constructing a secure financial future for the new millennium will depend more and more on a meticulously conceived and implemented plan.

THINK AND GROW RICH

The motivational message of Napoleon Hill's classic *Think and Grow Rich* reinforces the theme of the value of financial planning in the successful pursuit of financial independence.

Hill's book was inspired by steel baron and philanthropist Andrew Carnegie, who challenged the young journalist to undertake a lifelong pursuit of interviewing and chronicling 500 successful individuals, including such greats as Thomas Edison and Henry Ford.

From this comprehensive life study, Hill discovered certain hidden secrets and formulas that he distilled into principles and steps. When rigorously applied, they were said to enable individuals to achieve financial and life goals.

According to Hill, the starting point is to know what one is looking to accomplish. He frequently referred to this notion as a definiteness of purpose. Other traits common to the makeup of successful individuals include having a willingness to take control, setting clearly identified goals—financial or otherwise—developing a definite, organized plan, and mastering procrastination. Hill believed we need a vision and the courage born of self-confidence.

> "There are no limitations to the mind except those we acknowledge. Both poverty and riches are the offspring of thought."
> —Napoleon Hill, *Think and Grow Rich*

Hill was a contemporary of Thomas Edison, who conducted 10,000 failed experiments before he succeeded in producing the electric light. Hill claims the inventor finally achieved success when he committed his objective to writing and formulated an organized plan to proceed. Like Edison, auto titan Henry Ford possessed very little formal education, yet succeeded due greatly to vision and persistence.

Although *Think and Grow Rich* has been in print since 1926 and its success stories are based on a bygone era, its material and advice have withstood the passage of time. Its tenets have relevance today as we prepare for life in the 21st century.

Venita VanCaspel, popular personal finance author in the 1980s, suggested that one primary cause for lack of financial success could be the failure to develop a winning mentality about money, or, put another way, the lack of PMA, positive mental attitude. Hers is an updated version of an attitude espoused by Hill.

> "Is it true that people with a financial plan sleep better at night?"
> —Merrill Lynch advertisement

"Financial planning" is a widely used but frequently abused term. Too often it is a cloak to promote or push financial products, with little or no actual planning involved. Financial planning is a process. Product promotion, when and where necessary or appropriate, comes down the road when individuals can make reasoned decisions based on their unique circumstances.

Certain high-level financial planners seek to elevate the status of their practice by referring to themselves as wealth managers, and even using the term "wealth management" in the names of their firms. They describe a holistic approach of factoring in dreams, aspirations, and anxieties to help clients achieve life goals through proper management of financial resources.

I do see recent encouraging evidence that the financial services industry is placing a higher priority on the process of financial planning than on product promotion. For example, industry leader Merrill Lynch has moved from being bullish on America to proclaiming: "The difference is planning," as in financial planning.

Studies have tracked the lives of individuals after a financial windfall, such as winning a lottery or receiving an inheritance. It may come as no surprise that in many cases there was little trace of wealth to be found after five years. The younger the recipient, the sorrier the outcome. The windfalls had dissipated into depreciating luxury cars and a few years' worth of spending sprees.

Compare this outcome to a 25-year-old investing $100,000 in a long-term growth portfolio. The young investor assembles an investment account using a handful of well-chosen diversified stock mutual funds. The account includes small-, medium-, and large-capitalization funds, plus an international fund for good measure. This investment is left intact to allow the miracle of compound growth to take place over time.

Assuming a feasible, long-term, average annual compounded return of 12.25%, this portfolio would grow tenfold every 20 years, reaching the magic million-dollar mark in 20 years when the individual is age 45, and going on to reach—amazingly—$10 million by age 65:

$100,000	$1,000,000	$10,000,000
Age 25	Age 45	Age 65
	20 years	20 years

Average annual compounded return on investment (ROI) = 12.25%

PLANNING PAYS OFF

The International Association for Financial Planning (IAFP) is a professional organization that is conducting an awareness campaign to impress upon the public the value to be derived from financial planning.

When done well, the planning process is an important tool to help increase your probability of achieving financial objectives and mapping out a route to successfully reach your destination.

Figure 1-1

Informed financial consumers these days evaluate all products and services for their capacity to offer value. In the planning process, value is derived primarily from investment performance and tax minimization, which can be measured in terms of many thousands of additional dollars over a lifetime. But the most important attribute of planning is to help you reach the goal line.

Successful financial planning is not the product of a complicated mathematical formula. It requires:
- rigorous savings and capital accumulation
- intelligent asset management
- patient discipline
- a basic knowledge of related tax and financial matters

Yes, it requires elementary analytical skills, basic arithmetic, and the previously identified heavy doses of common sense, but the best plan need not be complicated. It involves:
- asking oneself some pointed questions
- defining a desired outcome

- putting pencil to paper on specifics
- gaining the necessary insight to make informed decisions

Financial planning involves taking a look at your entire personal financial picture and focusing attention on income and expenses, asset and debt management, and risk management. In virtually every financial situation, the areas that need to be addressed include: tax, estate, retirement, and investment planning.

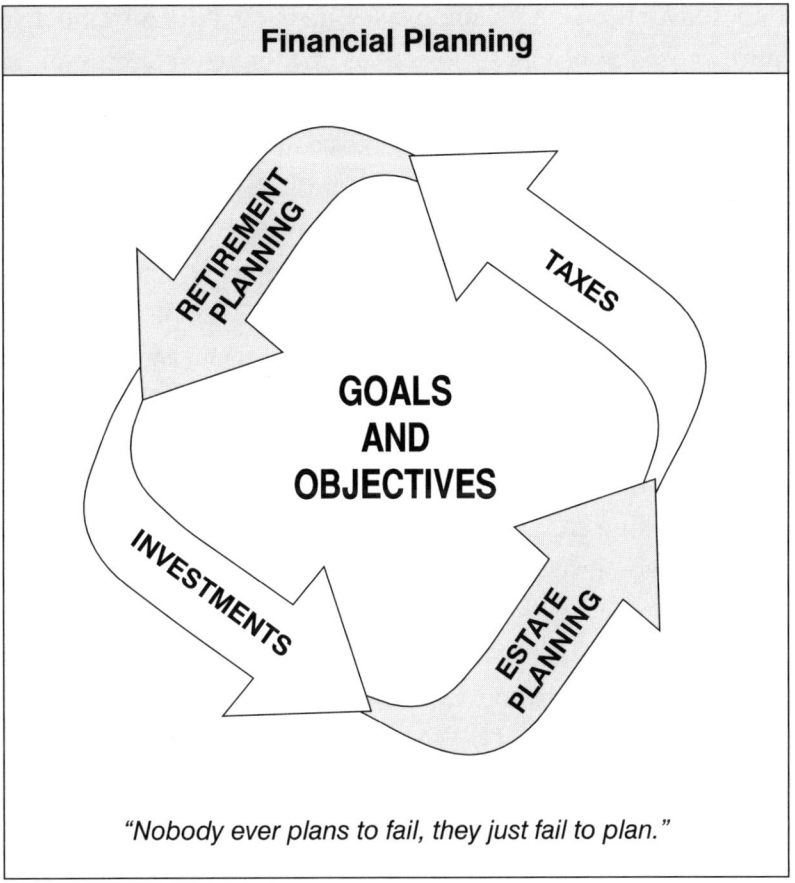

Figure 1-2

Financial independence can be defined as the freedom to enjoy a desired lifestyle without relying on employment income. As shown in Figure 1-2, goals and objectives are the heart of the planning equation. Investments are the foundation of many planning issues, for they add wind to your sail and determine how fast and far you go before you reach a given destination. Tax planning is integral to the planning process, and each move must be examined for its tax ramifications.

I contend that all financial planning revolves around the twin pillars of retirement and estate planning. In the preretirement years the goal is to accumulate a large enough nest egg so one no longer needs to work. In the postretirement period, retirees desperately hope they do not run out of money before they run out of breath. Financial security is paramount, with lifestyle issues somewhat secondary. Beyond that, they hope to also leave something to their children, grandchildren, or a favorite charity.

Important retirement planning tasks are to quantify how much money you need to accomplish these objectives, to monitor your progress, and to provide a sufficient contingency reserve. In the preretirement years you are looking to build an estate; during the postretirement years, to manage, consume, control, and ultimately transfer the residue of that estate.

Financial planning cannot be done in a vacuum, because all aspects are interrelated, as the arrows in Figure 1-2 indicate. Each aspect is covered in a later chapter of this book. Take the example of the planning surrounding a retirement account. As a participant, you are responsible for the investment management of that money, aiming for the best risk-reward balance. Tax planning is crucial for this tax-deferred account, especially at the time of distribution. Your retirement plan is likely to be your prime funding and accumulation vehicle during your working years. At retirement you face decisions about whether to roll it over to an individual retirement account, where to generate income, and which money to spend first—deferred or after-tax accumulations. Estate planning is forced into play because all retirement plans, including IRAs, require you to name a beneficiary. The estate tax ramifications of inherited retirement accounts are particularly complex and merit sound planning before and after the death of the benefactor.

If you are like most people, you need to be probed before your true objectives start to surface. I have noted the tendency for individuals and couples to be most open when we are sitting around the kitchen table in the comfort and privacy of their homes. It is in this familiar setting I am most likely to discover their aspirations and fears and understand what they would most like to accomplish.

The most powerful—and in many respects the most difficult—part of the planning process is capturing what is important in one's financial life.

"Our plans miscarry because they have no aim. When a man does not know what harbor he is making for, no wind is the right wind."

—Seneca

The first step, then, involves clearly defining your desired personal financial objective. It is worthwhile to be able to say simply what you want to achieve financially. Corporations and organizations formulate mission statements to put into words their organization's primary purpose. As business leaders have been scrutinized for their capacity to offer vision, individuals would be well served to think of their own financial well-being in visionary terms. Therefore, composing a personal finance mission statement is a useful first step.

PLANNED LIVING

Bob, a physical therapist from Chicago, has taken stock of his life and financial situation and has exciting plans for what he wants from the rest of his life.

As we look in on Bob, a productive strategic planning meeting is taking place involving his CPA, his estate planning attorney, and his CFP. As this meeting concludes, all parties on his team are seen smiling and congratulating each other on the plan they have mapped out for him.

It is a little over a year since Bob's dear wife, Dorothy, passed away at age 70. She had lived the last 30 years of her life with the challenges of multiple sclerosis (MS).

Bob just turned 64. He has decided to take his company's early retirement offer. This package contains continuation of health insurance coverage until age 65, when he becomes Medicare-eligible, group life insurance to age 70, six months' salary continuation, and a slightly enhanced retirement plan.

His three major assets are a large paid-up home, a sizable retirement plan, and a substantial blue chip stock portfolio that Dorothy inherited from her mother in 1980. Owing to these resources, Bob finds himself in a very comfortable financial position, a condition verified by his assembled team of financial advisors.

Bob has spent the last few months thinking hard and huddling with his trusted friends and advisors to define what he wants to accomplish in life and achieve from his wealth. He settled on the following four primary financial/life planning goals.

GOAL #1. To continue to live life to the fullest, while making a difference in the lives of others who are less fortunate.

Bob will attend training courses at his community college so he can learn to serve as a volunteer counselor affiliated with his church. He is also making plans to hike the entire Appalachian Trail over the next 15 years, and he has compiled a list of 100 great books he intends to read by the time he turns 70.

GOAL #2. To ensure his retirement financial security and be a good steward of his money.

As a by-product of the financial planning process to assess his net worth, income, and expenses, Bob has become convinced of his financial security. He discovered surplus wealth, and room to spare and share.

His plan calls for selling his house, taking advantage of the new capital gains laws. He will invest the proceeds and rent a comfortable, affordable apartment close to his church and agency. His Social Security income will cover his rent and utilities.

Since he will not require current income from his retirement plan, Bob has been advised to roll over this lump sum directly to an IRA, letting it continue to compound tax deferred. The IRA will be invested in a balanced portfolio projected to double in value over the next 10 years, allowing for the required minimum distributions starting at age $70\frac{1}{2}$.

Bob is able to draw a generous income stream from his investment nest egg. He is capable of easily meeting his cost-of-living needs by repositioning his investment portfolio to achieve an optimum risk-reward balance. He has updated his estate plan and has a strategy in place to minimize taxes.

Bob's biggest fear at this stage is the potential cost of lengthy convalescent care. Once again his thinking is drawn from personal experience—in this case the cruelty of Alzheimer's, which has completely erased the nest egg of his 84-year-old aunt.

His insurance agent and good friend, Jim, has been extolling the merits of long-term care (LTC) insurance. Jim counsels that LTC is an estate planning matter that can help protect Bob's estate in order to fund his charitable giving.

Bob is considering this LTC proposal because he must restructure his overall risk management (insurance) plan to conform to his changed financial realities.

GOAL #3. To finance his niece Jamie's college education.

Bob and Dorothy were never blessed with children but enjoyed a close and loving relationship with their niece and godchild, Jamie. A dedicated and gifted student, Jamie is looking forward to attending her Aunt Dorothy's alma mater next year. Bob has given Jamie some of Dorothy's favorite jewelry, along with a pledge of $25,000 each year to help cover the cost of her private school tuition. This amount will not be subject to gift or estate taxes because it is being directed toward tuition and will be paid directly to the institution. Jamie has her eyes set on a Ph.D. and a career in medical research. Bob has named Jamie as beneficiary of his life insurance policies to ensure realization of this mutual dream.

GOAL #4. To make a difference in the lives of the thousands living with the challenges of multiple sclerosis.

The seed for this goal had been planted at a presentation Bob and a wheelchair-bound Dorothy had attended some two years earlier as part of a regional National MS Society luncheon. Detailing real advances being made to combat the devastating effects of this cruel disease, the presenter discussed the goal of unlocking the mystery of this disease by the year 2005 and the impact of breakthrough drugs. The audience was reminded that polio was arrested in 1955 by the introduction of the Salk vaccine.

Bob and Dorothy were inspired to help fund this vital research. Dorothy named the National MS Society beneficiary of her $50,000 life insurance policy. Since her passing, Bob has been working with his advisors to formulate a plan that integrates his financial, retirement, tax, and estate planning with his charitable intent. The charitable and financial planning communities refer to these initiatives appropriately enough as *planned giving*. Bob's plan calls for establishing a charitable remainder trust (CRT) funded with his highly appreciated stock. This strategy neatly offers many retirement planning and tax benefits. He has also named the National MS Society as a beneficiary of his IRA and updated his will to make the society and his church equal beneficiaries of his trust.

As we check in with Bob six months later, we discover him relaxing in a handsome apartment, a great book on his lap, trail maps sprawled out on the dining room table, conversing by e-mail with Jamie at college, and feeling fulfilled with his ministry work.

FINANCIAL PLANNING GOALS AND OBJECTIVES

The following common financial planning objectives are not intended to be all-inclusive, nor is any one goal exclusive of others. It is likely that individuals have more than one objective and that goals will overlap. This list is meant to stimulate thought with an eye toward what you are looking to accomplish from your finances.

COMMON FINANCIAL PLANNING OBJECTIVES

- ❏ To enjoy a financially secure retirement.
    - ♦ This is the number one goal for many people.
    - ♦ Stated another way, reaching financial independence (security) by a certain age.
    - ♦ It encompasses preretirement plans, in which accumulating a sufficient nest egg is a goal.
    - ♦ It also includes postretirement planning, where the objective is to generate sufficient supplementary retirement income without running out of money.
- ❏ To finance the education of children, grandchildren, or other significant individuals.
    - ♦ Possessing the financial resources to provide for their desired levels of education.
    - ♦ Using education financing to transfer wealth from estate.
- ❏ To accumulate the necessary down payment to purchase a home or business.
- ❏ To establish a liquid cash reserve.
    - ♦ A contingency fund, the cushion for a rainy day.
    - ♦ Funding a short-term goal.
- ❏ To build (assemble) an investment portfolio of a certain size by a specified time.
    - ♦ Perhaps you like the sound of millionaire or multimillionaire and desire to reach this magic dollar mark by the time you reach age 55.

- ❏ To pass along a healthy estate to the next generation.
  - ♦ Providing estate liquidity and a sizable estate.
  - ♦ Planning in the event of incapacity or incompetence.
  - ♦ Minimizing estate taxes.
  - ♦ Caring for a child, family member, or friend with special needs.
  - ♦ Developing, if feasible, a gifting strategy both for individuals and qualified charities.
- ❏ To create financial order in your affairs.
  - ♦ Specific objectives are apt to include organization, consolidation, savings discipline, risk protection, diversification, timing, liquidity, and tax sheltering and documentation.

Stephen Covey, author of the best seller *The Seven Habits of Highly Effective People,* cites the number one habit as being proactive. He goes on to describe definiteness of purpose, taking initiative, and making things happen as valuable habits in the pursuit of financial success.

As a financial planner, I have come to the conclusion that my most vital role is one of catalyst, assisting in the identification and fulfillment of financial goals and objectives and spurring client action.

Individuals by nature are reactive rather than proactive, especially when it comes to personal financial planning. Many people express frustration when discussing their personal finances. Often they describe themselves as being lost, spinning their wheels, on a treadmill, or slipping backward. They are desperate for assurance they are on the right track and headed in the right direction. A good road map (financial plan) would assist them in reaching the hoped-for destination (goal).

Failure to identify and state your financial goals stands in the way of successful personal financial implementation.

I remember hearing an Englishman at a financial planning conference quote a survey that showed the number one goal in his country was a financially secure retirement. The second most common response shown by the same survey was, "I don't know." I strongly suspect this same pattern of response would hold true on this side of the Atlantic. Knowing what you want—that is, having clearly defined goals—is the strongest key to financial success.

In a relationship, a healthy situation develops when both partners approach personal finance matters as equals. Ideally, each individual brings different perspectives, anxieties, and dreams to the discussion. In a marriage, a formal, legal, and financial partnership exists. Disagreement over money has been identified as the top cause of marital discord and dissolution. The truth is that the root problem is not necessarily a shortage of money, but rather a deep-felt disagreement over how funds should be used. Divorce is rarely a positive solution for either party. The real solution is obvious: open communication, joint decisions, compromise, and a shared understanding of individual and family goals.

Open communication was definitely not apparent in an incident that occurred while I was leading an investment seminar. I announced I would be available at the break should anyone have a personal investment question. Sure enough, a fellow rushed up and proceeded to speak directly into my ear. "I have a little money, but I don't want the wife to know."

As it turned out, "the wife," as well as scores of other attendees, became fully aware of his secret intention. You see, I was wearing a lapel microphone and had not yet had an opportunity to remove it at the start of the break. Perhaps it served him right.

THE FINANCIAL PLANNING PROCESS

Generally, financial planning is expected to follow a six-step process carried out in a logical sequence. We must identify our objective and act upon it as we move from general to specific goals.

SIX-STEP FINANCIAL PLANNING PROCESS

1. Identify your goal.
2. Quantify your goal.
3. Identify constraints and resources.
4. Prioritize your goals.
5. Take action.
6. Monitor and adjust.

1. IDENTIFY YOUR GOAL

Look at the list of common financial planning objectives (pages 18–19) and turn your attention to your own primary goals. Condense your financial goal to capsule form. Be as specific as possible. You'll benefit from having tunnel vision. State your goal orally, then write it down.

2. QUANTIFY YOUR GOAL

In this step, add detail as you move from the general nature of your objective to a narrower definition. I suggest you quantify your goal by placing a dollar sign in front of the goal you have specified so you can know when you have reached a certain dollar plateau—your destination.

Let's say your objective is to finance a college education. Are we talking Harvard or the local community college? The cost differential is substantial, to say the least.

Or, assume the goal is to accumulate enough to put a 10% minimum down payment on a home. Are we looking at a million-dollar mansion or a hundred-thousand-dollar homestead?

Maybe your goal is to accumulate a sizable retirement nest egg. What size nest egg are you looking to build: $100,000, $250,000, $1 million, or $5 million? Your goal might be to retire on an income stream to support your current lifestyle. This could be $500 a month or $20,000 a month.

When thinking in terms of income requirements, it is a good idea to quote it in monthly as well as in annual terms.

In quantifying your objective, use a percentage figure to add perspective to your analysis; for example, an 8% return on investment as your target; a 5% expected inflation rate; the need to provide 50% of income from your retirement nest egg; the establishment of a 25% down payment on a house; or the accumulation of an emergency fund equal to 15% of current net income.

Paint a mental bull's-eye on your target to give you something to aim for and to provide satisfaction when you hit your goal.

Next, add a time frame to your plan. You might decide to categorize your planning objectives into short-term (one year or less), mid-term, and long-term goals, possibly using a cut-off at five years.

Say your goal is retirement. Is this sometime, anytime, or at a specific age, such as 55, 60, 62, 65, or 70? You need to develop a timeline and thereby add a planning horizon in pursuit of your objective. Once you retire, are you projecting a further period of income required for 5 years, 15 years, or 25 years?

The time factor is integral to the planning process because—as I shall continually stress—it has a major impact on the dynamics of the time value of money, such as a rate of investment growth and the impact of inflation.

Once you set a target, you automatically become more focused and better prepared. Continuing with your retirement objective, say your stated goal is to retire in five years on your 62nd birthday. You can further add a reference point such as a calendar year. The year 2005 provides a nice target. Another plan might call for semiretirement in seven years at age 60, with sufficient resources and income so you have to provide only 25% of needed income from part-time or transitional employment.

When someone is discussing an education funding goal, the first question I pose is, "How old is the child?" The implications of planning for a newborn versus planning for a 16-year-old are as great as the difference in relative costs of a Harvard degree versus a community college education.

3. IDENTIFY CONSTRAINTS AND RESOURCES

Your next step is to run a quick reality check on your goal. You have to assess your resources first, primarily income and assets. You might desire to retire next year at age 45, but this is unrealistic if you have yet to establish a nest egg or cannot expect adequate income sources without maintaining a full-time job.

We should be able to dream our dreams, but they do need to be filtered through a financial reality test. All but the truly wealthy have a ceiling on their financial ambitions. Factors such as income, assets, and time frame act as constraints. Their absence should not automatically shut the door on our dreams, but rather help us to find reasonable alternatives.

4. PRIORITIZE YOUR GOALS

Those in managerial positions understand that hard choices and difficult decisions need to be made. Also, anyone who has ever worked through a budget process understands that limited resources must be allocated carefully. Such is the task we as individuals face in our personal financial lives. Both organizations and individuals need to set priorities.

Frequently, different financial objectives collide. Perhaps the desire to fully fund a retirement savings program runs counter to the costs of higher education. Just think how old you will be when your youngest child enters college. It helps to ask yourself what financial objective you are committed to beyond all others.

Most individuals have several competing financial goals. I have counseled individuals who face such a dilemma to think in terms of allocating resources into different buckets corresponding to each objective. Devise a formula and pour a certain dollar amount into the retirement funding budget and a certain amount into the education savings budget.

Another approach is to visualize a dollar of discretionary income, then to determine what percentage (how many cents) of that dollar you wish to allocate to each account. This method should assist you with priority ranking.

5. TAKE ACTION

The best laid plans are useless unless we implement them. In the game of basketball, no scoring takes place unless you put up a shot. We need a basis for action.

"Plan your work and work your plan" was the motto of a successful sales manager for whom I once worked.

Many times, this involves putting your money where your intentions are. Are you willing to make the commitment to fulfilling a goal? Are you willing to write a check?

Action could involve establishing a mutual fund account, signing up for an elective deferral in a 401(k) plan, formulating an estate plan, adding a life insurance policy, refinancing a mortgage, or instituting an automatic monthly investment program. The emphasis is on action: open, increase, add to, start, complete, or improve. Listen to the popular Nike Corporation tag line: "Just Do It!"

6. MONITOR AND READJUST

No plan can or should be carved in stone. I go so far as to say use a pencil when writing down goals. We manage our personal and financial lives in a highly dynamic environment. The one constant is change. Hence, we must be prepared to change course occasionally.

Your income and expenditures go up and down. Tax laws change.

Investment returns fluctuate. Inflation heats up and cools down. As individuals we grow older, have children, and experience marriage, death, retirement, divorce, relocation, etc. A financial life can be compared to a piece of machinery. For best results, each needs to be fine-tuned and recalibrated from time to time.

As we progress through various passages of our lives, we experience a gradual change in our primary financial objectives and in the design of our financial status. This is in keeping with the concept of life cycle financial planning.

In the early years of our working lives, we are looking to establish a foothold, put together a cash reserve, and start to accumulate a down payment on a house. As we progress along the chain, we tend to focus on sheltering money from taxes, furthering education, and building an investment portfolio. Later, our concern turns to providing for a financially secure future through building a nest egg.

Once retired, we reverse our attention—from asset accumulation to income generation and consumption. Over time, the relative importance of liquidity, tax sheltering, and risk, growth, and income factors all undergo a transformation. Increasingly, life cycle planning spans multiple generations.

FAMILY FINANCIAL MATTERS

In my practice, I have noticed an increase in clients in their sixties planning their estates around aging parents, grown children, and grandchildren. The plan is to encompass the entire family and address wide-ranging financial needs in a coordinated fashion.

Examples of family financial challenges include issues such as:
- Adding separate living quarters to a personal residence for semi-independent, aging parents.
- Purchasing a "water hole" such as a lake or vacation property for far-flung family members to gather at and enjoy.
- Setting up a charity or foundation board to actively carry on a family philanthropic mission.
- Structuring a plan that keeps a family heritage alive, such as keeping a business, farm, or ranch in the family without causing disharmony.

- Establishing education trusts, perhaps funded with an irrevocable life insurance policy.
- Employing sophisticated estate planning techniques, including family limited partnerships and generation-skipping trusts to design an estate plan that works for multiple generations.
- Holding a multigenerational family annual meeting where financial issues are openly discussed and communicated and plans made to take care of family members when the need arises.
- Staging a 25-year, 40-year, or 50-year wedding anniversary event that has a communication component. (I am aware of a family that staged a multigeneration family celebration at a Disney complex. Another family held a cruise. It is sad when it takes a funeral to bring a family together.)
- One definition of financial success is to make a major gift to your parents for all they have done for you. Generosity does not always have to follow a top-down generational direction.

We have all heard of star athletes purchasing homes for their mothers after signing mega-contracts. I am aware of children paying off the balance on the family home or farm. Others have purchased a car for their parents or a dream vacation—ideal demonstrations of love and support.

Many parents and grandparents desire to foster financial planning awareness and thrift habits for younger generations.

There exists a well-founded fear that a traditional education, no matter how expensive, is devoid of much, if any, relevant and practical personal finance education.

It is ironic that we gain an education in order to learn how to make a living, but rarely are we educated on how to handle that income.

Ben Franklin's quote, "an investment in knowledge always pays the best interest," holds true in terms of increasing one's financial literacy.

AN INVESTMENT IN A LIFETIME

Dan and Sheila are bright, energetic teenagers, busy with school, activities and part-time jobs. They are each encouraged by their parents to open a new American Dream IRA with $2,000 from their respective earnings and to continue annual investments going forward.

The hope and plan is that these impressionable 16-year-olds will start on a financial planning and investment course that will pay handsome dividends over their lifetimes. The lessons to be learned include:

- the value of saving
- knowledge of investments
- importance of goal setting
- power of compound growth
- tax awareness

To get the ball rolling, Dan and Sheila each invest in a diversified asset allocation mutual fund, 80% weighted in stocks, capable of producing a growth-oriented 10% to 12% average annual return.

These Internet-savvy young people will track their investments on the World Wide Web, reviewing the portfolio makeup and current allocation, checking their returns, and being brought up to speed by reading the annual reports and investment commentary on their holdings.

This account, popularly known as a Roth IRA, gives them no immediate tax deduction, which is no big deal without a tax liability. However, their earnings will be growing on a favorable tax-deferred basis. The flexibility found in this type of account paints a picture of a real American dream. It will provide each of them with a sum of $10,000 for a down payment on their first houses, accessible funds to pay for their children's educations, and finally a means to build a substantial tax-advantaged nest egg to ensure their retirement security.

Let's assume these young investors are able to average a 12% return from their professionally managed portfolios, which include portions in international and small-cap stocks to boost performance.

In 10 years, Dan and Sheila are each 26, married, and looking to purchase first homes. Their $2,000 annual Roth IRA investments are now each worth about $39,300, from which they are eligible to withdraw $10,000 tax free to make down payments on a starter home.

Over the next 20 years they each continue their regular $2,000 annual investment. At age 46, their accounts have mushroomed in value to some $444,000 each, when they decide to pull out $50,000 to pay for their own children's higher education.

Fifteen more years pass and these childhood friends are 61 years old, gray, and eyeing retirement.

Over the 45-year span from age 16 to 61, Dan and Sheila have each put a total of $90,000 into their Roth IRA kitty. From this pot, they used $10,000 for a home purchase and tapped $50,000 for education expenses, and yet—amazingly—each is left with a retirement nest egg of $2,240,000 at age 61.

At this time they discontinue their combined $2,000 annual inputs and decide to continue to allow this account to accumulate tax deferred. They also decide to ratchet down their risk a notch and switch to a more moderate growth portfolio with a 10% annual return expectation. In this vein, these accounts are projected to grow to the astounding sum of $5,810,727 by age 71.

The great thing about a Roth IRA is that—unlike a traditional IRA—Dan and Sheila are not required to take distributions at a particular age, and when they do take income, having made their contributions with after-tax dollars, the entire income will be tax free.

Now that is what we call a smart move.

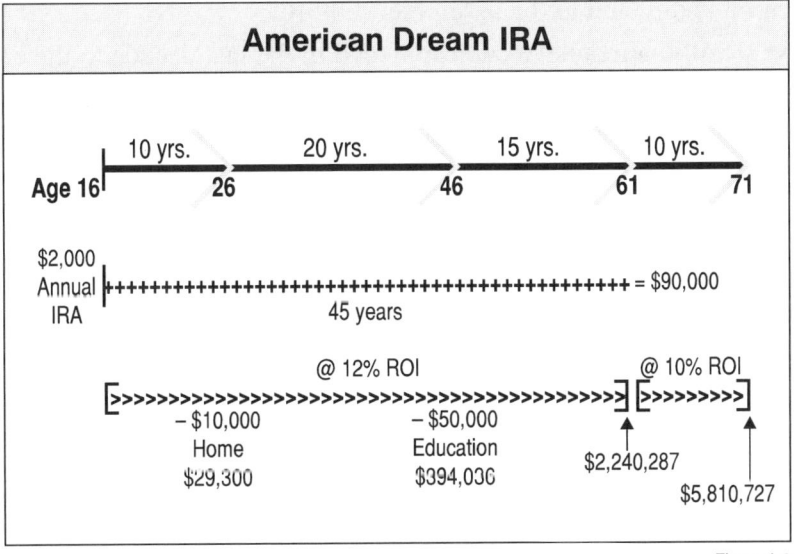

Figure 1-3

CHAPTER 2

SECRETS TO BECOMING A MILLIONAIRE

Any time I address groups on financial planning topics, there is an underlying question: "Can he show me how to become a millionaire?" The allure of amassing a seven-figure net worth is a goal synonymous with financial independence, and a million is still a magic number.

People often exhibit a sense of disbelief—a feeling that reaching this lofty level is an unrealistic goal. But the truth is, many folks attending a financial planning or investment seminar already are millionaires. Millionaires are the type of serious money managers who invest the time to be informed. These seminars are similar to a church service in which the preaching is directed to the assembled faithful.

New millionaires have been spawned in the last decade to the extent that 3.5 million households, or roughly 3.5% of the total population, have ascended to this lofty level. They don't necessarily consider themselves rich, nor are they comfortable with the label "millionaire."

Contrary to popular belief, the vast majority of this nation's millionaires do not lead the lifestyle of the rich and famous. You cannot pick out millionaires by the neighborhoods in which they reside, the cars they drive, or even the cut of their suits. They live below their means and don't look the way we think millionaires look.

The late Sam Walton, founder of Wal-Mart, offers the perfect case in point. No one would have guessed this unassuming Arkansas gentleman, attired in off-the-rack clothes from his stores, pumping his own gas, dogs frolicking in the back of his five-year-old pickup truck, was fabulously wealthy. Happily married his entire adult life, Sam Walton was a verified billionaire; one of the wealthiest men in the country.

At the other extreme, real estate and casino magnate Donald Trump, often photographed in a tuxedo entering limousines or exiting jets, is popularly believed to be one of the richest men in America. The fact is he has skirted bankruptcy and at one point probably had a negative net worth, his liabilities exceeding his assets. Appearances can be deceiving.

James Stowers, founder and president of Twentieth Century Mutual Funds, has an unswerving belief that anyone can achieve financial independence. He authored a book devoted to this topic, entitled, appropriately enough, *Yes, You Can...Achieve Financial Independence*. Stowers clearly took his own advice, for he is now on the Forbes 400 list of wealthiest Americans.

In contrast to his flashier counterparts, Stowers describes family habits of thrift and frugality that include taking a brown-bag lunch of a peanut butter sandwich to work daily, and using on-street parking over the convenience of a garage structure. His wife, Virginia, speaks of resisting the temptation to purchase a beautiful fur coat she admired.

Reading his account of his own financial success, we discover it is due also to a visionary's patience, the compounding of superior equity investment returns, and ownership of a growth business he loves, an investment management firm.

> "The best time to plant an oak was 20 years ago.
> The second best time is now."
> —James Stowers, *Yes, You Can . . . Achieve Financial Independence*

Stowers claims that the fruits of financial independence include peace of mind, along with the freedom to do what one wants to do when one wants to do it. We can't all achieve the magnitude of success of a Stowers or a Trump or a Walton, but we can all improve our financial conditions. By postponing high consumption today, we can draw ever closer to realizing the dream of financial independence.

DOWN AND OUT

JamesRodney Richard was found living under a Houston freeway in 1995. In 1980 J.R. Richard had been a superstar pitcher for the Houston Astros. His annual salary of $850,000 placed him among the highest-paid athletes of that era.

So intimidating was the six-foot, eight-inch tall fastball pitcher that opposing hitters were known to come down with a case of JR-itis and bail out of the batter's box when facing him.

J.R.'s misfortune started when he suffered a stroke in the heat of the 1980 season. Things went from bad to worse for the former high roller as he suffered further from an expensive divorce, a string of bad business ventures, and the loss of his showplace Houston home.

While tragic, this loss of wealth and fame is not an unheard-of phenomenon. Modern-day athletes and entertainers are capable of commanding astounding incomes at a relatively young age. Such affluence affords a lavish lifestyle but does not necessarily equate with the accumulation of wealth. Some years back, Dallas Cowboys star running back Tony Dorsett was holding out for more money. His main argument for an increase was not his ability or comparative worth, but rather his financial problems. He was making $800,000 a season but spending $1 million a year. Dorsett's deficit spending was brought to light when the IRS confiscated his cars and boats as payment for back taxes.

Then there is the case of Las Vegas casino headliner Wayne Newton, who filed for bankruptcy in 1992. At the time he was pulling down over a quarter of a million dollars a week singing "Danke Schoen" and "Daddy, Don't Leave" to packed audiences.

In a *People* magazine article, Newton admitted he had grown disconnected from his money. He confessed to readers, "I had never signed a check in my life." While his situation was lamentable, it may have been hard for anyone living paycheck-to-paycheck to sympathize with the plight of someone whose annual income exceeded $10 million.

The misfortunes of J.R. and Newton and others aside, academicians ThomasJ. Stanley , Ph.D., and WilliamD. Danko, Ph.D., set out to discover how America's rich amassed wealth, and they offer somewhat surprising conclusions in their 1997 best-seller, *The Millionaire Next Door*.

Their research is consistent with my own observations gathered as a practitioner, and I highly recommend a careful reading of this fine book for anyone who truly desires an easy-to-follow, proven recipe to attain wealth.

The authors find that today's millionaires are likely to be unassuming in many respects. This fact should give all of us aspiring millionaires inspiration that such a measure of financial status is achievable.

Stanley and Danko observe that most millionaires are first-generation wealthy, currently retired, and used to hold ordinary jobs or run mundane businesses. Their research discovered millionaires among the ranks of dry cleaners, auctioneers, mobile home park operators, rice farmers, and sandblasting contractors. I can add to this list a landscape contractor, maintenance supervisor, computer programmer, Christmas tree farmer, dairy worker, light bulb distributor, mid-level manager, nurse, cattle broker, and several school teachers.

Conspicuous by their absence on my list, as in Stanley and Danko's findings, are high-income professionals such as doctors, lawyers, and athletes.

Millionaire-authority Stanley still believes a million dollars represents the hallmark of prosperity, although the effects of inflation mean that today it takes $5 million to equal the $1 million of 30 years ago.

As we step into our third century as a nation, what constitutes real wealth in America? Many financial observers now believe you have to enter the more exclusive multimillionaire club before you begin to feel truly rich. A more telling measure of wealth is having at least a million in an income-producing portfolio, excluding a home and other assets.

It often comes down to the annual income flow that can be pumped out of a portfolio which provides some assurance along with a comfortable lifestyle.

For example, at a 6% return on a $3 million investment pot, much of it tax exempt, $180,000 could be pumped out annually without touching the principal; and from a $5 million nest egg, $300,000 annually.

At a certain level, most wants are satisfied and a point is reached when you realize you can't spend it fast enough. For most people, losing insecurity and feeling prosperous would perhaps occur when one's net worth is twice whatever it is now.

DOWN THE PATH

I first visited the beautiful country of Ireland in 1973. In centrally located Tullamore, famous for producing Tullamore Dew Irish whiskey, I stopped at a petrol station to ask directions to a family friend's farm on the outskirts of town.

A pipe-smoking, rosy-cheeked, mature gentleman sized me up instantly as a young Yank and declared, "If I was you, and I was headed to where you're headed, I sure wouldn't be starting from where you're starting from to get there!"

Then he drew me a crude map that included a tree marker supposedly used for a lynching some 300 years earlier. Needless to say, I stayed lost.

This experience illustrates the importance of knowing your present location if you want to reach your destination. Likewise, in the financial planning process it is difficult to determine where you are going if you don't know where you are.

To help ourselves identify our own starting points and assess our financial strengths and weaknesses, we can employ the same analytical tools that businesses use.

To begin to take control of your financial life, think of yourself as chief financial officer (CFO) of You, Inc.

Fundamentally, financial planning is about looking at one's resources and figuring out how to use them to meet identified life goals. A business uses financial statements, primarily the balance sheet and income statement, to keep score of and assess financial condition. As individuals, we use equivalent analytical tools, referred to as personal financial statements. The personal balance sheet and income statement represent the most fundamental tools in personal finance analysis, measuring financial condition and revealing financial strengths and weaknesses. Construction of these statements is a simple yet valuable starting point.

Many individuals admit to being too consumed with managing a career, family, profession, or business to pay attention to personal finances. Depending upon such factors as life cycle and compensation levels, it is possible that millions of dollars of income may come into your possession. If this revenue over your income-producing years is managed well, the result should be a substantial sum in the personal finance enterprise. Sadly, most people spend more time planning a wedding than the marriage, and more time planning a vacation than financial goals.

> "If you don't have a plan,
> you're planning on ending up being disappointed."
>
> —James Cecil

Chapter 2

The first part of any plan is to identify your current status. As an initial step, I recommend that you construct a *net worth statement,* also known as a *balance sheet,* similar to Figure 2-1. On a sheet of paper, draw a line down the middle. Head the left column *assets* and the right column *liabilities*. In the lower right-hand corner put today's date.

A net worth statement, also referred to as a statement of financial condition, can be thought of as a snapshot of your financial condition on any given date. *Assets* is financial jargon for those items you own. Take an inventory of all your assets and write down their value as of today.

Balance Sheet/Net Worth Statement

ASSETS		LIABILITIES	
LIQUID ASSETS		CURRENT BILLS	
Cash & Checking Accounts	_____	Household Bills	_____
Savings Accounts		Credit Cards	_____
Money Funds		Other	_____
CDs		Total Current Bills	_____
Cash Value Insurance	_____	LOANS PAYABLE	
Savings Bonds		Auto(s)	_____
Total Liquid Assets	_____	Bank Loans	_____
MARKETABLE INVESTMENTS		Installment Loans	_____
Common Stocks		Personal Loans	_____
Mutual Funds		Other	_____
Bonds		Total Loans Payable	_____
Total Marketable	_____	MORTGAGES PAYABLE	
NON-MARKETABLE ASSETS		Home Residence	_____
Business Interests		Other	_____
Other		Total Mortgages Payable	_____
Total Non-marketable	_____	TOTAL LIABILITIES	_____
PERSONAL PROPERTY			
Residence			
Other Property		NET WORTH	_____
Total Property	_____		
DEFERRED ASSETS		Date: _____	
IRAs			
401(k)/403(b)			
Other Pension Plans			
Total Deferred	_____		
OTHER PERSONAL ASSETS			
Autos			
Jewelry			
Collections/Hobbies			
Furnishings			
Other			
Total Personal Assets	_____		
TOTAL ASSETS	_____		

Figure 2-1

It might help to categorize your assets as liquid, marketable, nonmarketable, personal property, deferred, and other.

Liquid assets identify the current value of your cash equivalents, such as money market values. *Marketable* investments are so named because their value changes with market conditions. Let's say that as of today, ten shares of XYZ stock at $10 calculates to a current value of $100. One hundred shares of a mutual fund with a net asset value of $20 equates to $2,000. If the market goes up 10% in a period, the above valuations would rise to $11 and $110, and $22 and $2,200, respectively.

An example of a *nonmarketable* asset is a holding not priced in the financial section of the newspaper, such as a privately held business or perhaps a partnership interest. Its valuation has to be estimated based on a reasonable appraisal of worth. For most people personal property consists of the value of their personal home/residence. Again, you need to estimate what net value you could expect if you sold your home or second residence.

I like to refer to *deferred* assets as retirement assets. Include all tax-deferred retirement accounts, including IRAs, 401(k)s, SEPs, etc. The final categorization includes all personal items. For analytical purposes, I tend to deemphasize these values, which are dominated by nonliquid, depreciating items such as automobiles.

Once you have inventoried all your ownership asset holdings, it is a simple matter to do a tally to arrive at *total assets*.

Next, move across the sheet of paper to the *liability* column, or what you owe. It is a simple process to identify what it would take to completely satisfy any of these obligations, be it a credit card balance, auto note, or mortgage balance. Record on your statement current debt balances and add them together to get *total liabilities*.

Calculating your net worth is now a matter of simple arithmetic. The total of your assets minus the total of your liabilities equals your *net worth*. The net worth figure is basic to personal financial analysis and is the prime measure of wealth.

The net worth calculation also is a starting point for estate planning. Net worth represents your living estate. To find your death estate, add life insurance. In retirement planning parlance, I like to refer to net worth as the nest egg.

A net worth statement is a freeze-frame of your financial condition, accounting for both assets and debts and yielding a figure representing the difference. Put simply:

WHAT YOU OWN − WHAT YOU OWE = WHAT YOU'RE WORTH

As I mentioned, the net worth statement is also known as the balance sheet. Think in terms of the scales of justice, where both sides are in balance. The asset side of the ledger is balanced against the sum of liabilities plus net worth. Say, for example, total assets equal 100 and total liabilities equal 50. Net worth then computes to 50, providing balance on both sides of the ledger of 100.

In a business the net worth figure is referred to as a *book value* for valuation purposes. Book value is taken into account in any financial analysis to determine the wisdom of buying stock in a company or valuing a business for sale. As individuals, we submit our financial condition to analysis whenever we apply for credit, a loan, or a mortgage.

The net worth figure is critical in a personal finance analysis because it provides a clear measurement of financial wealth, a quick read on your financial condition, and a means to keep score and measure progress.

One's net worth is often subject to age and stage in the life cycle. I've identified three primary stages.

ACCUMULATION STAGE—AGES 25 OR 30 TO 40 OR 45

This first stage offers the initial steps toward building positive wealth. Perhaps a down payment is made on a first house at the same time as participation in a retirement plan begins. This period is likely to correspond to a heavy debt load, with a high ratio of debts to assets. It is important to get off to a good start with savings and investments to receive the tremendous benefit of compound growth through the coming decades.

ACCELERATION STAGE—AGES 40 OR 45 TO 60 OR 65

During this time frame, one is likely to experience the greatest growth in wealth. Financial condition is enhanced by taking advantage of the benefits to be derived from the momentum of a higher income and the ability to build an investment portfolio. Add to these the opportunities of compound growth, a substantial increase in home equity—even a mortgage payoff—a healthy balance in a tax-deferred retirement plan, and possibly an inheritance. Establishing a healthy nest egg during this period is crucial to assuring a financially secure retirement.

PRESERVATION STAGE—AGES 55 OR 60 TO 75 OR 85+

This stage corresponds to the postretirement period, and it might last 25 years or more. In the transition to this stage, wage income often has stopped and the retiree is focused on receiving supplemental income from investment assets. The financial planning emphasis is likely to be on protecting capital from the impact of inflation, market drops, and taxation. Estate planning becomes a central issue during this stage.

Construction of a personal net worth statement is a mandatory first step in the financial planning process. Tremendous value can be found from undertaking this simple procedure. I encourage you, as CFO of You, Inc., to take the time now to put pencil to paper, inventory your assets, and compile a list of debt balances.

Make sure to put the current date on your statement, and plan to update your net worth on an annual basis—at minimum. Many wise planners calculate their net worth at the start of each new year as they gather their tax information. You'd better believe they compare their current financial statements with the previous year's net worth, eager to document that this new scorecard shows progress and growth.

Compiling a net worth statement should be a wake-up call to address your overall financial planning. It facilitates analysis, forces you to accept the reality of your financial condition, and prods you to put your financial house in order.

Interpreting your net worth statement is a starting point for your financial planning. One simple exercise is to note the estimated average annual return of each item on the asset side and the cost of debt (interest) on the liability side. Ideally, you would like to see the larger percentage figures on the asset side and lower numbers on the debt side. Practically speaking, however, your cost of money is likely to be higher than a given investment return. As CFO, you would manage your finances to attempt to earn the highest feasible returns on your assets as you lower your debt load and the cost of borrowed funds. Those assets posting weaker returns, as well as expensive debt items, should be highlighted for further analysis and action in your quest to improve your overall financial condition.

GET A HANDLE ON DEBT

Conduct a debt analysis so you can answer the following planning questions. How much total debt are you carrying? What is the monthly cash flow burden? What types of loans do you have (tax deductible, mortgage or home equity loan, secured installments, or revolving credit)? What rate of interest are you paying? What percentage of your take-home pay is consumed by debt expense?

Debt Analysis

Type of Debt	% Rate	Date Paid In Full	Monthly Payment $	Current Balance $
		Totals		

Figure 2-2

The way you handle your debt load plays a major role in your financial success. A sign of a healthy balance sheet and a goal to work for is a low percentage of debts to assets. Every dollar you reduce in debt adds a dollar to your net worth and makes you stronger financially.

Perhaps the best investment one can make is to wipe out credit card debt. With rates of 16% to 22% that border on loansharking, the easy-money, plastic problem is choking too many already financially distressed individuals. If you carry a $2,500 credit card balance with a typical interest rate of 18% and pay only the monthly minimum, it will take you more than 20 years to pay off the balance at a total nondeductible interest cost of $3,366. Your best strategy is to pay off balances in full each month. Failing that discipline, seriously consider cutting up the plastic.

THREE STRATEGIES TO IMPROVE FINANCIAL CONDITION

As CFO of your personal enterprise, you have a job that demands continuous improvement of your financial position. Employ the same three-pronged strategic approach that financial executives use.

1. Work to improve the performance return on your assets. Seek to manage your investment portfolio for optimum returns.
2. Transfer income in excess of expenditures from the income statement and decide on the best way to accumulate appreciating assets (AAA) so you can invest them to enhance your financial condition. Remember, the principle of AAA is to build wealth.
3. Continually analyze your debt structure and employ careful use of debt. Pay down debt whenever possible.

Nest Egg Building	
Assets (Own)	Debts (Owe)
1. ↑ROI %	3. ↓Debt
2. ↑AAA	*Improve Net Worth*

Figure 2-3

INCOME STATEMENT

Another essential personal financial document is the income statement (Figure 2-4, next page). It complements your net worth statement by giving a different perspective on your financial condition. Unlike the net worth statement that measures your worth as of a given day, an income statement charts cash inflows and outflows over a calendar year.

If the net worth statement represents a snapshot of your financial condition, the income statement is like a motion picture. An individual's 12-month calendar year corresponds to the fiscal or tax year of a business. At the top of this statement write the year you are measuring.

Income Statement

For Year Ending _____

1. Revenues (Income)
    Salaries (W2)   _____
    Investments   _____
    Other   _____
      Total Income   _____

2. Expenses (Outgoing)
    Ordinary Living Expenses   _____
    Fixed Obligations & Expenses   _____
    Insurance Premiums   _____
    Taxes (Fed., St., S/S, R.E.)   _____
      Total Expenses   _____

Total Income − Expenses = Net Income**
**Balance is available for investments and savings

3. Annual Savings Components
    401(k)/403(b)   _____
    IRAs   _____
    Other   _____
      Total Savings   _____

Figure 2-4

An income statement is the same analytical tool on which any profit or nonprofit business places considerable emphasis. Constructing your income statement involves gathering the following information:

- most recent tax return
- checkbook register of last year's expenditures
- copy of year-end pay stubs
- annual income amounts from all other sources
- insurance policies with premium charges

The top section identifies the income or, in business terms, *revenue* that flowed in during the past year. List here all the income that passed through your hands in the last 12 months. For most individuals in the preretirement years, the primary source of income is derived from employment and is found on a W-2 form. In retirement, income usually comes in the form of pensions, Social Security, and investment income.

The middle section pinpoints the outgo or expense items for the year. A common question from individuals looking at their final earnings is:

"WHERE IN THE WORLD DID ALL THAT MONEY GO?"

> "More people should learn to tell their dollars where to go instead of asking them where they went."
>
> —Roger W. Babson

All businesses, as well as serious planners, need to get a handle on where the money is spent. To complete this task, I advise you to start from the bottom of the list and work up.

TAXES—If you want to learn where a large portion of your income is expended, look first to your tax returns.

- ♦ FEDERAL TAXES—Take this figure directly from your federal income tax return.
- ♦ STATE TAXES—This figure can be taken directly from your state tax return.
- ♦ REAL ESTATE TAXES—This significant expense is found on your annual tax bill. If you itemize, it can be picked up from Schedule A of your 1040.
- ♦ FICA (payroll taxes)—Commonly referred to as Social Security taxes, this sum appears on your W-2.

INSURANCE—The insurance premiums you pay for your protection (risk management) include life, health, disability, auto, home, long-term care, umbrella liability, etc., and add up to a significant outlay of money. You can ascertain how much protection you are purchasing by tallying your premium notices and reviewing your checking account registers. Perhaps some of these expense items are deductions from paychecks or are included in mortgage payments. Tabulate these figures on an annualized basis.

FIXED OBLIGATIONS AND EXPENSES—Expenditures that remain relatively the same from month to month are referred to as fixed. Prime examples of this large expense category include monthly mortgage, second mortgage, rent, and car payments. You might also have a set utility budget plan or other consistent monthly payment such as alimony, child support, or repayment of an education loan.

ORDINARY LIVING EXPENSES—This is a catchall for all other living expenses you incur throughout the year. If you are budget-conscious, this figure includes the most fat and deserves close scrutiny for reducing outgo. Unlike fixed expenses, many living expenses are variable in nature. For instance, utilities, home maintenance, entertainment, and clothing expenses may vary markedly from month to month, making the task of pinpointing total expenses difficult. To trace this category, break it down over a one-month period and multiply by 12. Sometimes you can work backward by filling in all other expenditures, including the money you put toward savings. Your ordinary living expenses can be imputed by subtracting your documented outgo from your income.

The third section of the income statement tells the story. The difference between inflows and outflows equals net income. In business jargon, the net income is referred to as the bottom line and is looked on as the measure of success or failure. If net is positive, the business has a profit and is operating in the black.

Having a positive bottom line is just as important to an individual. If income exceeds outgo, you are living within your means. Surplus dollars are available for savings and investment purposes. This sum can be converted into an asset in your drive to build your net worth.

> "If you're only making ends meet, you're running in circles."
> —Art Buck

I like to have clients think of their annual savings as a cost/expense item. Add to this figure new money you have saved over the course of the year. Identify, for example, your annual IRA contributions and retirement savings plan additions.

Analyze your completed income statement as a CFO would, monitoring and managing your financial ins and outs over the year. As you attempt to improve your bottom line, you face the same challenges as General Electric's CFO. Only the scale is different.

There are three basic strategies you can employ:

1. Increase income. GE could raise prices or attempt to sell more products or services. Both moves would increase their revenues. Individuals could push for a promotion with higher pay, work harder to derive higher compensation, or take a second job.
2. Decrease outgo. GE could look to cut costs by reducing expenses, increasing productivity, or paying less for raw materials and supplies. Individuals could try first to reduce discretionary expenses, then look to other opportunities to reduce outflows, especially taxes.

3. Strive for a combination of more income, less outgo. This two-pronged attack is the most beneficial strategy for both companies and individuals. Every dollar that can be added to income or reduced from outgo will flow directly to the bottom line.

On a personal finance level you need to quantify in dollars your desired lifestyle. Income is a less significant factor, because the cost of lifestyle expenditures drives decision making. Most of us have more wants than the income to provide for them. This creates the challenge of deciding which wants have priority. No one can hope to enjoy real independence unless expenditures are kept well within the limits of income. Do you want short-term gratification or long-term financial security?

"Most people look on budgeting as a nervous breakdown on paper."
—Unknown

Think in terms of a *spending plan* instead of a budget. A properly structured spending plan trims fat but allows you to have what you really want while you enjoy the peace of mind that comes from knowing you are achieving your financial goals.

NET WORTH AND INCOME STATEMENTS COMPARED

The early 1980s movie *Country* portrayed the struggles of a modern-day Iowa farm family. I was struck by the way the movie's theme illustrated the relationship between the net worth and income statements.

A local banker informed the farmer, played by actor Sam Sheppard, that he had a high net worth based on the market value of his farmland. Because of that perceived financial strength, money was lent. In fact, the assumption of debt was encouraged, and the farmer was given loans so he could plant his land "fence post to fence post." From an income standpoint, however, the farmer soon found himself operating at a loss. His outgo for fuel, fertilizer, loan interest, etc., exceeded his revenues because of low farm commodity prices. It cost $2.20 a bushel to produce corn that yielded a depressed $2 per bushel when sold.

In the movie, land prices fell as a direct result of these crop revenue losses. The banker became anxious as his customer's net worth (collateral) rapidly declined. The farmer was forced to liquidate the farm (sell off the assets and turn them into cash) to meet his bank debt. The drama culminated as family members, including the farm wife, played by actress Jessica Lange, stood by watching their home and livelihood auctioned at distressed prices. From a net worth standpoint the farmer had been considered wealthy because of the value of his land. But when that land no longer generated a profit, its value was driven down, throwing him into a severe financial reversal.

Farmers, ranchers, and small business owners share the plight of having their wealth locked up in illiquid assets such as real estate, inventory, and receivables. Though they might appear wealthy on paper, they face hardship unless those assets are capable of producing sustainable cash flow and income levels.

It's not how much you make, but how you manage debt and allocate the income you have that determines your net worth. Earmark a generous portion of your earned income for the purchase of investments that appreciate in value.

Company founder and multimillionaire Dick Heckmann contends that the way to wealth is through entrepreneurship. In a *Success* magazine profile on personal finance, Heckmann offers his belief that "wealth is never created by income. It's created by capital gains. If you can't let your profits run untaxed, you lose a huge compounding advantage. As a broker or a doctor or a lawyer, you are essentially paid by the hour. If you stop going to the office, you stop making money. The only way to wealth is to be an entrepreneur."

My favorite motivational speaker, Jim Rohn, observes that profits are better than wages. From wages you support a life, with profits you accumulate a fortune.

THE IMPORTANCE OF SAVINGS

Economically speaking, savings are income that's not spent. Accumulating savings is a prudent necessity if you are to reach your financial goals, and its importance cannot be overemphasized in building wealth, planning for retirement, or funding an education.

"We all make mistakes in life, but saving money is never one of them."
—Thomas A. Edison

Financial planners routinely advise individuals to save 10% of their income. If this target is met in a disciplined fashion throughout one's working life, most goals, including a financially secure retirement, will be achieved.

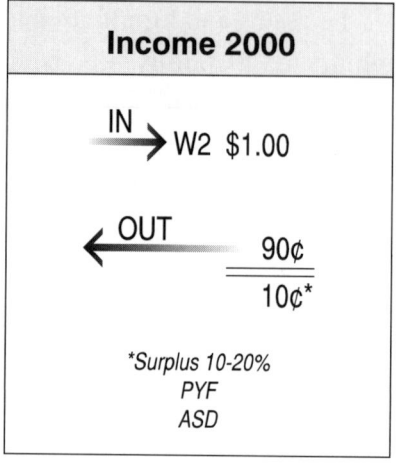

Figure 2-5

> "A major problem these days is how to save money for your children's college education while you're still paying for your own."
> —Anonymous

In many instances, it is reasonable to target a savings rate in the range of 10% to 25% of gross pay. Substantial capital put aside regularly can provide handsomely for the future. The real key to wealth accumulation is compounded savings. According to *The Wealthy Barber,* "Wealth beyond your wildest dreams is possible if you follow the golden rule: Invest 10% of all you make for long-term growth. If you follow that one simple guideline, some day you'll be very rich."

It is crucial to make a systematic savings program the foundation of your long-term wealth-building effort. As fundamental as saving is to financial success, it is not universally practiced. Failure to take this basic step can doom most planning efforts.

> "Wealth is largely a result of habit."
> —John Jacob Astor

People fail to save for a host of reasons, chief among them procrastination. What is called for is a sense of urgency and a saving mindset that recognizes the importance of diligent, regular saving.

SAVINGS-FIRST APPROACH

PYF is a helpful acronym for "pay yourself first." It suggests a saving mindset. Simply put, PYF means that when you allocate your income, you place the highest priority on saving. Adhering to PYF, you would channel X% of each dollar into a savings program before meting out funds for your other obligations. PYF automatically regulates your spending without requiring you to draw up a formal budget.

According to surveys, PYF is contrary to the spending habits of most Americans, who admit to saving only "whatever is left over." However, most of us place demands on our income that make it unlikely to have surplus funds at the end of the month. Paying yourself *last*—or PYL—awards the lowest priority to your savings dollars.

We know that if we fail to meet our debt obligations, we must be prepared to lose our car and even our home. If we do not meet our tax liability, we conceivably face penalties or jail time. If we don't pay our insurance premiums on time, we lose our protective coverage.

In the same way, if we do not implement a PYF program, we severely jeopardize our dream of financial independence. Savings should be considered a real cost and a budgeted obligation.

PYF, if exercised conscientiously, programs us to save even before we meet the mortgage payment. To aid in the process of PYF, I like to add discipline. The secret of financial independence is not brilliance, luck, or some complicated strategy, but rather a common sense discipline to save a part of all you earn and put it to work for you. Can you imagine how many people would be in a tax mess if payroll and FICA taxes were not automatically withheld from each paycheck?

To keep your resolution from flagging, put your savings program on automatic pilot using another acronym: ASD.

> A = Automatically deducted from paycheck or debited from checking account.
> S = Systematically accomplished on a regular basis, each paycheck or every month.
> D = Disciplined saving, putting some teeth into the PYF philosophy.

"A person who can invest systematically will accumulate more money in the long run than the person who writes a check when they have the money. It imposes a discipline that most investors are unable to impose themselves."

—Steve Norwitz, T. Rowe Price

Saving happens with a systematic program. If you were to count on your memory to write a check once a month to a fund company or a bank, you might forget—or come up with excuses for delaying or not writing it.

A companion benefit to systematic investing is *dollar-cost averaging*. Systematic investing reduces the cost of investing. You buy a set dollar amount of shares, say $100 a month. When prices are high, your $100 buys fewer shares. When prices are low, your $100 buys more shares. Studies show that over the long run you pay less for the same number of shares by dollar-cost averaging than by investing lump sums. This method also helps insulate you from emotional investing.

Signing up for an automatic investment program is an easy, guaranteed way to increase savings and maximize investments. If you don't see the money, you won't miss it.

Computer technology offers us the capability to pay many of our bills directly from our checking accounts. Take advantage of this convenient feature to manage your budget and to save and build your investment portfolio. Your financial institution will arrange to debit your checking account for bills and automatically funnel dollars into savings vehicles, including IRAs.

One common sense method to increase your nest egg is simply to boost your rate of saving. Instead of saving 10% of income, strive to save an additional 5%, a 50% increase. The rate of investing is often more crucial than the rate of return.

Following are some examples of how you can use an autopilot saving method.

- ♦ Contribute the maximum to 401(k)s or 403(b)s through an employer-sponsored payroll deduction.
- ♦ Contribute to IRAs with a monthly debit from a checking account ($166.67 per month equals $2,000 per year).
- ♦ Use mutual fund programs where you set up an automatic monthly debit from a checking account to purchase shares.
- ♦ Take advantage of automatic company payroll deductions for employee stock purchases.

A strategy is to build your investments and help your assets grow by adding discipline. Several methods are available to help force you into achieving this goal.

If you own stocks that offer automatic reinvestment of dividends, I encourage you to participate. More than 1,000 stocks now have a DRIP (dividend reinvestment plan) feature. Usually you can make optional cash payments that allow you to accumulate more shares without paying brokerage commissions.

An advantage of mutual funds is the ability to have all distributions, dividends, and capital gains distributions automatically purchase and accumulate additional shares.

Life insurance policies sometimes are sold on the basis of their forced savings element. Whole life policies accumulate a modest investment (cash value) interest that increases the asset side of your balance sheet.

Real estate, especially home ownership financed with a mortgage, also is a form of forced savings. Each monthly payment contains both a principal and interest component. Reducing the principal amount owed in this systematic manner, along with asset appreciation, increases your equity or ownership position, thereby building your net worth.

LONG-TERM WEALTH CREATION

You can be successful financially as measured by a million-dollar net worth even if you are not the recipient of high compensation, the holder of an advanced degree, the beneficiary of a substantial inheritance, or someone who was born clutching a silver spoon.

Financial planning, coupled with discipline, patience, thriftiness, and the compounding of assets, is the great equalizer.

In the book I referred to earlier in this chapter, *The Millionaire Next Door,* authors Stanley and Danko dwell heavily on the relationship between income and net worth. They refer to high income/low net worth individuals as UAWs, or under-accumulators of wealth.

Many people, I find, are curious about their financial position in comparison to others of the same age and income level. Stanley and Danko offer a quick method for calculating whether one is on track in accumulating wealth.

Expected net worth is equal to one-tenth your age times total annual income. A 50-year-old with an annual income of $100,000 should have a net worth of $500,000 ($\frac{1}{10}$ x 50 x $100,000). To be well positioned in your wealth building, your net worth should be approximately double the expected figure. In this example, net worth ought to be a million dollars ($500,000 x 2 = $1 million).

If your goal is to become financially independent, "your plan should be to sacrifice high consumption today for financial independence tomorrow." Listen to multimillionaire investor Jim Rogers, who—in his book *Investment Biker*—discusses his propensity for putting his money to work in the market when he was a young man in his twenties, rather than spending it. "I was convinced, and I still am, that every dollar a young man saves, properly invested, will return him twenty over the course of his life."

According to the authors of *The Millionaire Next Door,* the following traits describe those who demonstrate financial success. This list of traits reinforces the points I make in this chapter.

It should come as no surprise that most millionaires:
- use a pay-yourself-first (PYF) strategy
- operate on a budget
- invest a minimum of 15% of their income before they pay any other bills
- are goal oriented
- spend a lot of time planning their financial future
- take investment management seriously
- are masters at minimizing their income taxes

If you aren't wealthy, examine your lifestyle. Remember, you aren't what you drive.

THE EXTRAORDINARY POWER OF MONEY

Without a doubt, the best aid one can have in pursuit of financial success is to harness the tremendous power of compound growth. Compounding adds wind to your investment sail and provides the horsepower that drives your savings engine, thereby enabling you to reach your goal. An appreciation of the power of compound growth encourages the saving and investment efforts crucial to financial success.

Time truly is money, and the value of time forms the principle of the time value of money. All financial planning is heavily influenced by the time value of money. If you are to pursue the financial planning goals of a secure retirement or funded education, take the advice of Vanguard's

Chairman John Bogle. He advises, "Give yourself the benefit of all the time you can possibly afford."

The genius Einstein, when asked what was the most amazing thing available to mankind, purportedly said, "compound growth." It doesn't take a genius to understand that money has the ability to grow. To comprehend the time value of money is to understand what is meant by compound growth or compound interest. Although frequently referred to as magic or a miracle, compounding is simply the ability to *earn interest on your interest*.

Assume you start out with an initial principal sum of $1,000. If you earn simple interest of 8% annually, at the end of year one your account has accumulated $80 of interest to add to your $1,000 of initial principal—for a total of $1,080. If you allow this sum to grow, you start the second year with $1,080. If you earn 8%, your interest at the end of year two is $86.40, for a total of $1,166.40. The point here, of course, is that the second year interest figure is larger because you earned interest on the interest ($80 x .08 = $6.40) as well as on the original principal.

If you allow the original $1,000 to grow, or *compound*, over a period of nine years at 8%, your total interest earned would equal the initial principal—virtually doubling your money. Over long periods of time, the interest contributions come to dwarf the original principal. It might help to visualize this snowballing effect with each passing year. The sum grows at a greater speed over time, gaining momentum with each passing year.

The extraordinary power of compounding underscores the value of *time*. While compounding a problem makes things worse, compounding *interest* makes you wealthy.

JUST HOW POWERFUL IS THE EFFECT OF COMPOUND GROWTH?

It is commonly recounted in American history books that in 1626 some shrewd Dutch merchants purchased the island of Manhattan from Native Americans for $24 in trinkets. This event has not gone down as an evenhanded real estate transaction; yet we gain a different perspective by putting it in the context of the time value of money. If the recipients of this $24 had opened a Golden Savers Account at the local branch of the Pilgrim Bank and let it compound undisturbed at 6% for 374 years until the year 2000 and the new millennium, their account would be valued at an astonishing $64 billion. It is estimated this sum would be sufficient to buy back Manhattan today with all its improved real estate in place. Not a bad deal after all, when the time value of money is taken into account.

Suppose we expand upon the previous example in which $1,000 grows to $2,000 over a nine-year period, assuming an 8% annual return. Had our ancestors at Plymouth Rock the means and foresight to ante up $1,000 in 1620 and place it in a trust to compound untouched at the same 8% for 400 years, its value would grow to an amazing $2.3 trillion. That's enough to put a serious dent in our national debt. We could really have a Thanksgiving celebration in the year 2020.

THE RULE OF 72

A handy formula that demonstrates the power of compound growth is the Rule of 72, which simply approximates how long it will take you to double your money using different rates of return. Best-selling personal finance author Venita VanCaspel is widely credited with popularizing this rule in her book *Money Dynamics for the 1980s*.

The number 72 divided by the return gives you the approximate number of years it will take to double your money. For example, 72 ÷ 8% = 9 years. Knowing the rule of 72 provides you with a speedy answer to the question of how long it would take to double your initial $1,000 investment at an 8% return: 72 ÷ 8% = 9 years.

The Time Value of Money (TVM) involves basically three planning variables:

1. Initial dollar amount	$ PV (present value)
or	
Future dollar amount	$ FV (future value)
2. Rate of return	% i (interest rate as %)
3. Time periods	N (number of years or compounding periods)

Referring to our previous example:

PV	9 years (N)	=	FV
$1,000	8%	=	$2,000

$2,000 is the compounded result of $1,000 left to grow at an 8% return over 9 years
$1,000 is the present value of $2,000 discounted at 8% over 9 years

If you know three of the four variables, you can determine the unknown by using a financial calculator, time value tables, or—the best option—a personal finance software package. If you change any of the variables, the results change dramatically. An additional time value of money calculation deals with the use of a set sum of equal annual installments, as is the case of a $2,000 annual IRA investment (future value of annuity).

An important part of financial planning involves the use of time-value-of-money calculations to make projections, test what-if assumptions, calculate needs, and construct financial planning models. Billionaire Warren Buffett and his less visible right-hand man, Charlie Munger, are on record as sharing a deep appreciation for the awesome power of compounding. Munger is reported to always have a compound rate-of-return table handy. He says, "Understanding both the power of compound return and the difficulty of getting it is the heart and soul of understanding a lot of things."

When Asia's richest businessman, LeeShaw Kee, was asked his secret to success, he replied, "Trust in the magic of compounding."

MEET OSEOLA MCCARTY, SAVER EXTRAORDINAIRE

Oseola is a remarkable woman, eking out a living over some 70 years in the impoverished Mississippi Delta.

She labored those many years as a self-described washerwoman, earning about $9,000 in her best year. For her toils, she is collecting the minimum monthly Social Security check.

Her tale and life came to the attention of the public after she shocked the University of Southern Mississippi with a gift of $150,000. She directed that this substantial gift be used to provide scholarships for African-American students. How did this uneducated woman, who had to leave school after the sixth grade to care for a sick aunt, come to make such a substantial gift? By saving a little money over a long period of time. When asked her secret, she replied, "Compounding interest."

"Compounding 'tis the stone that will turn all your lead into gold."
—Benjamin Franklin

RALPH AND ALICE

Follow the story of twins Ralph and Alice, fortunate beneficiaries of $100,000 left to each of them by their wealthy great-aunt Avis. Avis had stipulated this substantial inheritance was not to be touched in any way until these young people reached age 65. Since they were 29 at the time, they were looking at a 36-year time frame for this sum to grow and compound.

Avis understood the time value of money (TVM) and credited the power of compound growth with allowing her to amass her fortune. While full of wit and wisdom, Avis was frugal. Alice remembers her aunt telling everyone at a wedding shower about the Rule of 72, and going on to describe how the surest and fastest way to double your money was to take the bill you had ready to purchase some frivolous item with, fold it over once, and return it to your pocketbook.

> "Those who are thrifty will grow wealthy,
> and those who are spendthrift will become poor."
> —John Templeton

The terms of Avis's trust stipulated that each beneficiary was solely responsible for the investment management of their $100,000 and could invest it in any responsible manner they saw fit.

As you can see, two out of three time-value-of-money variables were identical in this case; namely, the $100,000 present value and the time of 36 years. The ending value for each of these twins was a product of Ralph's and Alice's respective investment acumen.

Let's look at Ralph's situation first. Ralph invested according to the latest hot tips, took counsel from his bowling buddies, and was persuaded to employ market timing. For all his activity he managed to earn an average 6% compounded annual return over the 36-year period.

	PV		FV
Ralph	$100,000	6% ROI	$814,725
	Age 29	36 years	Age 65

Ralph's final tally is about what can be expected from his approach, and the $814,725 he ended up with is a respectable amount. He notes with pride that he had an eightfold return.

Alice is the more practical twin. She made serious money management choices to have her $100,000 grow to the highest figure over the long term, assuming reasonable risk. She learned from the likes of investment legend Philip Carret, who advised her to stay fully invested in the stock market at all times because "investing genius consists of one part patience and one part compound interest."

This counsel paid off handsomely for Alice, who was able to realize a 12% annualized compound rate of return to feather her retirement nest egg. Alice's 12% average result is in line with what patient, long-term investors could have expected over the period of 36 years in a well-diversified stock mutual fund portfolio. The fact is that most investors achieve results closer to the 6% ROI turned in by her brother.

	PV		FV
Alice	$100,000	12% ROI	$5,913,557
	Age 29	36 years	Age 65

Hooray for Alice. Her end result is an astounding $5,913,557, dwarfing her brother's result by more than $5 million. Alice is a multimillionaire, whereas Ralph, though far from poor, still hasn't quite reached that magic million-dollar mark.

Aunt Avis's early money lessons paid off well. Alice points out that her acquired stake grew 59 times, and that compound interest accounted for 98% of her final figure.

Alice is busy making plans with her own estate to similarly endow her 10 grandchildren and share this same wealth-building secret. Grandma Alice is in the enviable financial position of leaving a substantial sum to her church and charities and still enjoying the same financial security as Ralph.

Now an elderly retiree, grandpa Ralph is eager to instill into the minds of his own beloved grandchildren his hard-won knowledge on the magical power of compound growth.

Ralph reminds me of another grandfather, one who attended a seminar at which I illustrated the importance of time and starting early to build wealth. He told me he was so excited that he wanted to visit his grandchildren right away and wake them up to this "wealth-building secret." After all, he said, "Now that I finally learned how to grow a million, I just don't have the time."

FRED AND ETHEL

Newlyweds Fred and Ethel set out to build a retirement nest egg of $2 million by the time they reach age 65, 40 years away.

HERE'S THE FORMULA TO REACH THEIR GOAL

STEP 1. Put aside $100 each and every month in a disciplined, consistent fashion.

We can each look into our own spending habits and discover where we foolishly consume $100 a month, or, if you prefer, $3.33 a day. Fred and Ethel have mutually decided to kick their smoking habit and use the savings to fuel their goal. Fred points out this change in habit could help them live long enough to let them actually have retirement years. If Fred and Ethel put away $100 every month, that amounts to $1,200 annually. A couple who puts aside $200 a month saves $2,400 a year.

STEP 2. A healthy return on this money is needed to reach the lofty goal of $2 million. Fred and Ethel will need to average a 12% annual return.

The truth is that this rate of return is not easy to achieve. There is no easy way to accumulate a million dollars. But a 12% return is feasible and attainable for those long-term investors willing to accept reasonable risk. It should be pointed out that good quality stocks over the last 40 years have been able to post returns in the neighborhood of 12% when both dividends and capital gains are reinvested, as is the case with a mutual fund. The operative words to remember are *quality, long-term,* and *average*.

Ethel decides to use an S&P 500 index fund for her investment vehicle and persuades Fred to do the same. This passive (not actively managed) mutual fund will closely match the performance of the stock market. The Standard & Poor's 500 represents an unmanaged index of the 500 largest publicly traded domestic stocks—largest in terms of their market capitalization. The advantages of this investment choice include a pure stock play, broad-based diversification, predictable performance, low costs, and a low turnover that minimizes paying taxes on capital gains.

The Vanguard 500 Stock Index Trust offers these advantages and has a strong relative performance, and as a result has grown rapidly in popularity. In 1997, it is the second largest mutual fund, and it is within reach of being number one.

STEP 3. It is not enough to put away $2,400 per year and attain a 12% return unless it is done over a long-term working life, such as 40 years.

If Fred and Ethel stuffed their savings of $96,000 under their mattress, that's all they would have. But by harnessing the tremendous power of compound growth, they reach their 40-year goal with $2,061,580!

The three variables in this future value of an annuity are:

1. $200 per month, $2,400 per year (annuity)
2. 12 payments over 40 years = 480 payments
3. 12% average return on investment = $2,061,580

Not bad when you consider this investment fodder of $96,000 might otherwise have gone up in smoke.

Fred and Ethel, as a two-income couple, are also concerned with minimizing their tax burden. They wisely decide to contribute their $1,200 annual investments to IRAs. In this way, their future $2 million in investment earnings grow sheltered from current taxation, allowing their 12% average returns to compound at the full pretax rate.

Ethel reads an article about financially successful individuals who always purchase used rather than new cars. Fred and Ethel realize they could employ this method to better manage their capital, and they resolve to purchase high-quality, low-mileage automobiles and maintain them in good condition. They calculate this will lower their car expense by $300 each month.

Their plan calls for channeling this additional $3,600 a year ($144,000 over the next 40 years) into their stock portfolio. Instead of splurging on flashy, depreciating vehicles subject to rust and damage, they will invest more in financial enterprises with the potential to appreciate over time.

How much potential? Consider this: If they can realize the same performance-driven 12% long-term average annual return, Fred and Ethel will accumulate in excess of another $3 million. Fred calculates that the smell of a new car is vastly overrated.

We've all been drawn to chancy, get-rich-quick schemes. Here you see a get-rich-slow plan of action that can actually produce results.

CHAPTER 3
COMMON SENSE INVESTMENT PRINCIPLES

"I believe that successful investing is mainly common sense."
—Sir John Templeton

This chapter reinforces my theme that a common sense approach is urgently needed in all financial matters, especially investing. It is the most valuable attitude one can adopt. But I have observed that common sense in investing is an uncommon trait. Too often, good judgment is clouded by ignorance, greed, and impatience. For many people, common sense investing is another oxymoron.

"Common sense is perhaps the most equally divided, but surely the most underemployed talent in the world."
—Christine Collange

Management of risk can mitigate the pitfalls. In fact, risk management is the most fundamental aspect of common sense investing, and it underlies every one of the common sense points that follow.

NOBODY CARES AS MUCH ABOUT YOUR FINANCIAL HEALTH AS YOU DO

You are the steward of your financial resources. Naturally, you can and should consult with financial experts for guidance. You are also subject to vagaries of the economy beyond your control. However, you bear ultimate responsibility for your financial health in the same way you must take responsibility for maintaining your medical health. Although your doctor will continue to diagnose, prescribe, and perform surgery as needed, for you to maximize your lifelong health requires that you pay attention to key factors, such as diet, lifestyle, and exercise. So it is with personal finance matters. You are at the helm.

Trust your instincts. After all, it is your money. If you are uncomfortable following a product pitch, don't buy. I often hear frustrated investors vent their anger at themselves for going against their gut feelings. A wiser course of action is to develop self-confidence and follow your instincts.

WHEN RECEIVING INVESTMENT ADVICE, ALWAYS CONSIDER THE SOURCE

I continue to be amazed at the number of people who listen to experienced advisors and then act impulsively upon financial advice given to them by novices. I have witnessed foolhardy individuals who purchased investment products on tips from distant acquaintances.

Because it's your money, place your financial self-interest first. When you are being solicited to purchase an investment or insurance product, it is a good idea to ask both the method of compensation and the total amount the salesperson would receive. Be a good and wise consumer of financial services. If there is an agreement or disclosure statement, work to understand what you are buying. Inquire as to what level of service you can expect after your purchase.

THERE IS NO PERFECT INVESTMENT

A popular commercial printer's office displays a large sign behind the sales counter (Figure 3-1).

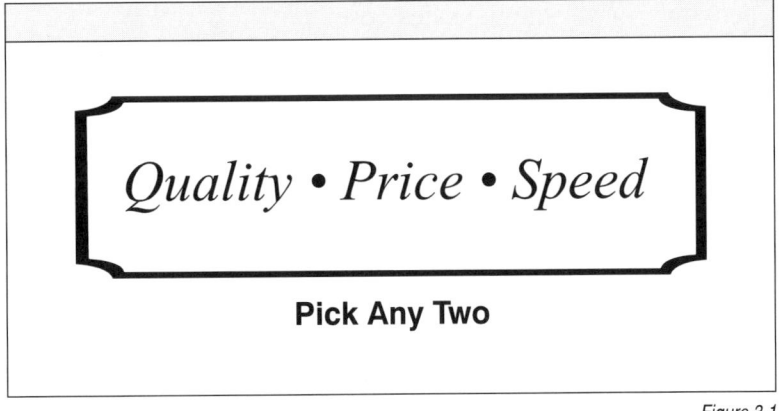

Figure 3-1

Obviously, when it comes to a printing job, you can't have it all. If you choose a high-quality job at a favorable price, expect a normal wait to get your job completed. If you insist on a rock-bottom price and want a rush job, the quality likely will suffer. Should you need the job yesterday and at top quality, expect to pay a premium price. The print shop analogy holds a lesson for investors.

There is no perfect investment, and each choice you make represents a compromise among various considerations. Investors are overwhelmed with the sheer number of investment offerings crowding the marketplace, a condition I refer to as *product pollution*. Thousands of different and often perplexing choices exist. To evaluate a given investment, I like to use a five-point investment matrix.

1. RISK—The most vital distinguishing feature of any investment involves its relative risk. Ask if this investment is considered a conservative or aggressive investment in terms of your potential to lose your principal. What is the magnitude of risk and probability of occurrence?
2. RETURN—Learn what the source of return is from an investment: dividend income, interest, projected capital gains, or some combination. What are the total return range expectations based on historical precedent?
3. TAX—Relative to the return, what is its tax treatment? Will it be taxed as ordinary income or capital gains, or is it treated as tax exempt or tax deferred?
4. LIQUIDITY—Ask how readily accessible the investment is. Would a redemption cause the possibility of loss of principal, trigger negative tax consequences, or impose surrender charges, penalties, or substantial sales costs?
5. MISCELLANEOUS—Is the investment subject to costs in the form of loads, fees, or commissions? Are there specific minimums to meet? Do tie-ins exist with other financial products, such as free check writing, or a higher interest rate?

All investing involves one big compromise. You must balance risk and return with liquidity and tax-sheltering features. Risk versus return forms the ultimate trade-off, while liquidity and tax advantages face off, especially in the retirement area. Be reconciled to the fact that these compromises are fundamental to investing, and choose what is more important to your financial goals.

Investment Characteristics	
Risk	FDIC Insured
Return	20%
Tax Treatment	Tax Free
Liquidity	Free Check Writing
Miscellaneous	No Charges
	Free Gift

Figure 3-2

If a perfect investment existed, it might resemble Figure 3-2: fully guaranteed 20% annual return; FDIC insured; ready access to your money; free check writing privileges; free of all taxes; no fees, loads, or charges of any kind; and offered by a financial institution that throws in a free microwave. Since this combination of features does not exist, I rest my case; there is no perfect investment.

Still, a whole parade of investments have been promoted as *the* perfect investment. Zero coupons, option income funds, single-premium whole life insurance, Ginnie Maes, global bond funds, limited partnerships, government bond funds, the current top-performing growth fund, home ownership, and high-yield bond funds. Through a closer analysis, their warts have now been revealed.

UNDERSTAND TOTAL RETURN

Total return. This oft-quoted term describes the cumulative returns of interest, dividends, and capital gains (or losses). For example, a stock selling for $100 could have a 5% or $5 dividend payout. This same stock could appreciate in value by 10% to $110. If this occurred on an annual basis, the investor in this case would be looking at a total return of 15%: a 5% dividend plus a 10% capital gain.

It is standard for mutual funds to quote their returns in this fashion on an annual basis.

Total return fluctuates, and one year's return should not be expected to be repeated. Total return is all-encompassing and could well be negative for a given period. Say, for example, this same stock or mutual fund with a 5% dividend yield suffers a decline in value of $10: going from $100 to $90. In this instance the total return for that period computes to a minus 5%.

UNDERSTAND AND ASSESS RISK INSIDE AND OUT

By far the most important of the fundamentals of investing is the risk-return trade-off. The risk-return trade-off is the basic investment principle and the framework within which all investment decisions should be made. If investors can manage to remember just one common sense investment principle, it should be this: *The higher the anticipated return, the higher the associated risk.* Even experienced investors sometimes fail to remember—or choose to ignore—this point. For novice investors, an appreciation of this crucial investment tenet is an absolute necessity.

The reverse also holds true: *A lower return or yield carries less risk.* This trade-off, or balance, is an investment law, a given. When a higher return is stated, quoted, promised, or assumed, the investor immediately should recognize a rising risk factor. With the promise of a high return, the investor's defense system should be on alert and common sense brain cells called into action. The investor should say aloud, *"Aha! High return equals high risk."*

Most often, the return part of this equation is given precedence. The message you get from a salesperson, agent, or advertisement is

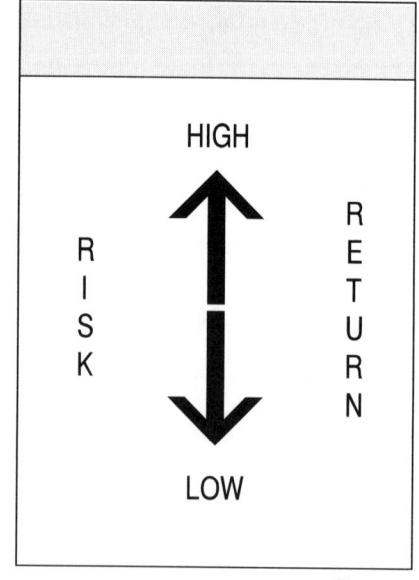

Figure 3-3

likely to dwell more heavily on the return. Investors would be wise to reverse this emphasis and concentrate first on the risk component.

Risk can be defined as the possibility that the return you anticipate will not be realized. I believe the most important aspect of investing is recognition of the risk involved.

My comfort level as an advisor increases when I know the client understands the risks involved. There is nothing wrong with going after the highest available return, provided the investor is making a decision with his or her eyes open to the associated risk.

Ask about the worst-case scenario for a given investment. Listen to your pessimistic impulse about the risk, rather than embracing return expectations that are too optimistic. Know the downside. Disappointment is in store for investors who have been blind to the risk and are surprised when that unanticipated risk inevitably comes into play. They then compound their predicament by acting impulsively and selling at a loss.

ALL INVESTMENTS INVOLVE RISK

Just as there is no such thing as a perfect investment, there is no risk-free investment. For you to assess risk, you need to broadly identify the element of risk carried in a given investment.

Four major categories of risk exist: *Market risk, interest-rate risk, financial risk,* and *purchasing-power risk*.

MARKET RISK—This risk is common to investments in stocks; it results whenever an investment declines in value. The marketplace, through supply and demand machinations, is constantly assigning valuation (pricing). Most individuals recognize that stocks carry risk and can go down in value, and that on occasion they are apt to suffer a loss. Basically, what is occurring is that the marketplace (stock market) is devaluing ownership. An individual stock, industry, or entire market can experience losses at any time or over a prolonged period known as a down market or a bear market. An example of market risk occurred during the October 1987 market meltdown.

INTEREST-RATE RISK—This risk is found in bonds; it is unquestionably one of the least understood forms of risk. All bonds, with the lone exception of U.S. Savings Bonds, lose value during periods of rising interest rates. Even supposedly conservative investments such as U.S. Treasury securities decline in value when interest rates rise. The reverse also holds true—bonds appreciate in value in periods of declining interest rates. The longer the maturity of the bond or bond fund, the greater the loss or gain if sold before maturity. The 1994 market saw the most recent example of this risk. Bond prices dropped as interest rates rose steeply, causing the worst bond market in 50 years.

FINANCIAL RISK—This risk, also known as credit risk, is associated with bonds other than treasury bonds. Corporate, municipal, and so-called high-yield (junk) bonds could run into financial distress and be unable to honor their debt obligation. Bonds can and do default, and higher-yielding bonds carry a proportionately higher risk of financial or credit risk. This is precisely what happened in the junk bond market in the autumn of 1989 and into 1990.

PURCHASING-POWER RISK—A federally insured (FDIC) bank money market account and bank CDs are among the most conservative investments, but they are not risk-free. During periods when the rate of inflation exceeds the rate of yield, investors are losing purchasing power. An example is a bank money market account yielding 2.5% when the general level of inflation is 3%, which happened during 1993. Factor in income taxes, and the negative yield becomes greater.

EXERCISE PATIENCE

Patience is a necessary virtue when it comes to investing. I recall the plight of a medical professional who failed to appreciate the value of patience. Around 1982, the gentleman used a significant amount of money to purchase undeveloped land in Florida. Although he didn't realize it at the time, this was a speculative investment. It wasn't long before he discovered the value of his land was falling dramatically. Panicked, he sold at a distressed price and parked the proceeds in what is perhaps the most conservative investment, a federally insured CD. The CD matured in 1986 during an interim of lower yields, so he looked for an alternative investment. Attracted by the higher yields advertised, he placed this sum into a well-recognized U.S. government bond fund.

The physician was reassured by the fund's reputation, unaware of the risk to principal of bond funds during periods of rapidly rising interest rates. Sure enough, he grew concerned about the steady erosion of his account's value as interest rates turned upward in the first part of 1987. What was particularly galling to him was the fact that during this same period, the fund family's growth fund was soaring, up 30% in a bull market that saw the Dow race from 2000 to 2800 during the first eight months of 1987.

He had considered the growth fund initially, but was dissuaded because it was, after all, a risky stock fund. He opted instead for the bond fund, persuaded by its safety and its 1986 performance. He put off his urge to switch to the hot-performing growth fund until October of 1987. Rotten timing for the hapless investor—the stock market crashed on Black Monday, October 19, 1987. The value of his growth fund tumbled 25%.

At the same time the U.S. government fund actually went up in value as nervous investors flocked to the relative safety of treasury bonds. The very next week, anxious to move once again, he and his concerned wife sought my counsel for the first time.

What had gone wrong? Here was an intelligent individual who over the relatively short span of five years saw his nest egg shrink substantially. He had been in all four asset categories: real estate, cash, bonds, and stocks. But his lack of patience and perspective, his failure to have an objective, and his tendency to chase what was hot at the moment had seriously eroded his capital. All this had happened during a period generally favorable for financial assets.

THINK LONG-TERM

How long should you maintain (hold) a mutual fund investment?

There is no pat answer. It depends on many factors, including personal circumstances. Many investors are apt to switch, a condition that routinely results in negative consequences. The beauty of a mutual fund is that it is a marketable investment, so you can sell or transfer your shares quickly. However, this is often shortsighted and reactionary.

Let me offer the following as a general guideline for a minimum holding period. With a bond fund, plan on holding your shares three to five years. Move closer to the five-year range if your portfolio holds more volatile, longer-term bonds. In a stock fund, I suggest you put blinders on for at least five years, ideally closer to 10 years. When you make an investment in a more aggressive fund, such as a small capitalization stock fund, my counsel is to think in terms of a minimum of 10 years. Allow the portfolio manager time to manage and be successful over at least a couple of economic cycles. That expertise is what you are purchasing.

Americans are accused of wanting instant gratification, and this holds true regarding investment performance. Our tendency is to look at quarterly returns rather than long-term performance. This shortsightedness proves to be a detriment to long-range investment success. Some Japanese real estate investors were once asked about their planned holding period. Their quick answer: 50 years. Contrast this to American limited partnership promoters who promised prospective investors they could hold a property five years and then sell at a fat profit.

Master investor Warren Buffett is on record for purchasing a stock with the notion that if the stock market actually shut down for 10 years, he would not be concerned. He does his homework before he makes an investment, and he gives it time to work.

I cannot recount the many times I have heard investors in mutual funds or stocks say they plan to carefully watch their investment so if it goes down they will immediately get out. This thinking is a recipe for investment failure. If your great idea is to get out the instant values decline, do yourself a favor and don't get in.

Investors ask just as frequently if I would let them know when the market is turning down just before it happens. Sometimes this request is an expected or assumed service. But it is impossible to predict the market with any consistency. Although I have the power to let you know after the fact from a historical standpoint whether the value went up, down, or stayed the same, no professional money manager, a mere mortal, possesses the power to protect you from market losses.

HIGH RETURN = HIGH RISK

The above equation is absolute. It is fact. But too many gullible investors mistakenly believe or are led to believe that lofty returns can be achieved without an equivalently high exposure to risk. If you ever come across a statement that equates low risk with high returns, dismiss the message and the messenger immediately. I cringe when I see books and articles entitled "Wealth Without Risk" and "Risk-Free Investing." One would like to believe these feats are possible, but don't be tempted or misled.

ITEM: A widow aged 60 sought to maximize income from her modest investment portfolio. Her broker placed the largest piece of her money into a high-yielding utility stock with an attractive 14% dividend. He assured her that utility stocks are the most conservative of stock choices.

What she was not told was the reason this particular utility's yield was so high. Public Service of New Hampshire was compensating investors for the great uncertainty of the status of its nuclear facilities. However large the dividend, when it was eventually suspended the loss of income proved painful. Tragically, this woman felt compelled to scale back her standard of living to a sustenance level. In retrospect, her plight builds a case for investors to consider proven utility stock mutual funds, in which diversification and professional management might have cushioned a similar event.

ITEM: An ad in the local paper promoted a $12^{5}/_{8}\%$ subordinated debenture (unsecured bond). The yield, heralded in bold type, compared well to the pale 8% yields offered at the same time for treasury bonds. Further, the offering was for Fort Howard Paper, one of the largest employers in the state of Wisconsin. During an investment talk I was leading in Green Bay, home of Fort Howard Paper, I held up this ad to ask the audience what type of investment was being offered.

My informal poll was met with blank stares and silence. "This is a junk bond investment," I informed them. At that, one angry woman demanded to know how I dared disparage the company.

My response was that I had no comment to make on the company, but this investment was definitely a junk bond offering. "How can you say that?" came her reply.

"It is very simple," I explained. "The high $12^{5}/_{8}\%$ yield compared to yields found in government and other quality debt makes it absolutely clear that my statement is true."

For background, Fort Howard Paper had earlier gone private

(bought back its own stock) in a leveraged buyout (LBO). The company used high-yield debt (junk bonds) to finance this purchase. Saddled with so much debt on its balance sheet, the only way it could attract financing was to pay the higher yields that accompany lower-quality debt instruments. So-called junk bonds carry a rating of B or lower.

When asked if I thought this was a good investment, I replied, "Very possibly, but I would much rather have this holding as part of a diversified portfolio of similar bonds through purchase of a high-yield bond mutual fund."

DIVERSIFY, DIVERSIFY, DIVERSIFY

Do you get the point? Investment master Sir John Templeton has preached to all who would listen, "Diversify, diversify, diversify." Diversification cannot be overemphasized, and in keeping with a common sense theme, it will be revisited throughout this book. Diversification is the proven best defense against risk. Can you be too diversified? I think not.

"To not diversify is to speculate," read the heading on a respected investment letter that recently crossed my desk.

Diversification takes many forms and levels. We are all familiar with the adage about not putting all your eggs in one basket. The opposite of diversification is concentration. Those eggs in that one basket run the risk of all being crushed.

LEVEL #1
DIVERSIFY BY THE QUANTITY OF YOUR HOLDINGS

History offers many examples of the wisdom of investment diversification. In 1986, the 30 large-cap industrial stocks that make up the Dow Jones average posted a composite 22% gain. One of them, IBM, considered at the time to be the bluest of the blue chips, was down 22%. The moral? If during 1986 you owned a weighting of stocks equivalent to the Dow, your IBM holding along with 29 other Dow stocks would have afforded you a very good year. If instead you had chosen to concentrate solely on IBM stock, you would have suffered a loss that year as great as the Dow composite's gain.

LEVEL #2
DIVERSIFY AMONG DIFFERENT INDUSTRY GROUPINGS

Philip Morris had been one of the top-performing stocks over the decade of 1983–1993. More than one investment manager proclaimed it the best stock to own in America. But on April 2, 1993, on a day now known in Wall Street lore as Marlboro Friday, shares dropped 20%. What caused this precipitous decline? Management had announced that to regain market share and compete with lower-priced tobacco products, it was discounting prices on its major cigarette brands.

The market swiftly reacted to the concern that in an era of generic brands, premium pricing for these major brand names would be unsustainable, eroding profit margins and income levels. Interestingly, many other major consumer stocks also declined. The market believed all stocks in name-brand retail consumer goods would suffer the same fate. However, stocks of chemical, cement, auto parts, and semiconductor companies fared better that year. Diversified portfolios weathered the storm.

LEVEL #3
DIVERSIFY AMONG DIFFERING STOCK INVESTMENT STYLES

The 1993 investment year is a textbook example of the virtue of employing an array of stock investment styles. You could categorize stock styles as: *value and growth stocks, large and small or medium-sized stocks, income-oriented (dividend paying) stocks,* and *international stocks.* Investment portfolios concentrated among traditional domestic, large-name growth companies trailed the other styles that year. Investors in Philip Morris and in the pharmaceutical giants such as Merck had been well rewarded over the previous decade. A diversified stock portfolio in 1993 that included quality international, small- and mid-caps, and value and equity income easily posted double-digit returns.

LEVEL #4
DIVERSIFY AMONG DIFFERENT ASSET GROUPINGS

To be truly diversified, one must choose asset groups rather than rely solely on stocks. Include bonds and cash equivalents as well as hard assets such as real estate. If you look back over investment performance tables, you find that in many years bonds zig while stocks zag, and vice versa. Among the four major asset categories of stocks, bonds, cash, and real estate, you find varying winners and losers and rankings over the decades. For example, financial assets such as stocks and bonds were the place to be in the 1980s. Real estate was the clear winner in the 1970s.

BE SKEPTICAL OF EXPERT ADVICE

November 1990 was an ominous time. Dark clouds shrouded the economy, and the prospect of war in the Persian Gulf threatened. Against this backdrop I listened to an economist's analysis of the situation. Her forecast was predicated on what would happen as a result of the Kuwait crisis. She was fairly confident that if a shooting war erupted in the Middle East, the Dow immediately would fall anywhere from 200 to 400 points. Provided the war effort was successful for the West, she felt the stock market would gradually recover. But if we were forced to engage in a ground war, the implications were even bleaker.

As we now know and CNN confirmed minute-to-minute, a shooting war was initiated on January 16, 1991, followed shortly by a ground war. So what happened? The very next day the Dow posted its second largest one-day advance, up 179 points.

The economist was even more confident of her second point. If the hostilities resulted in damage to oil production facilities, we could reasonably expect the price of a barrel of oil to skyrocket from $25 to $40, $50, or even $60, depending on the severity of the disruption of supplies. Who can forget the images of hundreds of oil wells set ablaze and burning out of control in Kuwait? And what about the ecological nightmare that saw millions of barrels of sabotaged oil floating in the Persian Gulf? You might recall that in spite of all this, the price of a barrel of oil actually dropped to $20, its lowest level in some time.

If you solicit expert opinions on the economy's future direction and its impact on the stock and bond markets, you could guarantee one outcome: a complete lack of consensus among those polled.

It has been said that if you assemble a dozen respected economists to give an economic prognosis, you are likely to get 13 different opinions, as well as a chorus of "on the other hand." Now you know why economics, far from being an exact science, is at times called the dismal science.

I read a report in *USA Today* about a class of eighth graders at St. Agnes School in Massachusetts that actually beat the legendary money manager Peter Lynch in a 1994 stock-picking contest. Performance was measured at the end of the calendar year. Although neither group did very well, the 14-year-olds topped the master. St. Agnes turned in a -15.7% to Mr. Lynch's -15.8%. During this same period the S&P market index was up +1.3%.

What are we to conclude? That Peter Lynch has lost his magic? I suspect not. However, there are lessons to be learned from this stock picking exercise:

1. One year is too short a time period. Ask yourself: Who do you want managing your money over the next *decade?*
2. The 10 stocks in the contest represented too small a list. If Lynch had more names he probably would have done better compared to the S&P.
3. Lynch wasn't allowed to actively manage his portfolio. Also, he is a patient investor, willing to stand behind his picks, fully expecting that improvement may not be confined to a turning of the calendar.
4. So-called investment geniuses are not invincible, and even teenagers and amateurs can have the good luck to win in a one-year stock-picking contest.
5. Many similar contests are held from time to time with investment pros pitted against a dog, a cat, or a chimp. At least Lynch lost out to human IQs.

You can always find investment gurus who try to convince you the stock market is due for an imminent rise of 1000 points in the Dow. An equal number are just as certain stocks will head the other way.

It's the same story on the direction of interest rates. I contend no one can consistently predict the future direction of interest rates or the timing and magnitude of change. The champion interest rate predictor is right just 50% of the time. Differences of opinion are what make the markets go round and up and down.

As a devoted viewer of public television's *Wall Street Week* with Louis Rukeyser, I have observed with interest the weekly recap of the Technical Elves Index. This index collects the judgment of 10 qualified market observers on the direction of the stock market over the upcoming six months, giving a thumbs up, thumbs down, or neutral call.

Elves, for the uninitiated, are practitioners of a faith in market investment interpretation known as *technical analysis,* and they are technicians. They look at trends, patterns, and charts to guide their opinions.

Fundamental analysis, which applies to everyone but technicians, represents another camp altogether. Fundamental analysts seem to believe the Elves are just reading tea leaves. You rarely find consensus among Elves; more likely you have just as many thumbs up as down. The result is nearly always a mildly bullish or mildly bearish indicator.

DON'T BUY WHAT YOU DON'T UNDERSTAND

Financial services marketers have been packaging a barrage of new and often exotic product offerings for an investing public that increasingly feels overwhelmed and confused. We have LYONs, CATs, ZEROs, PALs, PIGs, GNMAs, CMOs, FNMAs, PERCs, and ARMs, to name just a few of the ever-expanding list. And to think it all started with CDs.

I find myself drawn to financial advertisements. From this preoccupation, I have gleaned another common sense piece of advice. Do not focus on yield or return. Turn your attention to the fine print. Take note of the footnotes. Follow the asterisks.

An example of this phenomenon is the promotion of *Collateralized Mortgage Obligations*. CMOs are debt obligations that break down the principal and interest components of a mortgage payment into several *tranches*. These instruments, with their AAA ratings, are touted as smart alternatives to the low rates found in traditional insured bank products. A brokerage ad quotes relatively attractive yields for short-, medium-, and long-term CMOs. But the fine print reads: **bond equivalent yield based upon a 4-year average life assuming a 165 PSA speed.*

The fact is these supposedly safe investments possess risk characteristics that escape all but the most knowledgeable fixed-income investment professionals. You might want to own CMOs, but let them be part of a professionally managed mutual fund portfolio—unless, of course, you can explain tranches and a 165 PSA speed to the rest of us.

I recall an advertisement heralding the 11.2% yield of a *global bond income trust*—a GBIT in the current parlance, I presume. Following the asterisk down to its related fine print, I discovered this attention-grabbing return was actually an *estimated long-term return* (ELTR). I had never heard of an ELTR before, so I continued to squint into the body of the compressed paragraph. I was relieved to learn the ELTR was derived from a formula that takes into account the amortization of premiums, along with the accretion of discounts. The one fact I comprehended was the offering's sales charge of 4.9% (slightly under 5%).

In another promotion piece, Merrill Lynch instructed readers to learn more about how LYONs offered the relative safety of bonds with the appreciation potential of stocks. As a financial consumer exercising common sense, you will want to emphasize and underline the words *relative safety* and *appreciation potential*. This investment's further merits were extolled as combining many (but not all) of the favorable features of traditional convertibles (bonds, not cars), along with the advantages of zero coupon instruments. In addition, LYONs are said to provide investors the flexibility to exercise a holder's "put" option.

I consider myself a fairly sophisticated investor, but the truth is I don't understand this investment. I've learned the term "flexible" should pose some concern, because it typically is a flag that a financial or insurance product is complicated, be it an adjustable rate mortgage, universal life insurance, or a LYON. By the way, LYON stands for *Liquid Yield Option Notes*. Perhaps you see why someone selected the moniker of the king of the jungle for this questionable product.

Recently the financial and mainstream press have been rife with accounts of the debacle arising from the use of derivatives. Orange County, California, reportedly lost $2 billion, and Proctor & Gamble and Bank One lost hundreds of millions of dollars from these exotic instruments. Many astute investors have admitted they cannot adequately explain what derivatives are all about, so I am not going to try. Again, stay away from investments you can't understand.

AVOID OPTIONS AND COMMODITIES

In November 1996 a Milwaukee radio station broadcast a constant stream of ad spots for Ken Wolf Company and Kenco Commodities, which offered limited-risk heating oil options over a toll-free telephone line. The ad played on the fears Wisconsinites face every gray November: that of a bitterly cold winter. Listeners were told oil supplies were at the lowest levels since the Gulf War.

An excited voice warned us to act now to see huge profits on this incredible investment. The selling point was a promised limited risk with unlimited return. A tag line disclaimer mentioned that trading options involve risk and to use only risk capital.

During the period this ad ran, I was leading a series of financial planning sessions for a local financial institution's valued customers. At each seminar site throughout the state, I asked the audience what they thought of this investment and, more important, what the term *limited risk* implied. In every instance, these intelligent, mature, safety-conscious investors told me limited risk meant not too risky ... lower risk ... conservative. Nothing could be further from the truth.

I always got a laugh when I informed groups, in all seriousness, that limited risk is similar to limited partnerships: you could only lose every dollar you invested and not a dollar more.

When asked what I thought of this incredible investment opportunity, I soberly replied it was a highly speculative investment, and I don't recommend speculation. As a suitable alternative I suggested a trip to Las Vegas, where you could see a couple of shows, enjoy a few meals, and spend time at your favorite gaming pursuit. Your chances of winning $20,000 or losing your initial stake of $5,000 are the same in the commodities market as they are at a gambling casino. In both instances the odds are stacked against you.

The fact is, options and commodities are at the highest end of the risk pyramid and inappropriate for the vast majority of investors.

> "I've never bought a future nor an option in my entire investing career, and I can't imagine buying one now. Actually, I do know a few things about options. I know that the large potential return is attractive to many small investors who are dissatisfied with getting rich slow. Instead, they opt for getting poor quick."
>
> —Peter Lynch, *One Up on Wall Street*

BUY LOW, SELL HIGH

This piece of advice—to buy low, sell high—was ridiculed as too simplistic by a participant in one program I was leading. True, it is a simple principle, but seldom followed. As evidence, let's review investor psychology during 1987. In August the stock market as measured by the Dow reached a peak of 2888 for the year. Money poured into stock mutual funds and brokerage accounts in record volume. Euphoric investors witnessed the Dow march upward an average of 100 points a month for eight months. Optimism (bullishness) reigned supreme. The consensus was it was only a matter of months before the magic 3000 mark would be conquered.

History confirmed that anyone committing money to the market that summer was purchasing at a peak. In other words, they were buying *high*. October brought a series of precipitous stock market drops, culminating in Black Monday, October 19, with a one-day loss of a numbing 508 points. When the dust had settled, a dazed market stood at 1765.

Investors deluged stockbrokers and overwhelmed mutual fund operations with sell orders and panic-driven redemption requests. One suspects many of the individuals anxious to sell were the same enthusiastic purchasers in August. They had bought *high* and sold *low*. Human nature explains why the herd acted the way it did. In August, investors thought they had better get on to catch the market's ride up. In mid-October, they were sure the market was in a free fall. As one analyst observed at the time, corporate America was on a 40%-off sale. Yet there were few bargain hunters.

On Sunday, October 18, 1987, I participated in a Personal Finance Fair. Frank Capiello, the respected money manager and frequent *Wall Street Week* panelist and guest host, was the featured speaker. The crowd that morning was still reeling from the October 16 Black Friday shellacking and wanted Frank to answer one question: What was the market going to do?

Capiello used the following analogy: "Assume a coat you were interested in purchasing was selling briskly at $28 just two months ago. The same coat is now priced at $23, a full 20% off." His suggestion was that the Dow, having surpassed 2800 and currently just under 2300, represented a good value. A markdown by a full fifth, he asserted, was a buying opportunity.

Several people were swayed by this insight and entered orders for the next trading day, which turned out to be Black Monday. Had they delayed one more day, they could have received another 20 percent off, as that imaginary coat went down to around $18. Perhaps some were disappointed with Capiello's analysis. But by my estimation it was sound advice. After all, $23 represented better value than $28. In retrospect, it was a good time to get into the market. Add patience to the rule of buy low, sell high. Had those who bought high and sold low held on when the market dropped, they would have recouped their paper losses within a few months as the market retested its old high.

In November 1987 I participated in a continuing education investment program sponsored jointly by financial planning and CPA professional associations. Acting as moderator for the panel that had done a financial case study, I had the duty of fielding questions and comments from the audience. One recommendation from the panel was that our hypothetical client could benefit from some exposure to stocks, specifically through an investment in a growth stock mutual fund.

One CPA in the audience took strong exception to this particular recommendation, observing, "A rational professional would have to be crazy to suggest such a reckless course of action." The Dow was laboring near the 2000 mark, with the market still nervous from the black days in October, and the CPA drew audible support and nodding heads. I countered that it probably would be better if we waited until the market advanced 30% before making such an aggressive recommendation. I was being facetious, but I am afraid many did not pick this up in my tongue-in-cheek remark.

Anyone who follows the suggestion to buy low and sell high could rightly be tagged a *contrarian* investor. Take this as a compliment and as an appropriate philosophy of investing. By going against the prevailing sentiment, you put yourself in a position to reduce risk and capture gains by buying the out-of-favor (low) offering and selling the overpriced (high) holding. Buying low and selling high requires conviction, common sense, patience, and discipline, but the rewards prove financially satisfying.

IF IT SOUNDS TOO GOOD TO BE TRUE

A story appearing in the *Milwaukee Journal Sentinel* on October 22, 1996, speaks volumes about the wisdom of common sense investing. It chronicles the sad tale of some 3,000 security-conscious savers and investors who are still owed about $50 million from a now-worthless "guaranteed" investment offering.

The young brokers of a one-office Milwaukee brokerage firm aggressively sold a complex security that targeted primarily retirees looking to boost their incomes. Their alluring pitch was for a double-digit (10%+) return at a time when traditional bank CDs were paying just 4%. When the subject of risk was raised, the brokers and their promotional materials comforted clients' fears by claiming this high return was guaranteed. The combination of high return and promised safety proved irresistible. Imagine the conversations between broker and the soon-to-be brokee as to the urgent need to convert their sorry FDIC-insured CDs into this clearly superior, risk-equivalent investment.

Investors who had purchased this now-bankrupt security had as a goal preservation of capital. It is especially distressing that, in addition to losing out on their promised 10% interest payments, they received just a penny return on each original dollar in principal.

> "You should be more concerned with the return of your money than the return on your money!"
> —Benjamin Franklin

Who made out on what turned out to be a very risky investment? Well, the selling agents received outsized compensation in the form of commissions and fees up to 11.5%. The principal officer of the firm was found to have owned more than 10% of the stock and was a director of the failed firm for whom this capital was being raised. An investigation by the Wisconsin Department of Financial Institutions is still underway as this book goes to press.

Each year one can find episodes in every community that sound remarkably similar to this tragic story.

BEWARE OF INVESTMENT FRAUD

> "A gold mine is a hole in the ground with a liar on top."
> —Mark Twain

This chapter would not be complete without alerting you to guard against unscrupulous, ill-informed, illegal, unethical, and fraudulent purveyors of financial services and products. According to the Bureau of Consumer Protection, Americans lose more than a billion dollars each year to so-called investment opportunities that turn out to be scams. Greed too often attracts an unsavory element adept at quickly and painfully separating you from your hard-earned money. This warning underscores all the common sense investment points discussed. The best protection against being victimized by investment or financial services fraud is to practice common sense, including:

- If it sounds too good to be true, it is not true.
- Never succumb to pressure to make a hasty decision.
- Don't purchase anything from anybody you don't instinctively trust.
- You have more protection when dealing with a reputable institution than with an unknown individual.
- Never act upon an unsolicited phone pitch.
- Ask for a prospectus and read it.
- Always insist on personally meeting (eyeballing) the salesperson/agent/broker at his or her office.
- Be suspicious of anyone overtly displaying the excesses of wealth or success.
- Use all your senses; give recommendations the smell test.
- Avoid entirely options and commodities.

COMMON SENSE INVESTING POINTS

- Nobody cares as much about your money and financial health as you do.
- When receiving investment advice, always consider the source.
- There is no perfect investment (or mutual fund, for that matter).
- Understand total return.
- Understand and assess risk inside and out.
- Exercise patience.
- Think long-term.
- High return = high risk.
- Diversify, diversify, diversify.
- Be skeptical of expert advice.

- Don't buy what you don't understand.
- Buy low, sell high.
- Be on guard against falling prey to investment fraud.

A MAN FOR ALL INVESTMENT SEASONS: ALBERT O. "AB" NICHOLAS

I met 43-year veteran money manager Ab Nicholas in 1983 in the reception area of his Milwaukee mutual fund company. He graciously introduced himself and inquired whether I was being helped. Reflecting back on this chance encounter, I recall how impressed I was by his gentlemanly demeanor and concern.

After that initial meeting, I came to know Nicholas professionally through a mutual friend, the late, former Wisconsin Governor Warren P. Knowles. Through the years as a Nicholas fund shareholder and interested observer, I have benefited from the man's investment philosophy. His thinking exemplifies the major thrust of this book and illustrates the wisdom of a common sense, rational approach to money management.

The flagship Nicholas fund has $5.6 billion in assets and serves some 156,000 shareholders. At the helm, Ab Nicholas ranks high in safety and performance in down markets as well as bull runs. He credits the brutal 1973–1974 stock market decline as instructive to him about risk, and its memory tempers his successful investment style today.

Most money managers—and investors—have yet to be battle tested in a severe bear market and likely would find it a challenge to survive a prolonged decline. The Nicholas fund, however, lands regularly on the prestigious *Forbes* Honor Roll. In addition to good performance in up and down markets, the fund has low turnover, low volatility, and low fees. Nicholas credits its staying power to the practice of what its literature refers to as *consistency in a world of change*.

How is this philosophy defined? *Don't chase the stock of the moment or current market momentum.* Discipline comes down to "sticking to your knitting" and concentrating on what you know. For example, Nicholas often is asked why he does not invest in the hot and cold technology sector. His straightforward reply is, he doesn't understand those businesses and is uncomfortable with their high valuations.

Nicholas makes no pretense of his ability to predict the market, so he stays fully invested at all times within his familiar niche of small- and medium-sized companies. Regarding market direction, he is fond of saying he is cautious and bearish for the short run but confident and bullish for the long term. Individuals would be well served to adopt the same disciplined approach to investing and managing their money.

As a keen observer of the burgeoning mutual fund industry, Nicholas frets that asset gathering appears to have superseded the quest for superior investment performance. He is alarmed by heavy advertising expenditures, which reflect the unfortunate fact that the best time to advertise and promote past performance is actually the worst time for investors to buy.

Nicholas was an early proponent of the value of running a low-turnover, tax-efficient portfolio. These attributes are beginning to gain prominence due to favorable capital gains tax rates and the heightened interest in after-tax performance measurement.

Another Nicholas tenet is to pay attention to the interests of shareholders. As Ab says, "we are a no-load fund family, always have been, always will be." On top of that, internal fund expenses are kept reasonable. We all need to be better financial consumers, more highly conscious of these value propositions when shopping for mutual funds. Nicholas and his son, daughter, and brother-in-law are on board, and they make up an organization recognized as dedicated to high ethical standards. Nicholas is on record that integrity and reputation are their most important assets. After all, it is his name that appears on the prospectus (fund offering).

Individuals planning their personal finances are counseled to limit their product and service purchases to those providers who have a strong track record and whom they explicitly trust.

Ab Nicholas readily admits that fortune has smiled on him. Investment management can be a very lucrative business. Nicholas also is a dedicated philanthropist and recently joined with his spouse to bestow a major gift to their alma mater, the University of Wisconsin.

CHAPTER 4
PATHWAY TO FINANCIAL SUCCESS

If sports are a metaphor for life, the annual Super Bowl football game offers an analogy for the value of planning and goal setting.

Football borrows heavily from the military for its terminology, with the Super Bowl hyped as an epic battle. Some rabid partisans place as much importance on this game as on any life-or-death struggle.

Just as a general prepares for war, a football coach devises a game plan that will map the way to victory. Two of Winston Churchill's favorite activities were designing and planning, with a premium placed on follow-up and action.

> "For everything you must have a plan."
> —Napoleon

The late, great football coach Vince Lombardi can be viewed as the sports equivalent of a hero-general. The game plan is a strategic effort developed to marshal team strengths and exploit opponent weaknesses in order to win, and teams are lauded for the successful execution of their game plans. Preparation, fine-tuned by adjustments made at halftime and as game conditions warrant, is recognized as the key to success.

A professional football team follows a clearly defined objective: to post a winning score in a Sunday afternoon competition the fourth week of January. Good players are highly motivated and goal oriented. They speak of staying focused, being on a mission, and keeping an eye on the prize. For them, to believe is to achieve.

Strategic planning is a necessity not just in football, but in achieving the desired outcome in any worthwhile pursuit.

"Begin with the end in mind."
—Stephen Covey, *The Seven Habits of Highly Effective People,* Habit 2

Top-flight organizations talk of being programmed for success. To earn their championship rings, Super Bowl competitors use teamwork, preparation, drive, coordination, execution, perseverance, balance, and adjustments while on the road. To be successful on the personal financial field requires nothing less.

PROTECTING YOUR RESOURCES: INCOME AND ASSETS

In a 1983 movie, *Places of the Heart,* Emmy-nominee actress Sally Fields portrayed a gritty young woman facing hardships in the cotton fields of Georgia in the thirties.

Field's character must cope with the tragic killing of her husband, the local sheriff. She is left alone to raise her young children without a breadwinner-father or manager of their farm. To keep her family intact, she is forced to bring in a cotton crop alone, all the while dealing with the prejudices directed against her as a woman. She perseveres to save her home and farm from demanding creditors. The added peril of a tornado that destroys the property doesn't diminish her resolve.

To survive and hold on to the farm and home, she takes in boarders, including a blind man and a destitute farmhand who suffers the indignity of KKK-targeted terrorism.

What struck me about this movie was how much better her fate would have been if she'd had insurance protection.

Risk is a way of life. Substantial risks are associated with asset ownership and income production. Managing these risks is a fundamental planning need. Of course, if our heroine had been insured, there would be no sad tale to tell.

In the financial planning field, we refer to risk management as the vital defensive component of any sound financial plan. Insurance planning and risk management are placid topics compared to the excitement of investing or the challenges of dealing with taxes.

Insurance is a means of protecting your assets and income against the unexpected. We need to think in terms of a contingency plan, asking ourselves some pointed "what if" questions. What if you die prematurely, become disabled and incapable of earning an income, injure someone through the operation of your car, see your house and contents destroyed by fire or other disaster, need long-term convalescent care, or have heart disease that requires a transplant? How would any of these possibilities affect the makeup of your net worth and income statement?

Each of us should take the role of personal risk manager, identifying our risk exposure, searching for gaps or overlapping coverage, and determining the most effective way to provide adequate protection.

Any risk that cannot be handled from personal financial resources qualifies as an insurable need. One primary method to manage risk is to transfer that risk to an insurance company through the purchase of policies covering the specified exposures. Insurance premiums represent the cost of this protection and amount to a significant expense outlay.

Every time you pay an insurance premium, you need to ask yourself what you are protecting. Adding up the costs of health, life, auto, home, long-term care, and disability insurance will open your eyes to this expense. What percentage of your annual income is expended on this defensive protection?

The objective in a properly structured risk management program is to marry the best value for your premium dollars with the most effective coverage. Think in terms of the military defense budgeting process, where the aim is to gain the biggest bang for the buck.

It is important to realize that insurance does not improve or enhance our financial condition but rather makes us whole after suffering a loss. Dollars overspent on insurance represent money diverted from investment purposes.

Returning to the plight of our fictional movie heroine, she and her family and their quality of life would have benefited greatly from a risk management plan. The death of her husband was emotionally devastating, but the economic loss of his income allowed the pain to continue long after his demise.

Life insurance in its most basic form is protection in the event of premature death and the financial hardship it would impose on the dependents of an insured. Not everyone needs life insurance, although in this case a clearly identified need for protection existed. This provider/father left young children, a wife with limited income capacity, no financial reserves, and a heavy mortgage on the house and farm.

A major goal in retirement planning is to build up a sizable living estate (net worth). If this financial independence has not been reached, a plan needs to be in place to provide for survivors dependent on the insured. Life insurance is unique in that it provides an instant liquid estate at precisely the time of need.

To determine if life insurance protection is necessary, and how much, snap a mental family portrait. Next, cut out the primary breadwinner(s), and imagine the financial reality of this absence. Conduct a capital needs analysis to compare assets and resources available against housing, education, and income needs.

If there is a shortfall between what you have and what you need, the result is the amount of life insurance coverage required to carry on. Confirm whether your family is eligible for any group life insurance coverage offered as a benefit of employment. Purchase what is needed.

Contrary to the often-heated argument, the question is not between term insurance (pure, temporary, escalating premiums) versus whole life (permanent, cash value element, fixed premiums); the question is what form is most suitable and affordable in each individual planning circumstance.

My wife and I are proud parents of a beautiful daughter who has a cognitive disability. A combination of term and whole life insurance suits our situation best at this stage of our lives. The term insurance provides an instant estate to meet the needs of mortgage, college, child care, etc.

Our young daughter is physically healthy and can look forward to a long life. With their fixed premiums, whole life policies are the most affordable option for our retirement plans to adequately fund a special needs trust for her.

Disability insurance protects against the loss of earned income that results from a disabling injury or sickness. For this reason, it is often referred to as income protection or income replacement. Some planners refer to a serious long-term disability as economic death. Many individuals have a plan in place in the event of premature death, but they are exposed to the risk of disability, which statistically is a much more prevalent occurrence. Protection against income disruption is vital, although too often it represents the black hole in insurance protection plans. This coverage is costly and the provisions complex. Many employees are fortunate to have some protection as a fringe benefit.

When planning for retirement, the whole issue of income protection should be looked at under a different light. Reaching financial independence means being free from the need for income protection. Indeed, you cannot purchase this protection without an earned income or beyond retirement age. But prior to reaching a financially secure retirement, you should be adequately protected.

For retired individuals or those on the verge of retirement, the single biggest fear is likely the financial devastation that would result from expensive long-term convalescent care.

With the aging of America, hundreds of thousands of us will suffer the cruelty of Alzheimer's or a massive stroke lurking in the final years. There is a legitimate concern that one's financial resources could be wiped out, perhaps leaving a survivor in dire financial circumstances; or, in the case of a single individual, not being able to afford a level of dignified care. Another often-expressed concern is that of a proud parent who desperately does not want to be a burden to offspring.

One increasingly popular solution to this dilemma is to purchase a long-term care (LTC) insurance policy. As the name implies, these policies kick in with supplemental income in the event of a catastrophic illness and its resulting expense. Many policies also cover expenses associated with home health care.

Some practitioners in the LTC insurance field refer to these policies as an estate planning product because they effectively place a padlock on estate assets.

It is possible that premium dollars spent on disability insurance and perhaps life insurance could be redirected to LTC protection at the time of retirement.

For many of us, the most important protection is health insurance. Even the wealthiest could be bankrupted without adequate coverage. A severe illness has an impact on both the income statement and net worth condition and raises havoc with the financial health of the individual or family affected.

Health care costs have accelerated at rates much faster than the general level of inflation. For many people, health insurance premiums exceed the mortgage payment. Often the real concern is not affordability but availability. Much attention is being focused on such issues as portability of coverage, insurability, and the onus of preexisting conditions.

Insurance amounts to protection of your major assets. Property and casualty (P&C) insurance guards your personal assets against loss. In interpreting your net worth statement, you will be well advised not to assign too much value to your personal assets from a wealth measurement standpoint. Yet these possessions should be sufficiently insured.

Your home and possessions represent a significant major asset. If you suffered a peril such as a fire, flood, tornado, or hurricane, how would you replace this housing and its value?

Your automobile could be stolen or extensively damaged (totaled) in an accident at a loss of $25,000 or more.

Take a good look at your personal collections such as art, antiques, coins, or stamps. Conduct a personal appraisal of the value of these items, and then move to protect them accordingly.

Liability coverage is an absolute necessity to protect one's wealth in our litigious society. Liability protection is a component of all home and motor vehicle policies. Operation of even a modestly valued car exposes you to a potential liability of millions of dollars.

Down-to-earth syndicated radio show host Bruce Williams tells his listeners he would not walk out the door without an inexpensive excess umbrella liability policy of $1 million on top of the standard home and auto policy liability coverage.

Each of us needs to assume the role of personal risk manager, with duties including the following basic common sense steps:
- ♦ Update your inventory of all possessions, including their description, identification (model numbers, etc.), and estimated value.
- ♦ Undertake a comprehensive risk-management assessment to determine the amount of insurance you really need.
- ♦ Conduct an inventory of your insurance policies to determine current coverage, premium costs, and features, and adjust as necessary.
- ♦ Reduce risk exposures:

- stop smoking
- exercise regularly
- never drink and drive
- always wear a seat belt
- lock your car
- install deadbolt locks
- use smoke alarms with fresh batteries

One common sense piece of insurance advice is not to sweat the small stuff. Rather, turn your attention to those risks that would be most harmful to you. For example, you might be able to "self-insure" against certain risks by "going naked" (without coverage) or by increasing your deductibles or extending the waiting periods on certain policies. In these ways, you reduce the cost of insurance to better spend the same premium protection dollars somewhere else.

FINANCIAL PLANNING IN TRANSITION

"Only change is permanent."

—Heraclitus

The need for financial planning is most often driven by change. From time to time we must cope with dynamic changes in our personal financial lives. A triggering event could affect our personal finances, either from an income and expense standpoint or on the asset and liability ledger (net worth).

Change could be a positive: being the beneficiary of an inheritance, profiting from the sale of a business or property, or landing a more highly compensated employment position.

On the other hand, one could suffer a financial reversal. Disruption of one's income is among the more devastating occurrences that can befall an individual. This could result from unemployment, business misfortune, crop failure, or an accident, sickness, or disability.

Divorce often precipitates a fracturing of financial condition. Retirement marks the biggest financial transition in our lives. Losing a spouse, getting married, having children and grandchildren, relocating, and changing jobs all translate into major changes in the makeup of one's personal financial statement.

The pace of change is accelerating as we take the first few steps into the 21st century.

> "An investment in life is an investment in change....When you are changing all the time, you've got to continue to keep adjusting to change, which means that you are going to be constantly facing new obstacles."
> —Leo F. Buscaglia, *Living, Loving and Learning*

Follow along with an exercise I use at the conclusion of my financial planning seminars to illustrate the massive changes that have taken place in the 20th century. Economic history is not strictly tied to the past but serves as a lens with which to discern the future.

To start, reflect upon each given time period and name the dominant industry of that era, as well as the recognized leading company or stock:
  1900...1920...1940...1960...1970...1980...1985...1990...1995

At the beginning of this century, agriculture was the major economic force, and the family farm was predominant. Fast-forward to today, when less than 3% of the working population is left on the farm, yet it produces an abundance that helps feed the world. The small family farm, then a staple of American life, has suffered much the same fate as the buffalo.

In 1900, the manufacturing sector was turning out products such as buggies, barrels, baskets, barbed wire, and bicycles.

By 1920, the railroad had become king of industry, and the Pennsylvania Railroad, although it was soon to be dethroned, ruled the railroad kingdom. Economic historians say that one of the biggest wealth transfers took place as British and European financiers poured in capital to finance America's rolling stock.

My Chicago birthplace was the fastest growing city in the world in 1910. Much of that growth can be attributed to its role as "Player with railroads and the Nation's Freight Handler," as described by Carl Sandburg in his poem "Chicago."

The real wealth was not made by railroad stock and bond holders, but rather by shrewd investors who owned real estate adjoining the tracks or industry benefiting from this efficient mode of transport.

The bankruptcy of the Penn Central railroad some 50 years later marked the final chapter in what was left of the great railroad legacy.

The year is now 1940, the giant industry is steel, and the company is U.S. Steel. There can be little argument that U.S. Steel was the most dominant industrial powerhouse of that time in measures of output, plants, profits, revenues, and employees. Now called USX, this company is a shadow of its former self.

Moving on to a more recent vintage, the year is 1960, the automobile industry has emerged as number one, and General Motors is its recognized leader. The saying went, "What's good for General Motors is good for the country." Decades later, GM faces brutally tough foreign competition, environmental concerns, lower employment ranks, lower market share, and tight profit margins. Although still a major player, this corporate giant is no longer identified as a growth engine.

By the year 1970, the industry was big oil and the top company was Exxon. During the inflationary decade of the seventies, Exxon was on the top rung in terms of worldwide revenues. It marked a period in which energy companies virtually minted money in the stock market. But supply and demand equilibrium eventually brought down prices, which, when coupled with energy conservation, environmentalism, and improved fuel efficiency, served to dampen this once-hot sector.

In 1980, the computer industry moved to the top, with the name IBM (Big Blue) synonymous with the word "computer." IBM was universally regarded as the bluest of the blue chips at this time. Virtually every institutional and pension portfolio held the stock. So dominant was Big Blue's position and market share within the computer industry that the government instituted antitrust action, claiming IBM bordered on a monopoly.

But fortunes inevitably change, and technology shifted from room-sized mainframes to desktop PCs. IBM began to resemble an aging athlete as it looked to regain a semblance of its prime.

In 1985, and for much of the eighties, consumer stocks helped propel the stock market. Pharmaceutical companies emerged as the hot performers and the flagship was Merck. During this time, Merck appeared often as the most admired company on top of everyone's favorite stock list. Once again, the winds of change appeared as the prospect of health care reform and cost containment became national mantras. This once robust and healthy industry fell ill.

By 1990 General Electric, an international conglomerate, had supplanted IBM and Merck as the darling of the institutional investor set.

GE's Chairman Jack Welch is lauded for ushering this old-line company into the new era by focusing globally and insisting on high quality, productivity improvement, and a commitment to be number one—or a close number two—in any product area in which it competes. GE's renewal was not rooted in light bulbs, refrigerators, or even jet engines, but rather such growth areas as medical systems and—especially—financial services. As we straddle the new millennium, GE is being electrified by the profits generated by its basic businesses to finance the hyper growth, high margin, GE Capital Services Division.

GE has quietly emerged as a financial services superpower. If it were an independent company, GE Capital's revenue would put it ahead of banking giant Citicorp and its profits ahead of Hewlett-Packard and even Microsoft. This move illustrates the growth potential of the now high-flying financial services industry in the new economy.

By 1995 high technology appeared in the investment and economic galaxy, and no star shone brighter than software power Microsoft. Honorable mention would go to chip maker Intel. It is interesting to note that Microsoft and Intel, the two premier growth stocks of our era, are not even listed on the New York Stock Exchange, preferring to keep their listing on the tech-laden NASDAQ market.

The emphasis on software over hardware has resulted in the same antitrust complaints about Microsoft that IBM faced just 15 years earlier. The conventional perception is that Microsoft and its enormously wealthy chairman, Bill Gates, will soon own the world. Recent history in the technology field tells us this fear probably is unfounded.

So there we have it—a century of monumental change.

Year	Sector	Company
1900	agriculture	small family farm
1920	railroads	Pennsylvania Railroad
1940	steel	U.S. Steel
1960	automobiles	GM
1970	oil	Exxon
1980	computers	IBM
1985	pharmaceuticals	Merck
1990	global conglomerate	GE
1995	high technology	Microsoft

Let's take a minute to reflect upon the lessons to be learned from the preceding exercise.

- The pace of change is not just accelerating, it is exploding.
- We went from an economy centered in agriculture to industry and then to information, communication, and technology.
- Look to the future, not to the past, for leadership and explosive growth.
- Nobody stays on top for long. Change is inevitable. Change is the rule. You can't sit with a pat hand.

Who will the winners be in the year 2005...2010...2015? A correct call and subsequent investment will result in phenomenal riches.

Wouldn't it be ironic if agriculture came full circle to become the most dynamic element in the early 21st century's global economy? Should that occur, it likely will be in the form of innovative biotech companies.

One such player is Monsanto Corporation, which has transformed itself from a chemical company into a leading-edge biotech firm. Monsanto has developed genetically superior potatoes, corn, tomatoes, and soybean food crops. These crops not only produce higher yields, but are more disease resistant and environmentally friendly than hybrids currently available. Most intriguing is that these high-tech crops possess health-improving properties, now called *nutraceuticals* in the trade.

As a stock performer, Monsanto already has benefited from this huge potential, with its stock price tripling in the past three years.

The preceding examples underscore the personal financial challenges we face as we tread into a new century full of change.

Life is filled with surprises, and sound planning dictates preparing for the eventualities we could face. There is the need to be a lifelong planner.

> "Obligations and responsibilities—every generation faces them.
> Hopes and dreams—every generation wants to achieve them.
> But to do so we must meet and overcome many financial challenges throughout our lives."
> —Federated Investors

The truth is, most individuals react rather than act and plan ahead—not a common sense way to proceed.

Astronaut crews in the NASA space program, in order to have a safe and successful mission, practice countless hours and use a simulator to learn how to react to situations.

As individuals, we would be wise to conduct a fire drill to practice in the event of a financial upheaval, such as the loss of a job or loved one.

How would you react to a stock market crash or failure of a business? Give yourself the benefit of a wake-up call. In this way, you condition yourself to coping should these events come to pass.

Just think back to all that has transpired over the past 20 years of your life. As individuals we have grown older, had children or grandchildren, and experienced marriage, loss of loved ones, retirement, divorce, relocation, and so on.

Tax and estate laws have been altered. The investment climate and interest rate environment are in a constant state of flux. Inflation heats up and cools down. Our individual income and cost of living expenses undergo ebbs and flows.

Ask what you would have done differently. What can be learned from the benefit of hindsight? Nobody ever regretted planning. In fact, most readily admit they could have benefited by more attention to their personal finances and money management.

Get set to prepare for the next 20 years with the resolve and benefit of preparation and a strategic plan. Take command of change.

One of the first planning moves in any real or simulated financial occurrence is to conduct an honest appraisal and assessment of your predicament and condition. Reconstruct your income and net worth statements as you did in Chapter 2 and take a hard look at how your income, expenses, and resources have been affected. Consider what your best course of action is.

LOSS OF A LOVED ONE

In addition to a profound emotional impact, the death of a spouse is sure to have a profound financial impact on the survivor. Because a marriage represents a partnership in a true sense, the loss of a partner cascades across the entire financial planning spectrum. From an income standpoint, one could face the loss of the deceased's employment income or a reduction in Social Security or pension income.

In some cases, one can live less expensively than two, yet certain major expenditures, such as housing, remain constant. To be addressed soon after a loss is the whole perplexing housing decision of whether to stay or move, buy or rent, get a house or condo, pay cash or pay a mortgage, live independently or with assistance.

In economic terms, divorce is similar in many ways to the death of a spouse. I refer to it as a fracturing of financial condition. Divorce is usually a negative in financial terms. Income, assets, expenses, taxes, and estate factors all shake up and divide personal finances.

CORPORATE REFUGEE

On a personal note, a couple of years back I made a move that resulted in major financial repercussions affecting my wife and family. I left the security blanket of a well-paid position as vice president of a respected trust company to venture out on my own, starting my own independent financial planning and investment advisory practice.

I had come to the conclusion that I am an entrepreneur at heart. I felt I possessed the right stuff to provide personal, objective, quality service, and I found the corporate bureaucracy suffocating to my independent spirit. But starting a business represents a gamble. You invest a couple of years robbed from the heart of the wealth-building years. The price is a period of financial stagnation traded for the dream of a prosperous payoff down the road. It is a classic risk-reward proposition.

If you wait for the ideal time to take the self-employment plunge, you never do it. Buoyed by support from my wife, I took the leap of faith that is the mark of all those responsible for making their own paychecks.

I am proud to say at this stage I am producing a sustainable income and deriving the satisfaction that comes from building a growing enterprise. I harbor no regrets.

Most employees fail to appreciate the value of their fringe benefits as part of their total compensation package. While employed, I had enjoyed as a fringe benefit a group life plan with generous coverage based on 2.5 times salary. During my transition, the first critical step involved not jeopardizing the financial security of my family should something happen to me as primary breadwinner: namely, premature death or disability. So I immediately contacted my insurance professional and added a new policy to adequately insure my life.

In addition, I purchased a disability (income replacement) policy to make up for the loss of the group LTD (long-term disability) coverage.

I opted to stay in the corporate health plan with family protection under a COBRA provision for 18 months. During this period my family and I actively looked to line up health insurance for when this transition coverage would expire.

All my efforts at protection resulted in a significant increase in my family's monthly cost of living, yet each was absolutely essential to the well-being of our family.

On the income side, I had to go about a full year with modest earnings while the expenses continued unabated—as if I were unemployed.

To survive over this period, I scrambled to find sources of money. I cashed in some company stock I owned, sold off all nonretirement mutual funds we held, surrendered for cash value a life policy on my wife, and finally borrowed against the equity in our home.

Running a business is a cash-flow adventure and drama. Judicious spending was called for due to the dearth of income. To keep business expenses down, I maintained an office in my home and leased office equipment and a car. One piece of good news is that with little in the way of earnings that first year, I eagerly awaited the tax refund of my previous year's withholding taxes.

Some say it takes two years in a new venture to realize any meaningful income from a personal services business. During this income drought you need confidence and staying power to survive economically until you get to greener pastures.

In my case, income started to flow during the second year that was sufficient to meet basic living expenses. The income statement is now significantly improved, and my plan calls for restarting savings efforts with tax-deductible additions to my retirement plan, resuming home improvement projects, and paying down accumulated debt.

The net worth statement basically froze for the two-year period of my business start-up. The home value and retirement plan assets continued to appreciate, but that was offset by the increased debt load from the home equity loan.

Looking forward, the master plan is to generate sufficient income to support a comfortable lifestyle, afford the education of our children, build a substantial retirement nest egg, construct a business succession plan, aim for financial independence, and have surplus available for charitable causes.

LUCKY LYNNELL

Lynnell feels obligated to purchase a raffle ticket hawked by her good friend Charlotte that benefits the local AIDS organization. She wins first prize, an all-expense trip for two to Las Vegas. Lynnell and Charlotte fly off to Vegas looking to have a good time.

Lynnell has never gambled in her life, but in the spirit of the moment is prodded by Charlotte to try her luck with the one-armed bandits: quarter slot machines for the uninitiated. Feeding her last quarter with her now-sore arm, she sees the machine suddenly erupting in bells, whistles, and flashing lights.

Casino managers appear in red jackets and surround the startled Lynnell to inform her she has hit the jackpot lottery game. Open-mouthed, Lynnell is informed she has won $1.5 million. It is Charlotte who does the screaming.

On the return plane trip Lynnell is still in the clouds as she reflects on her good fortune. Lucky Lynnell has never considered herself fortunate. She is 40, single, diabetic, renting, with no significant retirement savings. Her companion and coworker Charlotte naturally assumes her friend will quit her job. Lynnell makes $40,000 a year with good benefits, but she is stressed in a job that has grown stale and in which she feels under-appreciated.

Once home and on solid ground, she is brought back to reality by her brother, Dan, who is her informal advisor. Contrary to the proclamations of an excited Charlotte, she is not a millionaire. Brother Dan correctly points out there is no immediate improvement in the makeup of her net worth. What she won was $75,000 a year for the next 20 years, for a total of $1.5 million. Dan suggests her windfall is not that different from getting a job in which she is paid $75,000 to age 60. A major difference is she does not have to perform anything for this income.

Dan prevails upon his sister to meet with a financial planner rather than getting pulled in so many directions and bombarded with well-meaning but unsound advice. Accompanied by her brother to this introductory meeting, Lynnell is asked by the planner what it is she really wants from her improved financial condition. After considerable thought and further discussion, Lynnell comes to the heart of her plan.

- She seeks a less stressful, more rewarding job.
- She desires a home with a backyard and garden.
- She wants to be able to retire at age 55.

Their follow-up meeting involved dissecting the specifics of her stated goals.

JOB

Her planner, Susan, informs Lynnell that with her windfall income, she can afford to take a substantial cut in pay. Lynnell loves flowers and plants, and she comes to realize she can accept a position as a designer at the local flower shop, even though it pays $25,000 a year, or 40% less than her current salary.

Owing to her diabetes and a need to hang on to health insurance coverage, she had felt trapped in her current position. She discovers she can stay in the same plan, with her own doctors, even though her premium will double.

HOUSE

With $100,000 in annual income ($75,000 winnings, plus $25,000 earnings), Lynnell easily qualifies for a mortgage. She is ecstatic to purchase a comfortable home close to the shop with a large backyard to plant her garden.

She makes a 20% down payment from her initial winnings and finances the balance with a 15-year fixed-rate mortgage. The final payment on this debt coincides with her financial independence target age. Meanwhile, the write-off of mortgage interest will help to lighten the load on her six-figure taxable income. Her monthly mortgage payment turns out to be not much of a stretch when compared to her escalating rent outlay.

RETIREMENT

Lynnell directly rolls over her retirement plan into an IRA she establishes. She also plans to continue to fund an annual IRA contribution. More good news is that the florist is instituting a SIMPLE retirement plan that will further allow her to grow her nest egg.

With Susan's help, Lynnell implements an automatic savings program to funnel a full 25% of her total income, $25,000 a year, into long-term accumulation. She still does not fancy herself a gambler, and decides to take a moderate-risk course with her investing.

She is strongly encouraged to set up an estate plan, for which she names her trusted brother as executor with a durable power of attorney for financial and health care matters. She also names him co-trustee of a trust that is set up for her. Beneficiaries include her brother, her dear friend Charlotte, and the American Diabetes Association.

As the plan comes into focus, Lynnell starts to feel lucky after all.

BEWILDERED BOB AND CAUTIOUS CAROLE

Our couple is torn between the quality-of-life issues of moving to a new, larger, more expensive home in the country or staying put in their modest yet comfortable home in the city. Stepping up to their dream house would result in a long daily commute, a much higher mortgage payment, and adjustments to new schools, neighbors, and church.

The new house would also represent a heavier cost of living and larger expenses for real estate taxes, utilities, and upkeep. When Bob and Carole fret over being house poor, their real estate agent is quick to point out that they can readily afford this new palace.

They can reduce the monthly mortgage payment, but it would involve tapping out their investment portfolio. Bob is hesitant to go this route because that sum is earmarked to help supplement retirement, only 15 years away. Plus, he realizes that by selling his portfolio, he would incur some capital gains. On top of that, these financial assets have outperformed the couple's real estate appreciation over the past 15 years.

The higher housing and commuting costs (70 miles round-trip) would eat into their ability to continue enjoying family camping vacations. They had even given some thought to purchasing a recreational camper.

One obvious solution would be to increase the household income by having Carole go back into the workplace grind. She had opted out when her children were born, and in the ensuing years she felt fulfilled as a dedicated volunteer. Carole calculates that her potential income will be eaten up by high marginal taxes, child care costs, and work-related expenses. The decision comes down to the realization that a second income just isn't worth it.

The purchase of the new home is a major decision, and once made, the large, six-figure decision would weigh down the couple for the next 30 years like a boulder around their necks. Complicating their decision is Bob's recently picking up some vibes that maybe his long-term employment is no longer as stable as it once seemed. In addition, Carole's mother, who lives a mile away from their city location, just fell and broke her hip, and she could use some help. The final straw is that interest rates abruptly turn up, meaning not only a higher mortgage payment than anticipated, but also a less attractive seller's market for their current home.

Because of all these factors, they jointly weigh in with staying put for another year to see how things turn out.

The realtor is disappointed they didn't go through with their purchase offer. Then again, that camper trailer is looking very good to them.

THE PLANNING VOYAGE

A gentle breeze pushes their sleek vessel through the blue-green British Virgin Islands waters, as vacationers Hank and Betty reach safe harbor in Cane Garden Bay at the end of a perfect day of sailing.

They toast each other over dinner that evening, celebrating their 25th wedding anniversary. Later, they discuss their life together and focus on what the next few years will bring—unlike most people, who have hazy goals and never bother to think out in detail what they want their money to accomplish for them.

Recently, both Barretts reached their 50th birthday milestone. They would like to change course in five years upon reaching the age of 55. Although they plan to leave their jobs, they don't care for the term "retirement," for they believe it connotes an ending and a period of prolonged inactivity. The Barretts intend to remain fully active and prefer the term *financially independent,* or *non–wage-dependent,* to describe the status they'd like. They have a dream, and it consists of sailing and exploring the Caribbean for four to six months each winter, and sailing and actively volunteering in the Great Lakes region during the warmer months.

Hank and Betty have put much thought into developing their plan, the result of countless hours of discussion, reflection, and investigation. A case in point is the timing of the next chapter in their life adventure, five years from now in the new millennium when they reach 55.

Their time frame corresponds with:

- the younger of their two sons completing professional school, which they consider an investment and something they have committed to fund;
- the mortgage and a home equity loan being paid, for the Barretts' goal is to be debt-free;
- Betty's being fully vested in her pension plan;
- Hank's employer considering age 55 as an early retirement window and offering continuation of some benefits, particularly group health and life insurance.

Most of all, Hank and Betty feel the timing will be right. After working hard, building careers, and raising a family, they desire to throttle down, change gears, and move into the next chapter of their lives.

In quantifying their objective, they aim to accumulate an investment portfolio of a million dollars. It is a nice round seven-digit figure. They believe it to be an attainable goal and consider it sufficient to finance their dream. Hank suggests it will provide a good target—a carrot—and Betty says she for one likes the sound of it, too.

They have inventoried their current assets, which they list as follows:

Current Assets	
$150,000	Hank's 401(k) retirement plan
50,000	Betty's IRA
100,000	Joint growth stock portfolio
150,000	Company stock of Hank's employer
50,000	Inherited stocks from Betty's mother
$500,000	Total 50% of Goal

Figure 4-1

The Barretts recognize they will need to employ a rigorous savings program from current income, along with solid investment performance, to reach the magic million-dollar mark and double the size of their current portfolio in five years.

As a higher tax-bracket, two-income couple, the Barretts intend to continue to fully maximize pretax contributions to their respective retirement plans. They are increasing their regular monthly investment program in growth mutual funds, and Hank is purchasing additional company stock through a payroll deduction arrangement, as shown by Figure 4-2.

Annual Savings Plan

$ 6,000/year	Hank's 401(k) plan
$ 3,000/year	Betty's 403(b) plan
$ 9,000/year	$750 mo. growth fund purchases
$12,000/year	$1,000 mo. company stock investment plan
$30,000	Total Annual Investments**

**Represents 25% of combined annual income*

Figure 4-2

In this marriage partnership it is Betty who has taken a serious interest in investing and investments, having joined an all-women investment club, the Dow Janes, some years back. The club has since disbanded, but the association kindled Betty's interest in stocks. She has become a student of growth stocks, particularly those of medium-sized companies, and has developed an investment philosophy that the Barretts follow with their joint portfolio.

She believes in being fully invested (85% plus) in the stock market at all times. Results of numerous studies have convinced her that the best long-term performance record is found in maintaining ownership in stocks, and she realizes that reaching their targeted average annual return of 10% plus dictates stock ownership. Betty aims to be a patient, long-term investor and fully expects to maintain this portfolio allocation over the next 25 years.

The Barretts' Five-Year Projection	
Present Value	**Future Value**
$500,000 @ 10% for 5 years	$805,000
$ 30,000 @ 10% annually for 5 years	$201,600
TOTAL	**$1,006,600**

Figure 4-3

To translate, their plan for reaching their million dollar target (as shown in Figure 4-3) calls for getting an investment return averaging 10% on their current $500,000 portfolio over five years, plus putting $30,000 into new investments annually over the next five years—a total outlay of $150,000—also at a 10% average annual return.

Their master plan calls for selling their primary residence in five years, and using from $150,000 to $175,000 of the proceeds to purchase a sailing vessel. They have tested a new model but plan to buy one that was previously owned. Their boat will be state-of-the-art, sleep six, and be equipped with all the comfort features, plus the latest in safety and navigation equipment. Their plans call for ratcheting down their cost of living. Selling their home will reduce real estate taxes, utilities, upkeep, and maintenance. Once retired, they expect to revert to a one-car household, rather than maintain the two vehicles they now use to commute to their respective jobs. Once the house is sold, they will make a gift of their unneeded furniture and household goods to their sons and to charities. Also, they will have completed funding their sons' educations.

The Barretts recently bought a cottage in Door County, Wisconsin, the "Cape Cod of the Midwest." They have been continuously upgrading, expanding, and modernizing the property. Once retired, they intend to make it their primary residence. They just took out a $25,000 home equity loan to help improve this second home, a move that allows them to deduct the interest on their tax return. They look at this loan as an investment in an appreciating asset that also represents a place to live in and enjoy. Hank has been doing a lot of the work himself and figures his sweat equity will translate the $25,000 into a $75,000 increase in value.

The recent passing of Betty's mother has prompted them to take a closer look at their own estate plan. They have a much-outdated will that was drawn up when they resided in a different state and their boys were minors. They ask a friend whose guidance they respect for a referral, and he sends them to an attorney specializing in estate planning.

In their initial consultation, they are informed of the value of avoiding probate and having a plan in place in the event of incapacity. Actually, they had learned this lesson the hard way through their experience with Betty's mother. They also realize their estate is more complicated now, and that it would be wise to make plans to reduce or eliminate estate taxation, among other matters. They pledge to follow through with a comprehensive estate plan.

The Barretts estimate they will require about $5,000 a month, or $60,000 in total annual income, at the start of their new life. This corresponds to about 50% of their current combined incomes. Between them they expect about $1,000 a month in supplementary income from their separate pensions. Part of their plan revolves around turning their sailing avocation into at least a partial income-producing vocation. They have discussed an arrangement with an island marina captain they befriended to run charters of their own for a month each season.

Hank has discovered he very much enjoys working with his hands, and he will spend some time assisting in boat maintenance. In exchange for his labor, the Barretts can expect some mooring and dry-dock privileges. The summer months should not prove too expensive. For the past several summers, they have led outdoor excursions, taking special-needs children on sailing, boating, fishing, and hiking outings. These children are served by Betty's nonprofit employer, and the Barretts very much want to expand this outreach effort once they become non–wage-dependent.

As shown in Figure 4-4, the Barretts expect about $12,000 in combined pensions, $6,000 in charter income, $24,000 in stock dividends, and the balance of $18,000 provided from a $150,000 surplus they expect upon the sale of their home. The plan calls for them to continue to let their retirement assets grow and for their stock portfolio to continue to appreciate in value over the years. They have not factored in Social Security benefits, which could further boost their income at age 62.

Retirement Income Projections

Income	Month	Year
Pensions	$1,000	$12,000
Charter Income	500	6,000
Dividend Income	2,000	24,000
Home Sale Proceeds	1,500	18,000
TOTAL	**$5,000**	**$60,000**
Outgo		
Estimated Expenses	$5,000	$60,000

Figure 4-4

    The Barretts' aim is to plan in five-year increments over the next quarter century of their life cycle. The first or current phase is elimination of debt, rigorous tax-advantaged accumulation, and effective investment portfolio management. Hank and Betty are excited about fulfilling their dream. They have a plan to make it happen and are systematically financing their objective. As they finish their anniversary dinner, their thoughts turn to a suitable name for their sailboat.

CHAPTER 5

REDUCING YOUR TAX BITE: TAX PLANNING STRATEGIES

Financial planning is heavily tax driven. Taxes represent a significant burden, and ignoring their importance jeopardizes your financial objectives. Any dollars saved through tax-minimization strategies can be used to help meet your financial goals.

> "Anyone may so arrange his affairs that his taxes shall be low as possible; he is not bound to choose that pattern which will best pay the treasury; there is not even a patriotic duty to increase one's taxes."
> —Judge Learned Hand

The tax impact needs to be assessed in every major financial planning decision you make: managing capital gains treatments on an investment portfolio, using tax-exempt or taxable bond income, choosing the best way to build a retirement nest egg, rolling over a retirement distribution, determining which money to spend first at retirement, developing charitable and gifting strategies, formulating an estate plan, or deciding to rent or purchase a home.

TAX PLANNING IN THE WAKE OF CHANGE

This chapter highlights the provisions found in the Taxpayer Relief Act of 1997. As taxpayers, we are still adjusting to the massive changes brought by the Tax Reform Act of 1986. To the certainty of death and taxes, we can safely add a third; namely, continuous tinkering with the tax code. We must learn to operate our personal financial affairs in a constantly changing tax environment. It's a difficult task because we are dealing with a moving target.

The monumental 1986 tax act traded lower rates for fewer deductions. Two rates were offered: 15% and 28%. In the ensuing years, three additional tax bites were added at 31%, 36%, and 39.6%.

You should realize that tax legislation is a product of partisan gamesmanship, political compromise, and lobbyists' pressures. There is an old saying that you really wouldn't want to see sausage or tax legislation being made. Don't expect any tax bill to be necessarily equitable or to make much sense.

With the ink still not dry on the latest piece of tax work, we must learn how to cope. Venita VanCaspel, in her best-selling book, *The Power of Money Dynamics,* claims a prime reason individuals fall short in pursuit of financial independence is a failure to understand and apply tax laws. The challenge now is to uncover planning opportunities built into the new law.

> "Why does a small tax increase cost you two hundred dollars and a substantial tax cut save you thirty cents?"
>
> —Peg Bracken

THE ALLURE OF CAPITAL GAINS

The best news in the 1997 tax act is a reduction in the capital gains tax rates, sliced from a maximum 28% to 20%. For lower bracket taxpayers it falls from 15% to 10%. The lowest tax on capital gains in 16 years, it brings the promise of still lower rates early in the next century.

A QUICK PRIMER ON CAPITAL GAINS

A tax is applied on the appreciation (profit) realized upon the sale of a capital asset. Capital assets include stocks, bonds, mutual funds, and real estate. A capital gain is the difference between the adjusted purchase price (cost) and the sales price.

You report your taxable gains on Schedule D. Assets held for the long-term, 18 months under the new tax law, are subject to the favorable capital gains rate. Prior to sale, your gain/loss is just on paper and hence unrealized. A sale transforms a paper profit into a realized capital gain in the year of sale.

Capital gain income should be contrasted with ordinary income for tax planning purposes. Interest and dividend income constitute ordinary income, whereas capital gain income comes from the profit realized from capital (money) placed at risk of loss.

Capital gains are given preferential tax treatment to encourage long-term investment behavior and risk taking. Ordinary income, as the name implies, receives no special treatment and thus is subject to the full brunt of taxation. The tax rates on ordinary income remain unchanged.

To illustrate, let's say Al owns a stock he purchased for $100 a share a few years back. It has doubled in value and now is worth $200. Al sells his stock to lock in his $100 long-term capital gain. This gain is taxed at $20 a share, or at a 20% rate, instead of the 28% before tax relief, when $28 would have been owed.

In contrast, Sara, a top-echelon taxpayer, is getting hit with a stiff 39.6% rate on her salary, which is classified as ordinary income. For every $100 in ordinary dividend income received, she must fork over $39.60 in tax, almost double the tax hit Al took on his capital gain.

PLANNING IMPLICATIONS

- Investments capable of generating capital gains are favored over endeavors that produce ordinary income.
- Clear winners are those growth stocks and mutual funds for which the bulk of the return is expected from appreciating share prices and for which dividend payments are nil or minimal. Such is the case with small- and medium-capitalization stocks and funds. The 1997 tax cut makes the increased risk and volatility inherent in these holdings more palatable.
- This tax cut affects taxable accounts only, so that investments carrying high yields, such as equity income funds and utility stocks, might better be held inside a tax-deferred account.
- Patience and a long-term outlook are further rewarded. The holding period to qualify for the special capital gains treatment has been extended from one year to one and a half years. A

further reduction in rates is promised after the year 2000 for investors with a five-year holding period. The top rate is scheduled to drop to 18% from 20%, while lower-bracket taxpayers are supposed to see the rate go from 10% to a super-low 8%.

- Unfortunately, the indexing of capital gains to keep pace with inflation is not a part of the 1997 Taxpayer Relief Act.
- Income shifting (transferring the tax bite) should now receive more of your attention. Parents and grandparents might consider gifting highly appreciated stock to children or grandchildren. Perhaps your intent is for the proceeds to be used for education expenses. Presumably, upon sale of the transferred asset, a lower capital gains tax would be owed by the younger owner. Instead of 20%, the tax would be half, or just 10%.
- The Taxpayer Relief Act lessens the appeal of variable annuities, because once withdrawn, these tax-deferred accounts are taxed as ordinary income, no matter how earned.
- No change was made in the ability to offset gains with losses. Taxpayers are still allowed a net loss of up to $3,000 per year against income, with any excess carried forward.
- Changes in this area give further impetus to the popularity of so-called tax-efficient mutual funds. Tax-managed mutual funds are designed to minimize taxable distributions and preserve capital gains treatment. Index funds with their low turnover are further enhanced from the lower long-term tax rates. Taxable index funds can actually outdo variable annuities in paring taxes.
- One result of the 1997 tax act is increased attention to after-tax performance measurements. It means portfolios managed inefficiently through excessive trading and rapid turnover will slip in comparison to tax-efficient funds on the all-important after-tax basis.

Tax-efficient fund manager Ab Nicholas points out that one reason his flagship Nicholas Fund is heralded among fund offerings is a low turnover level, resulting in above average after-tax performance.

In conclusion, the aim more than ever is to receive capital gains over ordinary income, allowing you to keep more of what you reap.

GOOD NEWS ON THE HOME FRONT

For the most part, individuals are no longer subject to gains from the sale of a home. Under the new rules, single taxpayers will not owe tax on gains of up to $250,000, and married couples, $500,000. The only restriction is that the home sold must be the principal residence and have been owned and occupied for at least two of the previous five years.

Prior rules were more restrictive, allowing just a one-time exclusion limited to $125,000, and only to homeowners 55 or older. Before age 55, homeowners had been able to defer a gain only by purchasing a home of equal or greater value. To preserve the profit exclusion meant arduous recordkeeping to track capital improvements and cost basis adjustments.

Going forward, such paperwork filing will be virtually unnecessary because the exclusion is available every two years upon a sale, making it unlikely you will bump up against the new higher limits.

The new home sale rules provide a lot of planning flexibility. Individuals or couples, for reasons including divorce, job change or transfer, premature death of spouse, or early retirement, will no longer feel forced by the tax code to keep their current home or plow back their gains into a more expensive home. The new planning parameters allow for a sale at any age and as often as every two years without forcing a capital gain tax reckoning.

The equity locked up in a home could be freed up to meet pressing needs from a financial setback. In another scenario, capital could be redeployed from a personal residence by choosing to rent or downsize. Trading down to a less expensive property significantly lowers the overall cost of living, involving saving on mortgage interest, real estate taxes, utilities, and upkeep.

However, if you frequently turn over your homes, commissions and associated expenses could eat up any profit. Be forewarned that, unlike financial assets, you still cannot write off any loss incurred from the sale of a residence.

FORM 1040 AS A TAX PLANNING ROAD MAP

Because all financial planning has such a major income-tax planning emphasis, the best starting point is the gathering of your most recent 1040 tax return and taking a couple of minutes to study it. Involve your spouse if it's a joint return.

Even the most basic financial planning demands an analysis of the income tax return. Whether or not you have your taxes professionally prepared—perhaps especially if you do—it is valuable to have a basic understanding of the federal tax structure. This is not an easy task with the mind-boggling complexity of the tax code.

One conclusion that can be drawn from the biggest set of tax changes since 1986 is that true tax reform or simplification is but a cruel joke.

These latest changes are a boon for tax preparers and advisors skilled at navigating the maze of eligibility requirements and phaseouts. Criticism has been leveled at Congress because the extra dollop of complexity will negate much of the benefit by increasing the cost for filing assistance. In fact, the complexity found in this new tax legislation makes tax preparation firms such as H & R Block a sure-fire growth stock.

> "The hardest thing in the world to understand is the income tax."
> —Albert Einstein

As an advisor, I always carry 1040 tax forms with me so I can illustrate tax planning implications to clients. An analysis of the 1040 provides a road map for tax discovery. Note that the IRS divides the form into horizontal sections, which are found on the left side of the form in bold print.

Perhaps the best way to understand and interpret Form 1040 is to look at the income tax structure summarized in Figure 5-1.

Depending on which of the four filing statuses you declare—married, filing jointly, head of household, or single taxpayer—there are differences in the tax consequences and rules under which you operate. Because the "married filing separate" choice penalizes couples, when it is used it often indicates that a marriage is on shaky grounds. Other than this one elected status, not much choice is offered in the filing status section, which limits planning opportunities.

> "An income tax form is like a laundry list—
> either way you lose your shirt."
> —Fred Allen

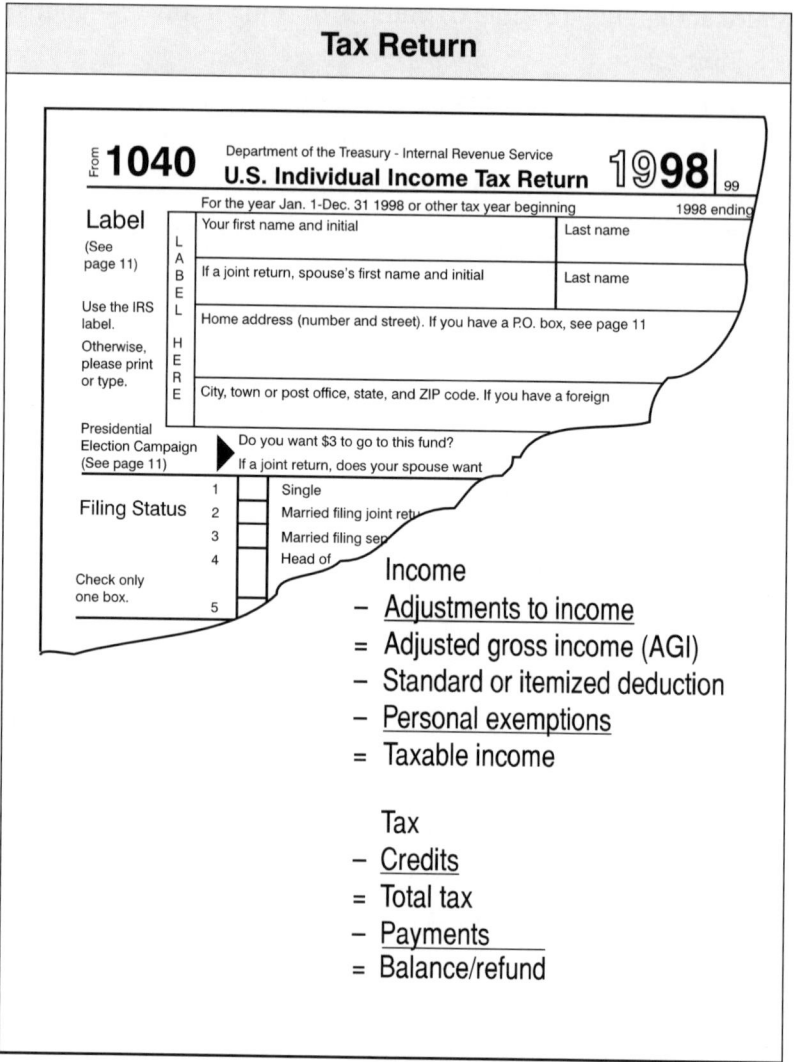

Figure 5-1

INCOME

The income section of the 1040 includes reported income from all sources, with the summation leading to the total income figure. The answer is quite simple as to what constitutes taxable income. The IRS defines all income from whatever source as taxable, and hence reportable, unless specifically excluded. The list of excludable items is short, and even then there are exceptions, whereas the list of reportable income items is exhaustive. It includes wages (W-2s), interest, dividends, capital gains, pensions, IRA distributions, and a host of other items, which are detailed

Chapter 5

in this section. There is even a catchall line (miscellaneous) for other income. This is the line on which you enter, for example, winnings from the lottery or even illegally derived gambling winnings.

ADJUSTMENTS TO INCOME

The adjustments section of the 1040 effectively adjusts (reduces) the total income figure. Examples of adjustments to income include alimony paid, allowable IRA deductions*, self-employed health insurance*, one-half of self-employment tax, and SEP contributions.

ADJUSTED GROSS INCOME

The very bottom section on the front page of Form 1040 shows a sole line item: adjusted gross income. As its name implies, this figure results from subtracting the total adjustments to income from the total income amount. It is quite possible you have no adjustments to income, in which case your total income equals your adjusted gross income. Also referred to as AGI, this figure forms the basis for a host of eligibility requirements, including education and child credits, and the new Roth IRA account. It also is likely to be used in the computation of state income taxes.

STANDARD OR ITEMIZED DEDUCTIONS

In this section on the back page of the 1040 you get down to the business of computing your tax. You are faced with either accepting the standard deduction or choosing the itemized total from Schedule A. Compare these two figures and choose the larger number, which is then subtracted.

Schedule A is used frequently, and can be best understood using the same procedure we recommend for the 1040 form. The form is segmented horizontally into eight distinct categories, with a total for itemized deductions. It has the effect of reducing taxable income by the amount that your total allowed itemized deductions exceed the standard deduction. You are most likely to itemize if you are a homeowner paying mortgage interest and real estate taxes, and are currently employed and pay state income taxes. Certain retired individuals could also benefit from itemiz-

---

*These adjustments have been altered as a result of the 1997 Taxpayer Relief Act.

ing with Schedule A. This would be the case for those who have high real estate taxes, pay estimated state income taxes, are generous to charitable organizations, and have high unreimbursed medical expenses and health insurance premiums.

Certain itemized deductions such as medical and miscellaneous have to exceed a threshold percentage of AGI in order to qualify for listing on Schedule A.

PERSONAL EXEMPTIONS

Each taxpayer (and spouse, if filing jointly) is entitled to one personal exemption. Additional exemptions (e.g., for dependent children) may be claimed if qualification tests are met.

Both the personal exemption and standard deduction rise slightly each year because they are indexed to help keep pace with inflation. For example, each exemption was worth $2,550 in 1996 and rose to $2,650 in 1997. Multiply the latest dollar amount by the number of exemptions claimed and subtract it to arrive at taxable income.

TAXABLE INCOME

This important line item is emphasized in bold print as *taxable income*. That figure is the result of all preceding computations. As the name implies, it refers to the actual amount of your income that is taxable. From a tax standpoint, the taxable income figure represents the bottom line, the dollar amount of your income subject to federal income tax.

TAX

The next line item after taxable income directs us to the tax tables or tax schedules to discover the moment of truth and amount of pain owed.

CREDITS

Credits are much more valuable than deductions or adjustments, which simply reduce taxable income. Credits erase tax that otherwise is owed. For someone in the 28% tax bracket, it takes $5,357 in deductions to cut a tax bill by $1,500. Credits are a dollar-for-dollar-reduction from tax liability.

A major plum of the new tax law for qualifying families is a credit of $400 in 1998 per child, and $500 in 1999 and each year thereafter. This credit is targeted to the middle class; it starts phasing out for single parents whose AGI reaches $75,000 and for married couples at $110,000.

Starting in 1998, credits are also available to offset college education costs. The credit varies depending upon the year of college, with different percentages applying. The maximum credit is $1,500 for the first two years, $1,000 for the final two years. Similar to the family child credit, this tax break starts to disappear for taxpayers with larger AGIs.

ARE TAX-EXEMPT BONDS AN ANSWER?

High-bracket taxpayers are often frustrated to see a third or more of their investment income go down the federal tax drain, particularly true with the 31%, 36%, and 39.6% tax rates. Tax-exempt income is an option to consider.

Municipalities are allowed to attract investors with bond income returns that are exempt by law from federal taxation. This tax advantage helps municipalities secure financing at a favorable cost, because high-income investors find these lower tax-exempt returns attractive on an after-tax basis.

To determine if tax-exempt bonds are the answer in your situation:
1. First, determine if your current investment income is necessary to meet living expenses, especially important if you are retired.
2. Check your tax return for the amount of taxable interest and dividend income you receive.
3. A taxpayer in one of the three highest tax brackets (31%, 36%, 39.6%) should compare the taxable yield with the equivalent tax-exempt return to see if a difference exists (see Figure 5-2).

A taxpayer in the 36% bracket would have to receive a taxable yield of 7.8% to match a tax-free return of 5%. Looked at in another way, a 7.8% return becomes 5% after a tax rate of 36% is applied. The higher one's tax bracket, the more advantageous is muni-bond income when compared to taxable corporate and government bonds.

Individuals sometimes let the reduction of taxes override other financial considerations. I have witnessed individuals so intent on avoiding

Taxable-Equivalent Yields									
Your Federal Tax Rate	\multicolumn{9}{c}{Tax-Exempt Yield}
	4.0%	4.5%	5.0%	5.5%	6.0%	6.5%	7.0%	7.5%	8.0%
	\multicolumn{9}{c}{Taxable-Equivalent Yield}
28%	5.6%	6.3%	6.9%	7.6%	8.3%	9.0%	9.7%	10.4%	11.1%
31%	5.8%	6.5%	7.3%	8.0%	8.7%	9.4%	10.1%	11.2%	12.0%
36%	6.3%	7.0%	7.8%	8.6%	9.4%	10.2%	10.9%	11.7%	12.5%
39.6%	6.6%	7.5%	8.3%	9.1%	9.9%	10.8%	11.6%	12.4%	13.3%

Figure 5-2

taxes they willingly accept a lower after-tax investment return. Taxpayers in the 15% tax bracket, for instance, are left with more after paying taxes than if they opted for a tax-free return. Tax avoidance for low-bracket taxpayers is not a common sense approach.

DISCOVERING YOUR MARGINAL TAX BRACKET

The first thing I do when analyzing a tax return—and I recommend that you do—is to isolate the taxable income line. Knowing both your filing status and taxable income means you can quickly identify your marginal tax bracket simply by referring to the IRS tax tables.

Knowing your marginal tax bracket and comprehending its implications are at the heart of tax planning.

The terms *tax bracket, bracket,* and *marginal tax bracket* are used synonymously. Most taxpayers have heard these terms, yet I find few who can tell me what their tax bracket is. Fewer still are able to express the importance of this percentage to their personal financial planning.

With your taxable income figure in hand, look at Figure 5-3 on the next page and find the appropriate schedule: Schedule X for single taxpayers or Schedule Y-1 for married taxpayers filing jointly. Proceed down the left column until you find where your taxable income fits. Then go to the right to the corresponding dollar figure and percentage figure. This percentage represents your marginal tax bracket.

Knowing your marginal tax bracket is important to comprehending the impact on your income. For example, Bill falls into the 28% bracket. If he receives a $1 raise, 28% or 28 cents of this income is eaten by

1997 Tax Rate Schedules

SINGLE FILERS — SCHEDULE X
If the Taxable Income line of 1040

Is Over	But Not Over	The Tax Is	Of Amount Over
$0	$24,650	............15.0%	$0
$24,650	$59,750	$3,697.50 + 28.0%	$24,650
$59,750	$124,650	$13,525.50 + 31.0%	$59,750
$124,650	$271,050	$33,644.50 + 36.0%	$124,650
$271,050	....	$86,348.50 + 39.6%	$271,050

MARRIED FILING JOINTLY — SCHEDULE Y-1
If the Taxable Income line of 1040

Is Over	But Not Over	The Tax Is	Of Amount Over
$0	$41,200	15.0%	$0
$41,200	$99,600	$6,180.00 + 28.0%	$41,200
$99,600	$151,750	$22,532.00 + 31.0%	$99,600
$151,750	$271,050	$38,698.50 + 36.0%	$151,750
$271,050		$81,646.50 + 39.6%	$271,050

Figure 5-3

federal taxes. If Bill is able to reduce his taxable income by $1, perhaps by making a deductible charitable contribution, he lightens his tax load by 28% or 28 cents for that $1.

It helps to visualize the concept of marginal tax brackets by thinking of a stairway, with each step representing one of the five steps or brackets in our progressive tax schedule.

Don't confuse marginal with average. Marginalism is an economic term used to define the impact on the next dollar. Note that as your taxable income increases, the tax bite on those dollars gets progressively higher. I like to refer to this phenomenon as: "The more you make, the more they take."

As you progress up the taxable income stairway, the air becomes heavier, with taxes choking a greater share of your income. Higher tax-bracket payers are naturally more inclined to seek relief from the voracious appetite of the tax collectors. But I like to emphasize that the edge of a tax rate increase is a step, not a cliff. Many taxpayers are desperately afraid of being pushed into a higher tax bracket.

Sue is single and reports a taxable income of $24,750 for the tax year 1997, which lands her on the 28% tax bracket step. However, she pays a flat 15% on the bulk of her income up to $24,650 ($24,650 x 15% = $3,697.50). Only on the last $100 does the 28% rate apply. She pays $28 in tax on this income above the 15% cutoff, for a total tax bill of $3,725.50 ($3,697.50 + $28.00).

Sue was reluctant to accept the raise that placed her in a dreaded higher tax bracket. I pointed out that in a 28% marginal tax bracket, Uncle Sam gets a $28 bite of *just that last hundred dollars*. Not all of her income was subject to this bigger mouthful.

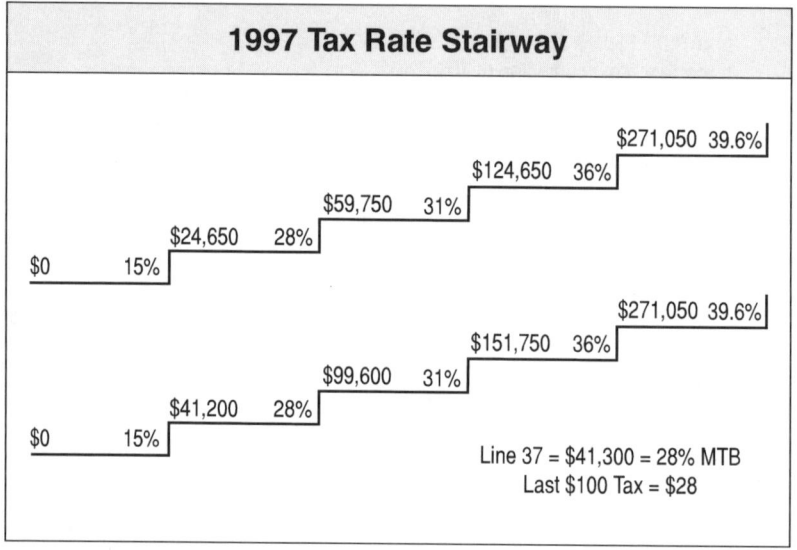

Figure 5-4

PLANNING POINTER

I hope that everyone appreciates the stark contrast between tax avoidance and tax evasion. Tax avoidance is perfectly legal and is an important aspect of tax planning. Tax evasion is illegal. Avoid tax evasion at all costs.

> "The avoidance of taxes is the only intellectual pursuit that carries any reward."
> —John Maynard Keynes

TAX-SAVING STRATEGIES

Tax planning turns to a search for ways to minimize taxable income. Retirement planning goes hand in hand with effective tax planning.

During the preretirement accumulation period, your focus should be on maximizing the benefits of tax-advantaged retirement plans.

Once retired, you want to shift your strategy to planning issues that include which money to consume first for cash flow, how to maximize tax-deferred growth, and how to manage capital gain assets. Charitable and gifting strategies may come into play to reduce your currently taxable income, to give you a tax deduction, or to shift your income.

THE IMPORTANCE OF TAX DEDUCTIBILITY

In your preretirement years, you are advised to accumulate your nest egg on a tax-advantaged basis. The best retirement savings plans possess twin tax advantages: namely, tax deductibility and tax deferral. Included in this select group are the popular 401(k) and 403(b) plans, SEPs, Keoghs, SIMPLE IRAs, and deductible IRAs. The ability to reduce your taxable income dollar for dollar with your retirement contributions provides a powerful tax incentive.

As an effective tax shelter, you receive a 1:1 tax benefit. Your contributed dollars are made pretax, or before taxation. Contributions to 401(k) and 403(b) plans are subtracted from W-2 gross income and are not included in income for tax purposes. SEPs, Keoghs, and deductible IRA contributions are subtracted (adjusted) on the tax return and derive an equivalent benefit. Their ability to reduce taxable income makes these plans the best retirement planning tax shelters.

Let's look at Sarah's example, which illustrates the power of tax deductibility on her earnings of $35,000, of which $1,000 is in the 28% marginal tax bracket.

A $1,000 tax-deductible saving in a 28% marginal tax bracket gives Sarah a $280 tax subsidy owing to deductibility.

Since she is in the 28% tax bracket, her federal tax savings will be $280 greater than if no qualified retirement savings plan is used. Another way of looking at it is that the federal government, through the tax code, has promoted the use of retirement plans. For taxpayer Sarah, the out-of-pocket after-tax effect is really the difference, or $720 ($1,000 - $280 = $720).

In addition, she can realize further savings from a reduction in state income taxes that otherwise would have been owed.

THE IMPORTANCE OF TAX DEFERRAL

The second tax advantage is just as important. All retirement saving plans offer the benefit of tax deferral. Investment returns, whether interest, dividends, or capital gains, are not reported on the current tax return.

Tax deferral allows your retirement savings to grow unencumbered by current taxation until these funds are withdrawn. Tax deferral is an important strategy in preretirement planning when you are looking to grow a substantial nest egg. Tax deferral is simply the legal postponement or delay of the taxation of investment earnings until some future date. Tax deferral does not avoid your legal tax obligation, nor does it exempt the taxes. It merely delays the inevitable payment of the tax. It represents one instance in which procrastination—or in this case, putting off tax due—is a positive.

Let's use a simple example. Suppose you have a $1,000 investment. If you could earn 10% before tax (BT), you would generate $100 in investment income. If this investment income were subject to current taxation, you would receive a Form 1099 at tax time and be required to report the full $100 on your 1040. Assuming you are in a 28% marginal tax bracket, the tax bite would eat in excess of a full quarter of this investment return, or $28. Taking into account this after-tax effect, you would be left with investment income of $72 ($100 - $28) and an after-tax return of 7.2% (10% - 2.8%).

In the first year, this 28% loss or $28 might seem insignificant. But let's look at a longer time frame of 25 years: $1,000 at 10% left to grow unburdened by current taxation would compound to $10,835 over a 25-year period. The same $1,000, using the after-tax equivalent annual yield of 7.2%, would grow to $5,687.

Comparing these two results demonstrates a sizable difference. The $28 initial difference on the $1,000 principal amount is now $5,148. The after-tax effect has produced a nest egg smaller than its tax-deferred competitor by 52%. This substantial difference is a direct result of the erosive effects of current taxation versus the dynamic power of compound growth. If we had used a larger initial dollar amount or illustrated the effect of additional annual investments, the dollar difference would have loomed much larger.

It helps to visualize tax deferral as an umbrella over your retirement

Figure 5-5

nest egg that shelters and protects it from the erosive effects of current taxation. Deferral can be considered a tax shelter because it protects your investment nest egg from the bite of current taxation. Deferral may be thought of as an interest-free loan from our government. Owing to the effects of inflation, when you do start paying these taxes it will be with cheaper dollars. Moreover, by then you are likely to be retired. At retirement, without earned income, you could well be in a lower tax bracket.

Another important planning benefit in the preretirement stage is that tax deductibility and tax deferral effectively reduce not only taxable income, but adjusted gross income as well. This benefit is valuable because a host of favorable tax programs are tied to AGI, including IRA deductibility, Roth IRA eligibility, and education incentives.

HOME SWEET HOME—
THE ULTIMATE TAX SHELTER

In addition to the shelter of a roof over your head, a home provides a major asset in securing a financial future in both preretirement and postretirement stages.

There are multiple advantages to home ownership:
- Unlike a car, a home is an appreciating asset.
- Your equity in your home (market value less mortgage balance) can represent the largest portion of net worth.
- As a real estate holding, a home diversifies the financial assets in your portfolio.
- A home has proven to be a solid inflation hedge.
- With a fixed-rate mortgage payment, you are paying off in cheaper dollars in the years down the road.
- It is a forced savings mechanism through a monthly mortgage obligation, which must be paid if you are to keep your home.
- Each payment contains a principal payoff component.
- Market value is likely to rise through the years, resulting in increased equity.
- If you time your final mortgage payment to coincide with the onset of college costs, you can direct the cash outlay you are in the habit of making toward tuition without taking on additional expense.
- Alternatively, a debt-free home can be tapped via a home equity loan to provide education funds.
- Increasingly, retired individuals are turning to reverse mortgages. These financial products allow them to stay put in their own home, yet tap the tied-up equity with regular monthly supplemental income payments from a financial institution.
- The sale of a home might yield a source of funds from which to construct an income-producing portfolio, if the home were replaced via downsizing to less expensive housing or renting.
  - Once the celebration of a mortgage-burning party takes place, new planning opportunities are present.
  - At retirement, a mortgage-free state helps keep the cost of living down and stable.

TAX SHELTER

A home is a tax shelter in the true sense. Tax incentives found in home ownership make it an appealing investment.

- ♦ Unlike federal, sales, and payroll taxes, real estate taxes assessed to your home count as an itemized deduction on Schedule A of your income tax return.
- ♦ The mortgage interest you incur on a primary or vacation home is also deductible, giving you a major tax write-off. Virtually every taxpayer carrying a mortgage benefits from itemizing this deduction over taking the standard deduction.

Ruth is a taxpayer and homeowner in the 28% tax bracket. She carries a large mortgage costing 8%, on which she incurred $10,000 in interest charges this last tax year. As a result of the mortgage interest write-off, her income taxes are reduced by $2,800. If she rented, there would be no tax reduction. She calculates the 8% mortgage note effectively costs her about 5.76%, after accounting for the 28% tax incentive.

- ♦ The interest incurred on a qualifying home equity loan is also a deductible expense, making such loans a popular form of tax-advantaged borrowing.

Sheldon and Susan are fortunate to be sitting on substantial equity in their home.

They are also in the market for a new car, which, even with trade-ins, will set them back $20,000. The dealer naturally offers to arrange financing to save the sale, but they are not enamored of the terms. They discover they can negotiate a much better deal on an all-cash transaction.

Susan voices concern about carrying another debt payment, but what really bothers her is a $5,000 credit card balance maxed to the limit and costing a sky-high 20% annual interest rate.

After careful consideration, the couple jointly decides to take out a home equity loan for the sum of $25,000. This enables them to purchase the car for cash and to erase completely their plastic balance.

In this regard, they not only benefit from a lower cost of borrowing, but the 10% interest on the home equity loan is fully tax deductible.

Sheldon understands that the reason they qualify for a lower cost debt is that their loan is secured. They have pledged their home and risk losing it if they don't honor this obligation.

One of the prime tax planning principles is to make every effort to refrain from assuming debt for which the interest is not tax deductible. Tax laws effectively limit this advantage to home mortgage and home equity loans.

Peter Lynch, in his best-selling book, *One Up On Wall Street,* extols the merits of home ownership and suggests it should be a prerequisite to venturing into the stock market.

He points out it is rare to get wiped out financially on a house, and that for millions it has been hailed as a great investment.

Lynch goes on to focus on the remarkable power of leverage available with a home. For example, a $100,000 home can be purchased routinely with just $20,000 or a 20% down payment. If the house appreciates in value at 5% a year, this amounts to a hefty 25% return on your invested capital. Leverage allows you to control a $100,000 asset with just one fifth of the value put forth. Think of how a heavy boulder can be moved by effectively employing the lever of a two-by-four board. When leverage is applied, you gain the appreciation on the home, and the mortgage interest is deductible to boot.

Comparing the virtues of home ownership to stock ownership, stock-picker Lynch gives the nod to the roof over your head. In addition to the previously mentioned favorable tax treatment, Lynch likes the long-term nature inherent in home ownership, an approach so beneficial to a successful investment. Another advantage is not being able to find the daily market value of your home, which means not fixating on it, as many people do with a stock holding. As Lynch says, "It takes a moving van to get out of a house, and only a phone call to get out of a stock."

I want to remind you at this point that home ownership is not for everybody nor an absolute essential for financial success. Renting, contrary to some biased real estate agents, is not throwing your money away. Nor is owning a home an unbeatable, sure-fire investment.

If you lead the life of a nomad, or prefer not being tied down with the demands accompanying ownership, renting is a viable option. But make no mistake about it, home ownership has a lot going for it. Included are juicy tax incentives, the discipline imposed from forced savings, the ability to use leverage, and intangibles, including pride of ownership, all of which make owning a home an attractive personal finance objective.

IRAS—A VITAL COG IN YOUR RETIREMENT PLANNING MACHINERY

Individual retirement accounts (IRAs), as the name implies, have been expressly designed for retirement savings accumulation. Their primary feature is a tax-advantaged buildup under the umbrella of tax deferral.

Unfortunately, more misconceptions surround IRAs than any other subject in all of retirement planning. I hope I can dispel some of the myths and spotlight the value of these tax-saving vehicles.

Understanding the tax aspects and opportunities of these accounts will shape your financial security and help trim your tax bill.

The Tax Reform Act of 1986 seriously wounded IRAs by restricting their deductibility feature to certain taxpayers, adding to the complexity and confusion in the process.

Nonetheless, IRA account balances, fueled by compounding effects, have grown magnificently—from inheritances and especially from rollovers from employer-sponsored retirement plans, which occur upon an employee's changing jobs or retiring. Intelligent tax management of these accounts is essential to your financial well-being.

One basic piece of IRA information to comprehend is that the "I" stands for *individual*. IRAs are not allowed to be joint accounts, and at death they bypass probate and go directly to the named beneficiary.

The Taxpayer Relief Act of 1997 repaired some of the inequity and pitfalls found in IRAs. Chief among them were:

1. a repeal of the 15% excise tax on plan distributions above certain levels; and
2. repeal of an additional 15% estate tax imposed on excess retirement accumulations.

Elimination of these so-called success taxes is welcome news for those possessing or planning to amass $1 million-plus retirement account balances. Under the 1997 law no tax disincentive lurks in the shadows for possessing or building a large-balance retirement account. Removing this onus should dispel the notion that IRAs are bad accumulation vehicles.

Additionally, the 1997 tax legislation finally increases the income ranges over which the $2,000 IRA deductibility is phased out. This income test applies only to active participants in an employer-sponsored retirement plan, such as a 401(k).

For single taxpayers this range jumps $10,000 beginning in 1998 to $30,000–$40,000, and for married couples, $50,000–$60,000. It slowly rises over the next 10 years to a doubling of the income range by the year 2007: $50,000–$60,000 for singles and $80,000–$100,000 for married couples.

In the past, if one spouse was in a retirement plan and the couple's AGI was above $40,000, neither spouse was allowed the more attractive deductible IRA. Under the new law this inequity is corrected, provided the AGI on a joint return is not more than $150,000.

Previously, the maximum for a spousal IRA when only one mate was employed was $2,250. Now couples can contribute up to $4,000 even if one spouse is not employed.

Unfortunately, the $2,000 maximum annual IRA contribution is stuck at the same dollar limit that existed at its inception.

TAX TIP: Although you have until April 15th to make your IRA contribution for the previous tax year, do it early in the year to gain the benefit of tax-deferred compounding.

TAX TIP: When you change jobs or leave your employer don't look at your retirement account as a windfall. Have the foresight to place this lump sum in your new employer's plan or in a direct rollover to your established IRA. A direct rollover (with the check made out to your new IRA trustee) avoids a 20% withholding tax that is otherwise attached.

LEAVE PLAN BALANCES ALONE

In other words, don't touch your plan balances until you're retired and use distributions for retirement income. This strategy allows your nest egg to grow on a tax-deferred basis and accumulate to a sufficient size to assure financial security.

I'd like to see a proper warning label on all retirement plans to the effect that premature distributions are hazardous to your financial security. Too many people casually dip into their retirement money for short-term purposes.

Negative tax consequences come into play, including the burden that all distributions are fully and immediately taxable as ordinary income.

This additional income could push you into a higher tax bracket, and, if you are under age 59½, cause you to incur a 10% penalty tax. Depending on the amount of federal and state taxes, up to half of this premature distribution could be eaten by additional taxes. Retirement sums receive tax incentives to build for retirement, but penalties are levied for use of this money for any other purpose.

LOOK OVER THE NEW ROTH IRA

Some taxpayers should consider a new type of IRA for which the contributions are not deductible, but the withdrawals, when taken, are tax free.

Named after proponent Senator William Roth, this back-loaded IRA is an improved version for those taxpayers previously eligible only for nondeductible IRAs. This new model is similar to the standard IRA in that the contribution limit is the familiar $2,000 for singles and $4,000 for married couples, and the investment earnings grow untaxed.

In addition to tax-free rather than taxable distributions after age 59½, the Roth IRA is differentiated by not requiring minimum distributions to start at age 70½.

This type of account, promoted as the American Dream IRA, also allows for accessible tax-free and penalty-free withdrawals prior to age 59½ of up to $10,000 toward the purchase of a first home or toward qualifying higher education expenses for the benefit of the taxpayer or family.

Unfortunately, the Roth IRA is not available to everyone, as there exists a phase-out range starting at an AGI of $95,000 on single filer returns and $150,000 on joint returns. My knock on this and the dozens of applicable IRA rules is that they are exceedingly complicated and inhibit people from using them.

For example, the appeal of tax-free withdrawals makes the Roth IRA attractive, but so is an immediate tax write-off for those who qualify for a deductible IRA.

High-income earners who participate in a retirement plan through their employers are locked out of deductible IRAs and possibly the Roth IRA as well. However, this group is still eligible to contribute to a nondeductible, tax-deferred IRA if they so choose.

Then again, taxpayers might find the recordkeeping requirements and restrictions of nondeductible IRAs to be too much bother. Some might opt to build a no-limit, fully accessible, tax-efficient capital gain portfolio instead.

	New Roth IRA	Deductible IRA	Nondeductible IRA
Eligibility starts to phase out at these levels of adjusted gross income	$95,000 single $150,000 joint	$25,000 single $40,000 joint (increases to $50,000 single by 2005 and $80,000 joint by 2007)	No limits
Earnings grow tax deferred	Yes	Yes	Yes
Earnings are taxed upon withdrawal	No (with restrictions)	Yes	Yes
10% penalty on premature withdrawals	In some instances	In some instances	In some instances
Tax-deductible contributions	No	Yes	No
Maximum annual contributions	$2,000	$2,000	$2,000
Subject to minimum withdrawal requirements after age 70½	No	Yes	Yes
Contributions allowed after age 70½	Yes	No	No

IRA Options

Figure 5-6

Confused? You should be. This hodgepodge points out the value of seeking objective and competent retirement and tax planning counsel. A CPA would be a good source to map out the best route for you.

If I had my druthers, I would like to see universal IRA deductibility reinstated and the contribution dollar limit quadrupled to $8,000 or even $10,000 a year per taxpayer. Such an understandable program would once again excite taxpayers to opt for an IRA to build a secure financial future.

PRERETIREMENT TAX-SAVING STRATEGIES GUIDE

In your employment years you are naturally inclined to maximize your wage earnings. Since the prime tax planning objective is to reduce taxable income, attention must focus on other than employment income. Every dollar reduction in taxable income translates to a tax saving that is equivalent to the percentage of your marginal tax bracket. Remember, only the last dollars of income provide any real tax planning capability.

The following six techniques reduce taxable income and minimize income taxation:

1. Keep income off the tax return and out of taxable income by maximizing pre-tax retirement contributions to 401(k) and 403(b) plans.
2. If you are eligible, contribute to plans such as SEPs, Keoghs, and deductible IRAs in order to take full advantage of tax planning strategies to reduce your current income.
   - By reducing your AGI in this manner, you could also be reducing your state tax burden, as many states use the federal AGI in state tax computation.
   - Two-income couples in particular would be wise to maximize their respective retirement plan contributions. Because a definite marriage penalty exists in the tax code, this method helps to justify both partners working. The second income is subject to a higher marginal tax bracket.
3. Postpone recognition of investment income through tax deferral found in all retirement plans and IRAs as well as in tax-deferred annuities, savings bonds, and cash-value life insurance buildup.
   - Note there is no limit on the amount of tax-deferred investments you may accumulate.
4. Itemize deductions to benefit from amounts exceeding the standard deduction. A good way to do this is to own a home, because mortgage interest, real estate taxes, and home equity interest all count as deductible items. Better yet, your home's appreciation in value amounts to a tax-free buildup at the time of its sale.
5. Be tax intelligent with your investment management by look-

ing to earn tax-favored capital gains over ordinary income and owning tax-exempt municipal bonds if your tax bracket warrants.
6. Employ the services of a tax planning specialist trained to uncover valuable tax-saving strategies.

DON'T FORGET STATE TAXES

Although your emphasis should be on reducing federal taxes with their higher burden, don't overlook state tax-saving opportunities to save on state taxes.

As discussed, federal tax reduction techniques such as pre-tax retirement contributions, tax deferral, and the special treatment accorded to homeowners also translate to state income tax savings.

Additionally, recognize that all U.S. government interest is, by law, exempt from state income tax. Included are U.S. Treasury securities, be they bills, notes, bonds, or U.S. Savings Bonds. Investors in mutual funds should inquire from the fund what percentage of investment income is from U.S. Treasury issues.

Residents of high-tax states should take a look at double tax-exempt (state and federal) municipal bonds. A word of caution: these bonds can carry higher risks. Look for quality and don't grab a bond solely because of tax considerations.

COPING WITH THE KIDDIE TAX

Children under age 14 are subject to a so-called "Kiddie Tax" on their investment (unearned) income. Its effect is to tax these young taxpayers at the same rate as their parents once their investment income exceeds $1,300 in a tax year. However, they can receive the first $650 of investment income tax free. Another $650 is taxed at the low 15% rate. Children over 14 are taxed at their own (presumably lower) tax bracket.

The Kiddie Tax was hatched as a result of tax reform to prevent parents from shifting investments into their children's names to avoid or reduce taxation.

Income shifting is the maneuver of having income taxed at the lower rate of another taxpayer, be that a child, grandchild, or parent. As such, it remains a valid tax planning strategy.

In financing an education, parents and grandparents frequently establish custodial accounts in the children's names. For younger children, consideration might be given to those investments such as stocks or index mutual funds which generate little in the way of current income. In this way, it is possible to build a sizable account without bumping up against the filing requirement. Once a child is over the age of 14 any income received is taxed at the lightest rate.

> TAX TIP: The start of a new year is the best time to plot out tax planning. Tax-saving strategies adopted at the beginning of the calendar year can save taxes year-round.
>
> TAX TIP: The rules, requirements, and eligibility associated with education planning are very complicated and technical. No clear-cut advice can be offered to cover planning implications of prepaid tuition plans, education IRAs, Roth IRAs, financial aid eligibility, deductibility of student loan interest, or education tax credits.

However, all these programs involve tax matters, and problems and backfires are lurking in all the complexity we face. This is another area where competent counsel could well be worth the cost. There also exists a business opportunity for anyone who wants to hang out a shingle as an education funding expert.

> "The taxpayer: Someone who works for the government but doesn't have to take a civil service examination."
> —Ronald Reagan

SAM AND DIANE PLAN TO TACKLE THEIR TAXES

Sam and Diane are in their early sixties, retired for a year, and in need of some postretirement tax planning.

Sam gets all worked up every quarter when he writes out an estimated tax payment for $2,500 made out to what he derogatorily calls the Infernal Revenue Service.

I have noted the tendency for self-employed and retired taxpayers who actually pen checks to the IRS to be very aware of their tax burden, whereas employees and retirees who have taxes automatically withheld are less likely to be concerned about taxation.

Sam and Diane are typical in that their $10,000 federal tax bill is actually much less than what they used to have withheld from their paychecks, including some $5,100 in FICA payroll taxes. When Diane points this out, Sam retorts that he wouldn't mind this extraction (he equates taxes to tooth pulling without anesthesia) if he thought the government spent the money better. Diane suggests they quit their complaining and seek some tax planning assistance. Sam is pessimistic, but has learned from 39 years of marriage to trust the instincts of his mate.

Diane contacts Colleen, a CPA who has earned a solid reputation as a tax planning specialist. Diane wisely makes the appointment for November in order to unearth any year-end planning opportunities and to be ready to start out the new tax year with the full benefit of tax-minimization strategies.

At their initial consultation, Colleen asks to see their last three years' tax returns to help her get a feel for their tax picture. Her analysis zeroes in on sources of income, income requirements, and the makeup of their investment portfolio.

Colleen informs Diane that postretirement tax strategy commonly revolves around which income to spend and consume first.

Sam and Diane's income sources are identified as follows:

- They receive $20,000 in taxable interest and dividends from a $250,000 portfolio, which consists of $75,000 in money funds yielding 5.5% and $175,000 in a high-yield bond fund yielding 9%. These funds represent a lifetime of savings and an inheritance from Diane's grandmother.
- They own $100,000 of a single stock they inherited years before when it was a glamour growth stock. It is now stuck at the same value it reached a decade ago and pays no dividend. They would like to sell it and move on, but because their basis in it is just $20,000, they are hesitant to incur the $80,000 capital gain.
- Their IRAs are worth a total of $240,000, from which they have been taking distributions of $2,000 a month, $24,000 annually. The bulk of the IRA assets reside in aggressive growth stock mutual funds which Sam boasts have performed well. Diane does harbor concerns over the risk of these holdings at this stage in their life.

- Diane owns two tax-deferred fixed annuities for $10,000, for which she paid $5,000.
- Diane receives a monthly pension of $646 totaling $7,750 a year. She elected not to have taxes withheld.

From this information-gathering session Colleen draws up a portfolio listing as follows:

$	75,000	Money fund
$	175,000	High-yield bond fund
$	100,000	Out-of-gas, low-basis stock
$	240,000	IRAs invested in aggressive stock funds
$	10,000	Tax-deferred fixed annuities
$	600,000	TOTAL

Their taxable income sources as of their most recent tax return are:

$	20,000	Interest/Dividends
$	7,750	Pension
$	24,000	IRA Distributions
$	15,300	Social Security (gross: $18,000)
$	67,050	TOTAL

Sam becomes irritated when Colleen points out that the maximum 85% of their Social Security benefits has been included in the taxable income column. She points out that this is a prime reason their tax bill is heavy. A priority in retirement is to keep Social Security benefits from being taxed.

Diane would like to gift more to her church and charity, but Sam has resisted. Since the mortgage is paid off they use the standard deduction, and he sees no direct tax benefit from any charitable intent.

Both Sam and Diane would like to reduce their investment-risk exposure, but are hesitant to make any moves because of the presumed tax consequences.

With their $10,000 annual tax liability, Sam and Diane feel constrained from carrying out their dream of traveling.

Diane thinks it would be great if someone else took on the tax-preparation chore, which a harried Sam has insisted on tackling himself. Ideally, she would like to remove the need to make quarterly estimated tax payments, which are a source of aggravation and anxiety over missing any payments and being subject to a penalty.

Sam's ideas for tax savings have included purchasing tax-deferred annuities and tax-exempt municipal bonds, buying income property, and tapping a home equity loan. Colleen politely points out that these are all sound tax planning measures but not appropriate in their situation.

Armed with this information and now fully aware of their wish list, Colleen goes to work on her laptop computer, crunching the numbers and projecting various outcomes using a tax planning software program. She presents the following recommendations, confident they are in line with Sam and Diane's objectives:

1. There is no real reason for Sam and Diane to be tapping their IRAs at their current ages. Sam had felt they needed this income because he has no pension, and no penalty is incurred because they are over age $59\frac{1}{2}$. However, each dollar of distribution is fully taxable, and the $24,000 causes their Social Security to be pushed into the tax column. Colleen points out that they can generate income from other sources and allow their IRA to continue to grow tax-deferred until age $70\frac{1}{2}$. Her first recommendation is to immediately discontinue their $2,000 monthly distributions and erase $24,000 from taxable income.

2. The non-IRA and IRA investment portfolios are mismatched in terms of tax and investment makeup. An advantage of IRAs is that changes can be made in portfolio composition without triggering tax consequences. Colleen shows that the high-yield 9% bond fund is better held under the umbrella of tax deferral. Sam and Diane can redeem the volatile stock funds inside their IRA without having to ante up for the big gains earned from these funds.

Colleen recommends they rearrange their portfolio as follows:

Their IRAs would hold $70,000 in a high-yield bond fund balanced by $170,000 in a more conservative GNMA mutual fund. These higher-yielding investments would then be sheltered inside the IRA and not spill out to the tax return.

The nonretirement taxable account would then look like this:

$	75,000	Money funds	@ 5.0%	$ 3,750 Income
$	100,000	U.S. Treasury notes	@ 6.0%	$ 6,000 Income
$	75,000	Stock index fund	@ 3.0%	$ 2,250 Income
$	250,000	TOTAL	@ 4.8%	$12,000 Income

For now, the couple would hold onto the $100,000 low-basis shares of "dead stock" and Diane's $10,000 in tax-deferred annuities.

The result is a more tax-efficient portfolio, with a lower level of risk because of a more conservative asset allocation, but without immediate negative tax consequences being triggered.

Sam asks Colleen how they would replace the $2,000 monthly supplementary income now coming from the IRAs. Her plan is to spend down the money fund balances and then the Treasury notes. At $24,000 a year, this source will last about eight years, at which time Sam and Diane will be 70½. They will then turn the IRA spigot back on.

Sam voices concern that they will run out of money. The CPA illustrates that a $240,000 IRA left to grow at 8% over an eight-year period will be worth some $444,000.

The money market and treasury notes provide an income generator from which $2,000 a month is automatically deposited to their checking account. Because this income source represents a return of principal, taxes are minimized. Another advantage of the treasury notes, in addition to relative safety, is that the earnings are exempt from state income taxes. The index fund, by design, has a low turnover and will throw off little in capital gains distributions and just minimal dividends.

Tax Planning

	Before	After
Interest/Dividends	$20,000	$12,000
Pension	$ 7,750	$ 7,750
IRA Distributions	$24,000	$ 0
Social Security $18,000	$15,300	$18,000 $ 0
TOTAL	$67,050	$19,750
Standard Deduction	$6,900	Itemized $12,450
(2) Personal Exemptions	$ 5,300	$ 5,300
	($12,200)	($17,750)
Taxable Income	$54,850	$ 2,000
Tax Bracket	28%	15%
Tax	$ 10,000	$ 300
Tax Savings		$ 9,700

Figure 5-7

Diane's pension and their combined Social Security income streams can't be altered, but the tax bite on Diane's pension is significantly lowered. Social Security income is no longer taxed.

In analyzing Schedule A, itemized deductions, Colleen discovers a total of $5,000, primarily because of charitable contributions and real estate taxes. As Sam had mentioned, this figure falls short of exceeding the standard deduction.

Colleen suggests one tax planning technique to consider is bunching deductions and itemizing one year, and settling for the standard deduction the next. This involves accelerating (pulling) deductions into a calendar tax year, while deferring (pushing) income into the next year.

Colleen also suggests they collect into one targeted tax year deductions such as charitable gifts, real estate taxes, and, where possible, state income taxes and medical deductions.

Given Diane's desire to be more generous to her church and charities, the $100,000 stock holding that Sam calls "dead" now merits a closer look. Colleen recommends that they consider gifting $10,000-worth of shares of this stock at year-end and going forward to donate to their favorite charities. In this way, they get a charitable deduction at full market value and are able to itemize. They avoid the capital gains tax that would have been imposed had they sold this low-basis holding. Diane appreciates the fact that this option beats writing out a check. The qualified charitable beneficiaries can turn around and sell the stock without facing a tax consequence.

Sam is getting itchy to learn the result, while Diane appreciates the positive moves Colleen is putting in place.

Touchdown! Sam can't believe his eyes or ears, and Diane flashes a smile of relief. Sam asks Colleen, "You mean to tell me that our total tax bill for next year will be only $300? Won't the tax authorities be suspicious if our taxes go down by so much?"

Colleen has heard this concern dozens of times by shell-shocked taxpayers. She assures them their plan is perfectly legal and offers to prepare and sign off on their tax return. Sam is quick to take her up on the offer. Colleen asks if they want to have $25 in taxes withheld from Diane's monthly pension or just pay the balance due at filing time and say goodbye to the dreaded quarterly estimated tax payments.

Finally, Colleen asks Diane how much their dream trip to Scotland to celebrate their 40th wedding anniversary would cost. Recalling the $2,500 quarterly tax bite they'll save, Diane smiles at her husband and replies, "about $10,000." Sam then does something out of character for him: he leans over and kisses his bride.

PLANNING POINTERS

"The income tax has made liars out of more Americans than golf."
—Will Rogers

The best approach toward the IRS and your tax obligation is to follow these guidelines:
- file timely and accurate returns
- maintain good tax records
  - cost and purchase information
  - documentation to back up deductions
- seek professional tax help when warranted
- be prepared to fully support your filed return
- if challenged by the IRS, verify that their figures are correct.

CHAPTER 6

MANAGING YOUR NEST EGG: PORTFOLIO MANAGEMENT & ASSET ALLOCATION

"Investing is the focal point of financial planning."
—Jonathan D. Pond

The successful pursuit of financial objectives is certain to be tied to how well the investment process is aligned, on an individual basis, with our purpose. The return and performance from an investment portfolio is most critical to reaching goals. Unfortunately, I have found too many investors hitting potholes, taking detours, and being slowed by delays in the drive for investment and financial success.

These problems include neglect and disregard of the value of portfolio investment management. This inattention is underscored by the inability of many to recognize even the size or makeup of their holdings. The typical portfolio amounts to a hodgepodge collection of components.

Most lack a clear idea of what is to be accomplished from a pool of money. Instead of a concrete plan or policy, we discover a mishmash puzzle. It is no surprise that investment direction is out of control, paralyzed in a state of indecision. One investment counselor highly visible on local TV and radio frequently conducts seminars entitled, "Investing in Uncertain Times." The allure of this presentation is that it can be delivered at any time. After all, when is there any certainty in the investment climate? "Now" is always the most difficult environment in which to invest. If the market is down, we tend to believe it will continue to falter. When the market is rising we are dejected, thinking any moves are too late. Indecision and its companion, procrastination, add up to a costly mistake.

The tendency when making investment moves is to routinely follow the wrong path, such as:

- misunderstanding the folly of market timing;
- believing you can consistently select superior investments;
- being misinformed about risk;
- lacking an appreciation for the virtue of patience,
- overlooking the rewards from effective diversification.

"It is not the volume of money, but the activity of money that counts."

—W. Bourke Cochran

It has been my experience that a majority of investors cannot identify the current value of their portfolios, missing by a full 20 to 25%. The tendency is for younger investors with smaller portfolios to grossly overstate their investment holdings, while older folks with more sizable portfolios seem to miss the mark on the low end. Which brings us to a common sense check: How can money be adequately managed without knowing what is being worked with?

A couple of years back, I was counseling a retiring business executive and his soon-to-be wife. We sat together in the comfortable new home they had recently purchased. After some discussion about what they were looking to accomplish, I used a management term he was fond of and suggested we proceed to "get our arms around" his investment portfolio. This called for inventorying his scattered holdings.

Prior to tabulating his portfolio on my adding machine, I made the remark that I had found many investors in similar stages to underestimate their investment pot by a full 25%. He concurred with the probable truth of this finding, but countered that he is, after all, an executive with a strong financial background, and he personally wouldn't expect anywhere near that disparity. He could, for instance, discuss in detail any financial measurement of his business enterprise.

At this point, his curious future wife asked him what he thought the final tally would be on his personal portfolio. I proceeded to write down the figure he confidently offered. Once I hit the total button, I shared this number and wrote it right above his estimate. The result was almost exactly a 25% underestimate.

Smiling, we all had reason to be satisfied with the result of this exercise. He owned a substantially larger investment portfolio than he had previously imagined. His new partner felt more comfortable knowing the exact measure of his wealth. I scored some points while confirming the value of portfolio management.

Therefore, the first step in managing your portfolio is to identify what you have. Any good manager should fully assess all assets. This is equally true of a business manager, athletic coach, or you—when acting as your own personal money manager.

MANAGING INVESTMENT RISK

The investment world is full of uncertainty and risk. As I pointed out in Chapter 3 on common sense investment principles, elements of risk exist in every investment. Although you can't eliminate risk, you can and should act to reduce, minimize, and manage it. We must accept risk as a precondition of investing in the stock and bond market if we are to gain the superior return potential that exists there.

Theoretical and statistical discussions of risk seldom sink in. A decline amounting to tens of thousands of dollars hits home.

As of this writing, a sustained bull market has masked the element of risk for too many unaware or naive investors. It has been too easy to dismiss and underappreciate risk in a generally rising market. What is called for is a downsizing of expectations and getting back to more historical returns for both stocks and bonds.

Biloxi, Mississippi, had been spared the devastation of a major hurricane for more than a quarter of a century. For some recent residents of this gulf town, and for the younger generation, the dangers of such a violent storm seemed remote. So it was not entirely surprising when a portion of the local population dismissed the warnings of an impending storm. Rather than taking the necessary precautions, this element decided to stay and hold a hurricane party instead.

When the storm hit it destroyed much of the town. It also ruined the party. Similar was the effect of the brutal bear market that toppled the stock market in 1973 and 1974. The lesson is not to be blind to risk, but rather to recognize its existence and appreciate its ability to topple values and inflict pain. Down years and difficult market periods should come as no surprise, and should be expected and anticipated as part of the normal cycle.

Because volatility is a major part of investing, it is useful to take a closer look at it. Very often when speaking about risk, the reference is actually to volatility. *Volatility* is not a measure of performance, but rather the magnitude and frequency of fluctuations of a given investment.

Learn to live with some degree of volatility, because stocks tend to rise slowly yet drop fast. Take the 1987 market, for example, in which five months of steady 100-point gains were wiped out in one 508-point October trading day free fall.

The most recent expression of volatility was the startling 554 point loss on October 27, 1997, equating to a hefty 7.3% decline in stock prices.

In an attempt to dampen expectations, the Royce Funds in its annual report to shareholders warned:

"Volatility, which has always been a part of the investment equation, is likely to resurface and resume a more normal course as background conditions change. In summation, the natural laws of gravity and market cycles have not been rescinded."

Realize that your time and planning horizons are closely interwoven. The time horizon is directly related to the level and amount of risk you can assume.

Figure 6-1 builds upon these three variables and is instructional for your formulating a retirement investment strategy. In this analysis, we illustrate a lump-sum investment of $10,000. Use a multiple of this figure for your own purposes; e.g., multiply by 10 for $100,000, or 100 for $1 million.

Time periods appear as columns across the top, measuring projections of 5, 10, 20, 30, and 40 years.

Down the left side of the chart are shown annual returns of 6, 8, 10, and 12%. For assumption purposes, 6% is what might be expected from a five-year treasury note; 8% steps up to the average yield from a long-term corporate bond or mortgage; 10% is the historical return from a

Return Expectations					
Investment $10,000	5 yrs.	10 yrs.	20 yrs.	25 yrs.	40 yrs.
@ 6%	$13,382	$17,908	$32,701	$42,919	$102,857
@ 8%	14,693	21,589	46,609	68,485	217,245
@10%	16,105	25,937	67,275	108,347	452,593
@12%	17,623	31,058	96,463	170,001	930,510

Figure 6-1

common stock; and 12% corresponds with the potential average return of a small-cap stock fund.

Use the chart to project growth for a given investment return over a certain time period. Important lessons are to be learned from analyzing this intersection of return and time.

If you want to reach a given level faster (in less time), you must either assume a higher level of risk to capture this return potential or increase the amount you save. If you have a 20-year time frame, common in retirement planning, you can afford to take on greater risk for the higher rewards. The probability of the various expected returns approaches 100% if you have in excess of 20 years; 75%, if 10 years; and roughly 50%, if 5 years.

This chart also shows that at the end of 20 years, a corporate long-term bond could grow 25% more than an intermediate treasury note, a stock could grow in excess of 100%, and an aggressive small-cap fund could grow 300%. With a small-cap at the 20-year mark, the growth on initial investment is almost tenfold.

Over a 40-year term (remember that retirement planning is a long-term proposition) the treasury note could grow tenfold, while each step-up in asset class almost doubles, culminating in an amazing 93 times for the most aggressive small-cap investment.

THE IMPORTANCE OF ASSET ALLOCATION

Asset allocation is the hot topic in the investment community these days. However, it would be a mistake to dismiss it as just another fad that will fade away. The concept of asset allocation is as valid as anything in the investment field. The roots of asset allocation lie in modern portfolio theory (MPT), a simple concept, but one built on a foundation of Nobel prize-winning economic analysis.

The essence of successful investing is to seek to maximize (push up) return on the one hand, and at the same time minimize (push down) risk (volatility) on the other. So a successful investment portfolio must be capable of meeting this challenge.

To assist you in understanding how asset allocation works, it helps to think of a silver dollar. This coin equates to 100 cents, which easily converts to percentages, and its circular shape can depict a pie chart.

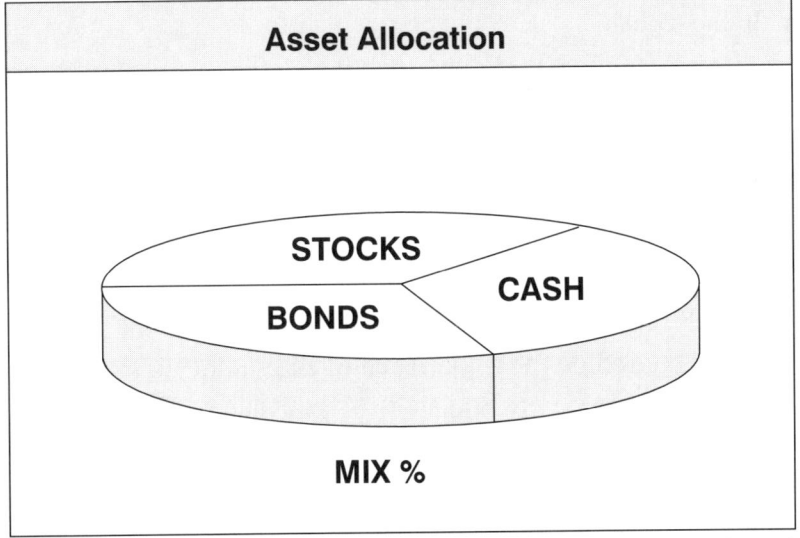

Figure 6-2

Asset allocation has to do with the relative amount you assign to various asset classes. This relative amount can be expressed as how many cents or what percent you allocate. Asset classes represent types of investments: stocks, bonds, and money markets (cash). Stocks are further classified into subclasses: large and small, U.S. (domestic) and foreign, and those with a value or growth orientation. Mutual funds provide packaged ingredients from which to assemble tailored portfolios.

Asset allocation is the planned division of your capital among various classes of investments, such as stocks, bonds, and cash equivalents. Such planning is important because study after study has shown that successful investing is much more than picking individual stocks or bonds.

Modern portfolio theory has convincingly demonstrated that the asset mix of a given portfolio is the prime determinant in investment return. By blending asset classes in a proper allocation, investors can achieve higher returns while managing risk.

Most experts come out firmly for asset allocation as an effective long-term approach to investing.

Modern portfolio theory uses statistics to demonstrate that asset classes behave differently. Bonds are likely to be zigging while stocks are zagging. Research shows that you can actually achieve a lowering of overall risk to support higher return potential if you add a normally riskier asset class, such as mutual funds invested in international stocks, junk bonds, or small-cap stocks.

Studies have shown that more than 90% of investment performance is a direct function of how you allocate assets. The truth is that other factors such as market timing and security selection (including mutual funds) are insignificant contributors, accounting for not much more of an effect than sheer luck.

Gary Brinson, president and chief investment officer of the Brinson mutual family, appeared on a PBS investment series in the fall of 1997. His episode focused on the importance of asset allocation in the investment process, appropriately titled "90% of the Game."

If you accept the compelling evidence of the value of asset allocation, it follows that this strategy is where your focus and attention should be.

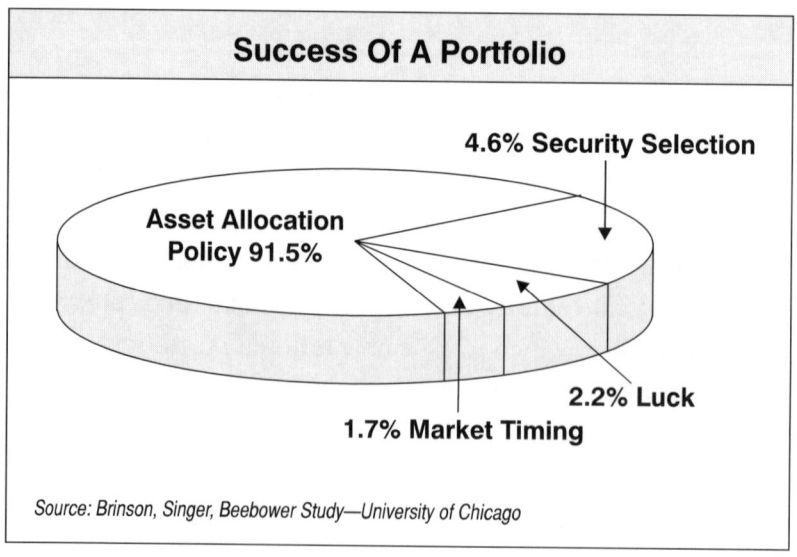

Figure 6-3

Of course, this focus is contrary to the actions of the majority, who chase the hot fund in a futile attempt to beat the market. Asset allocation is frequently misconstrued. It goes beyond diversification and should not be confused with market timing.

> "Yet, despite the highfalutin' name, asset allocation represents a fairly simple idea: The Big Picture."
> —New York Times News Service

Roger Gibson, author of the authoritative text *Asset Allocation—Balancing Financial Risk*, sums it up well:

"Traditionally, money management has been equated with market timing and security selection. Ironically, it is because of the tremendous intelligence and skill of the investment professionals engaging in these activities that the probability for success in these areas is so low. Yet, the choice of asset categories and their respective weights in a portfolio has had, and will continue to have, a large impact on future performance. To many it is surprising that over time investment policy decisions regarding the choice of investment asset categories and their relative long-term weightings within the portfolio have a much greater impact on their portfolio's future investment performance than does the shifting of money among the asset categories and the selection of securities within asset categories."

THE FOLLY OF MARKET TIMING

Investors yearn to enjoy the sweetness of bull markets without having to suffer the bitterness of a bear market. We desperately want to believe the ability exists to reap the rewards of the stock market without the pain, and we follow any strategy or advisor who appears to have a crystal ball. Resist being seduced by this notion, because market timing does not work.

The appeal of nimbly jumping in and out of the stock market at just the right time is a dubious strategy, unlikely to prove successful. The fact is, it is nearly impossible to consistently outguess the market. It is *time in the market*, not *timing the market*, that creates wealth. There is more risk of failing to meet your financial goals by being out of the market than by being in the market.

Among the opponents of market timing is Lynn Hopewell, editor of the *Journal of Financial Planning*. He says, "It's a discredited proposition. I wouldn't dream of using it."

Roger Gibson offers this view: "In the aggregate, market timing does not work, and most investor experiences have been and will be negative." Gibson, although unable to place its source, recalls seeing this statement: "Market timers make astrologers look respectable."

The major problem with market timing is that even if you are fortunate enough to get out of the market at the opportune time, you also need to be able to climb back in at precisely the right time. You have to be right twice, and your timing must be impeccable. If market timers are so smart, why aren't they all super-rich?

The volatility of the market poses a major obstacle to timing the market successfully. The best returns are likely to be concentrated in a few months, weeks, and even trading days. The 1991 stock market offers a good example. That calendar year the stock market as measured by the performance of the S&P 500 had a great year, posting a 30% total return. But upon closer examination, 95% of that substantial appreciation was bunched in the middle two weeks of the month of January and in the last week of the year. If you were out of the stock market for those few weeks, you missed almost the entire upside.

Forbes columnist David Dreman, author of *The New Contrarian Investment Strategy*, is unequivocally opposed to market timers and market timing, which he derisively labels "mistiming." His succinct advice is that the way to make big money is to buy and hold quality stocks, not to try to outsmart the market. He pointed out in a January 13, 1997, column in *Forbes* that in January 1995, many market timers and market letter writers were warning that stocks looked toppy, having run up 71% from a 1990 low. Anyone heeding the call of those gurus missed out as the stock market roared ahead another 71% in just the following two years, 1995 and 1996.

Market timing is a poor substitute for a long-term investment plan. In fact, it can severely penalize you for missing the market. Consider the behavior of mutual fund shareholders in the August 1982 to August 1987 bull market. Those who stayed put the entire five-year run averaged a whopping 26.3% a year. As I said, there are "risks" associated with being out of the market. Those who were out of the market just the 40 best performing days in those 1,200 trading days averaged a comparatively paltry 4.3%, less than the return of a money market fund. If one missed just the 20 best days over the same period the performance was cut in half to 13.1% on average. To keep up, you have to invest through thick and thin, as no one can predict the next big move.

> "But we know market timing doesn't work.
> A market may indeed be 'overpriced,' but it can stay overpriced for years. Bull markets come in all lengths. Your only defense against every sort of market jitters is to think like a long-term investor. If you stare the monster down with focus, patience, and a calm eye, you will be rewarded in the end."
> —Ralph Wanger, *A Zebra in Lion Country*

According to an Investment Management Council 1993 study, it is extremely difficult to improve on an investment strategy of buy and hold. You would have to have an accurate forecasting call 71% of the time to outperform the tried and true buy and hold strategy. If you add the tax consequences and transaction costs associated with market timing, it should become evident that the odds of its success are long.

Nor should investors believe that Wall Street investment professionals possess any special ability to time the market by tactically switching a portfolio between stocks, bonds, and cash. All the major brokerage houses tout their recommended blend, and yet a recent 10-year study found only a tiny advantage from their wisdom when compared to a conservatively fixed blend at 55%-35%-10% (for stocks, bonds, cash). Again, if fees, taxes, and transaction costs are taken into account, the experts' advice is worthless. Always remember to be an investor and not a trader. Dr. Henry Glaudiet, an economist with Federated Investors, opines: "If you are too aggressive at the top, you can recover. If too defensive at the bottom, you can recover. However, if you do both simultaneously, you can't recover."

Market timing is often sold as a risk-avoidance technique and foisted upon the unsophisticated. If you are panicked at the prospect of a market turndown, you are better off staying with more stable investments than attempting to time the market. David Dreman is fond of referring to market timers as false prophets, and he points out that with so many forecasts in the pipeline some are bound to get lucky and be right. We have all seen promotions touting some guru who correctly "called" the stock market crash of October 1987.

Mutual fund investors are apt to want to switch funds, follow the cult of performance, and chase last year's winners. This temptation is widely followed, yet it rarely is a winning approach to investing. According to a study profiled in *Investor's Business Daily*, mutual fund investors stayed in the average no-load growth stock fund an average of fewer than 22 months. This is an alarming statistic. Listen to the advice of Vanguard's Chairman John Bogle: "Giving way to the emotions of the moment is the reverse of the common sense approach."

THE BENEFITS OF DIVERSIFICATION

> "Let every man divide his money into three parts, and invest a third in land, a third in business, and a third let him keep by him in reserve."
> —Hebrew Proverb

Diversification is a critical part of the investment process precisely because it reduces risk.

Too many investors believe their portfolio is adequately diversified when in fact it is not. Diversification involves more than the quantity of investments. True diversification is not achieved if the holdings all tend to move together with the same tide. Such would be the case with a portfolio consisting of a dozen utility stocks or a half-dozen aggressive growth stock mutual funds heavy in technology issues.

> "Money is like muck, not good unless spread."
> —Francis Bacon

There is no better risk reduction technique than effective diversification. Such a portfolio is achieved by commingling assets (investments) whose returns don't always move in the same direction. In the language of investment professionals, they possess low *market correlation*. As with a teeter-totter, one asset class moves opposite to the other. The lower the market correlation, the higher (better) the portfolio diversification.

The time-honored truth is that diversification among asset classes is the best asset allocation investment policy.

THE IMPORTANCE OF ASSET ALLOCATION

From a financial planning standpoint, I find that engineers make the best clients. By nature of their profession, makeup, and training, they are true believers in the merits of disciplined planning. As a whole, they are inclined to be rational decision makers who base their investment actions on sound analysis. They are uniformly good at assessing risk and particularly good at comprehending the risk/reward equation—all valuable traits for success in investment management. Dealing and working with engineers, I observe that they love charts, graphs, and presentations of facts.

The following chart on asset allocation (Figure 6-4) contains a wealth of information. It is so full of investment and portfolio management knowledge that a graduate-level course could be designed around this one page. My purpose in presenting this copyrighted material is to highlight and illuminate the important investment points found in a quick analysis.

This chart verifies the importance of asset allocation, graphically depicts the risk/reward trade-off, offers return expectations, presents a worst-case scenario for stomaching risk, shows real (inflation-plus) returns, and reflects the banner performance returns of 1995.

The analysis covers the $46 1/4$-year-period between January 1950 and March 1997, constituting observations over 555 months. This long-term measuring period proves statistically valid.

To interpret this chart, note that it consists of 10 rows down the left side and six columns, A through F, across the top.

Each of its 10 boxes portrays a different portfolio mix, allocating a different percentage to each of the three primary asset classes of stocks, bonds, and cash. The stock component represents the S&P 500 index, the bonds reference intermediate five-year treasury bonds, and cash is represented by 90-day treasury bills, the equivalent of a money market fund.

The composition or mix of the portfolio goes from the most aggressive to the most conservative. The most aggressive composition is shown in box #1 by a stock weighting of 90%, bonds 0%. With each step down this column, another 10% is shifted from stocks into bonds. The most conservative mix is found in box #10 with a makeup of 0% stocks, 90% bonds. Ten percent of each portfolio is fixed in a cash holding (money market) for each of the 10 model portfolios.

Column A illustrates the average annual total return over the entire

Risk, Reward, and Asset Mixes
One-Year Returns January 1950-March 1997

Portfolio Mix	A Average Return	B Largest Loss	C Average Loss	D Percent Negative	E % of Returns Greater Than Inflation	F 1995 Total Return
1. 90% Stocks / 0% Bonds / 10% Cash	12.8%	-34.3%	-7.0%	20%	72%	34.4%
2. 80% Stocks / 10% Bonds / 10% Cash	12.1%	-30.2%	-6.0%	19%	72%	32.4%
3. 70% Stocks / 20% Bonds / 10% Cash	11.4%	-26.2%	-5.4%	17%	72%	30.3%
4. 60% Stocks / 30% Bonds / 10% Cash	10.6%	-22.2%	-4.5%	15%	72%	28.3%
5. 50% Stocks / 40% Bonds / 10% Cash	9.9%	-18.2%	-3.5%	14%	71%	26.3%
6. 40% Stocks / 50% Bonds / 10% Cash	9.1%	-14.1%	-3.0%	11%	71%	24.3%
7. 30% Stocks / 60% Bonds / 10% Cash	8.4%	-10.1%	-2.3%	8%	70%	22.2%
8. 20% Stocks / 70% Bonds / 10% Cash	7.7%	-6.1%	-1.9%	6%	68%	20.2%
9. 10% Stocks / 80% Bonds / 10% Cash	6.9%	-3.9%	-1.3%	5%	68%	18.2%
10. 0% Stocks / 90% Bonds / 10% Cash	6.2%	-4.2%	-1.4%	11%	61%	16.2%

Sources: Standard & Poor's Corp.; Ryan Labs, Inc.; Lehman Bros.; Bureau of Labor Statistics Stocks; Standard & Poor's 500 Stock Index; Bonds: 5-Year Treasury Bonds; Cash: 90-Day Treasury Bills; Inflation: Consumer Price Index; © 1997 by Crandall, Pierce & Company (1-800-272-6355), used with permission.

Figure 6-4

46-year-plus period. The first point to comprehend is that history shows that by assuming a higher risk profile (a greater percent of portfolio assigned to the stock market), you can expect to be rewarded with a higher average return.

Place your finger at the top of column A and proceed down the column, noting that the average return goes down at each successive step. Conversely, proceed back up the column, and you find the average total return increasing with heavier allocations of stock.

The risk/reward equation is clearly illustrated by Figure 6-5, which demonstrates a straight-line correlation where average return is shown as a direct function of the amount of stocks employed.

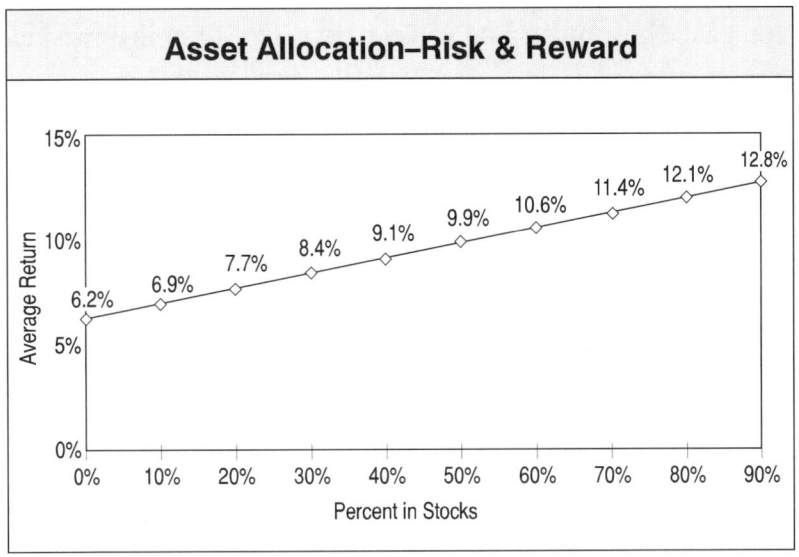

Figure 6-5

Columns B, C, and D in Figure 6-4 depict the inherent risk found in a given portfolio over the 46¼-year time frame.

Column B can be thought of as a sobering worst-case scenario of the largest loss for each portfolio. These projections provide a useful exercise in coming to grips with risk in real terms and determining your downside risk temperament.

For example, if you own a $100,000 portfolio, would you be able to accept (survive) a nightmare yearly performance of minus 34.3%? This is the worst-case performance that accompanied a fully weighted 90% stock portfolio during the past 46 years. Imagine your state of mind if your investment account statement at the end of this type of year read only $65,700.

One way to use this exercise is to plug in your own dollar portfolio value and look for the worst-case return you could live with. Then choose your asset allocation accordingly. Say you are retired and were raised in the throes of the Depression. Perhaps you know you couldn't sleep with the thought of incurring any more than a 10% annual loss. If that is the case, the most risk you should assume is a stock allocation of 30%.

Continuing with the analysis of portfolio risk, Columns C and D should be viewed together. Column C shows the average loss in down performance years while Column D shows the percentage of years you could expect a year of negative total return. Taken together, these projections help you gauge how much pain you can expect to suffer in down years as well as how often you can expect to post a year's loss.

As an example, with the most aggressive portfolio you could expect a down return year about one in five years, with the average loss amounting to 7%. A balanced portfolio with a 50% stock allocation cuts the expected average loss in half to 3.5%. The expectation to be in positive territory is about 86% of the time.

Once again, this analysis shows that greater risk is harbored in the more aggressive portfolios in which a direct risk-reward relationship exists. The lone exception lies in the ultraconservative portfolio shown in box #10, which I will discuss shortly.

Column E shows the percentage of times a given annual total return is likely to beat the inflation rate (that is, to register a real return) as compared to the consumer price index.

At the far right, Column F highlights the banner performance turned in during 1995 on both stock and bond portfolios. It reveals the risk of being out of the market. Every portfolio looked great and healthy in 1995.

The downside from this well-above-average performance is multifold:

- ♦ It seemed too easy to make money.
- ♦ Investors tended to feel smug and smart.
- ♦ Market risk was buried by the euphoric returns.
- ♦ Expectations were raised to unrealistic levels.

Take a minute to note how an ultraconservative portfolio, absent any position in stocks such as shown in box #10 of Figure 6-4, not only posts an expected lower average return, but also has worse risk measures than a portfolio with a moderate 10% stock position. This allocation scores poorly in terms of average loss, largest loss, negative return years, and by far the worst performance on inflation protection.

The key ingredient in successful investing and financial goal attainment comes from first mixing the assets well, creating a suitably diversified portfolio among stocks, bonds, and cash. This important recipe escapes most investors, even those who might have a handle on investment size.

Once all the investment assets have been summarized on one sheet of paper, the next valuable exercise is to figure out the current allocation, because you need to comprehend the current makeup of your asset weightings before any changes can be considered. A haphazard accumulation pattern makes for a misaligned portfolio in terms of risk tolerance and return expectations.

I suggest you develop your own investment policy to mirror your situation and investment expectations, then design a long-term, disciplined, strategic asset allocation investment plan. Construct the portfolio with the right overall mix, seeking optimum returns subject to your risk tolerance.

EXPAND YOUR INVESTMENT HORIZONS

To truly and effectively diversify your portfolio, it makes sense to not overlook two-thirds of the world's equity market. International investing actually lowers your overall portfolio risk in terms of reducing volatility. This is because domestic and foreign stocks tend to follow the beat of a different drummer; in other words, they move in different directions.

International stocks have often been viewed as risky and were to be shunned in a traditional, prudent portfolio. It is true that international investing, including foreign stock funds, carries extra elements of risk because of currency fluctuations, political risks, and uneven financial reporting and accounting standards.

However, foreign stocks have also rewarded long-term investors with higher returns than domestic equities.

> "People look at a fund and say, 'how risky is it?'
> But it's not the risk of the individual fund that counts, but what the addition of that fund does to your overall portfolio."
> —Gerald Perritt, editor, *Mutual Fund Newsletter*

The value of asset allocation is seen in studies that convincingly demonstrate that the addition of international stocks to a portfolio leads not only to a higher return, but also to a lower measure of risk. All in all, history provides a compelling case to look beyond the border and utilize an international stock fund or funds when constructing a portfolio.

Fickle investors enamored of the latest hot asset class make the same mistakes while chasing international stocks as they do with their domestic counterparts. During the 1993 calendar year, international stock funds shone with returns north of 30%, while U.S. domestic stocks stayed in the shadows with a 10% return. The year 1995 witnessed the reverse, as U.S. stocks barreled ahead at a lofty 37.5% clip while international stocks cooled in single-digit return territory.

A CLASS OF THEIR OWN

A good case can be made for considering a junk bond fund in your portfolio makeup. This unique asset class is something of a hybrid: stock return potential from a bond coupon.

This uniqueness makes for a pronounced inclination to move in the opposite direction of stocks or treasury bonds. Remember, the lower the market correlation, the higher the portfolio diversification.

Many people would be surprised to find that in addition to increased diversity, these bonds in the period from 1980 to 1995 actually turned in higher average returns than did domestic stocks, international stocks, or long-term treasuries. In a stock market correction, these high-yield bond funds have usually performed better than equities.

Junk bonds provide ammunition for one of the important truths of asset allocation; namely, that the inclusion of a more volatile security does not necessarily increase the overall risk of the portfolio. *The Wall Street Journal* headed a special report on investing, "For a calmer portfolio: Just add a little risk."

It used to be that no "quality" portfolio would ever hold junk bonds, international securities, or small-cap stocks. New standards of the "prudent man rule" have now come to the realization that a suitable portfolio can contain more than strictly high-grade bonds and blue chip stocks.

I routinely place junk bond funds inside IRAs where their higher yields are shielded by the armor of tax deferral. Federated Investors points out that the considerable risk of high-yield bonds can be managed by portfolio managers who do not get piggy over yield, stay with the most creditworthy of this lower-quality debt pool, and truly diversify.

CHAPTER 7
THE IMPORTANCE OF PLANNING YOUR ESTATE

There is no area within the financial and retirement planning field where more misconceptions are held, mistakes are made, and myths abound than in estate planning. This is unfortunate, because estate planning is integral to a sound financial and retirement plan, and much value can be derived from the estate-planning process.

Too many people look upon estate planning as unimportant, unpleasant, or unnecessary. Virtually everyone can benefit from undertaking some form of estate planning, yet far too many avoid it, for a host of reasons:

- I'm too young!
- Estate planning is a morbid topic.
- I prefer not to contemplate my ultimate demise.
- I'm too poor.
- My estate is too small.
- I plan to leave it all to my wife, and she'll just leave it to the kids.
- I'm single, so what does it matter?
- Estate planning is just too expensive and too hard to understand, so it's not worth the bother.

Each of these common excuses for refraining from estate planning loses its validity upon closer inspection under a rational light.

Despite the importance of estate planning, 70% of people leave this world without a will in place. Their estates are likely to be subject to unnecessary expenses and taxes, and there is no legal assurance their wishes will be followed.

What is an estate? How can you plan it?

Your estate consists of a storehouse of wealth and includes all assets, property, life insurance, and other financial interests. If you have a dollar that you don't plan to spend, you have an estate.

Estate planning is an active endeavor, a lifetime process of wealth accumulation, conservation, control, and transfer.

THE FATE OF THOMAS JEFFERSON

Founding father Thomas Jefferson died July 4, 1826, on the 50th anniversary of the Declaration of Independence, the famous document he so eloquently authored.

But his passing also marked a final tragedy. His beloved Monticello estate was put up for auction to pay down his sizable debt. When Jefferson died at the age of 83, he was mired in debt of $100,000, the equivalent of several million in today's dollars.

We know from his correspondence with former President James Monroe that he was deeply depressed about his financial predicament and lamented his lack of attention to estate planning.

"To keep a Virginia estate together," in Jefferson's words, "requires in the owner both skill and attention, skill I never had and attention I could not have, and really when I reflect on all the circumstances, my wonder is that I should have been so long as 60 years in reaching the result to which I am now reduced."

We should step back and note that in Jefferson's era there was no life insurance option to help save his property for the generations that followed. On the other hand, in 1826 there was no federal estate taxation, a burden contrary to Jefferson's philosophy.

DO YOU HAVE AN ESTATE PLAN?

I had an enlightening experience while presenting a joint retirement and estate planning seminar together with an attorney, who presented the merits of estate planning. He started by asking members of the audience to raise their hands if they had an estate plan.

Observing the response, I noted a lot of puzzled looks, open-mouthed glances between spouses, and other body language that clearly indicated these seminar participants did not know how to respond. If they had a will, did that qualify them to nod in the affirmative? What about a trust? Did a trust mean they possessed a written sheaf of documents they'd had prepared by an attorney for a generous fee?

The attorney then went on to state that whether they realized it or not, everyone in attendance had an estate plan. If they didn't know whether or not they had an estate plan, they had obviously not played an active role in creating their plan.

To illustrate his point, he asked who was a participant in a 401(k) or 403(b) plan, owned an IRA, had group and/or individual life insurance, a home, mutual funds, checking account, or personal property. Because everyone in the room possessed at least some of these, he said that even those without a will have an estate plan in place. If one dies without a will, it is referred to as dying *intestate*, and the state of residence steps in to apply the rules of intestacy to determine how property will be distributed and how any minor children affected will be provided for. The point is, by not acting and taking responsibility for your own estate, you are abdicating control.

Your heirs could suffer unnecessary delays, expenses, taxes, and other negative consequences. In fact, the very individuals you may wish to protect may not benefit at all.

He pointed out that a critical part of any estate plan is to name beneficiaries on retirement plans, life insurance, and annuity contracts, as well as to choose the type of ownership (titling) on one's residence and other financial assets.

10 COMMON ESTATE PLANNING GOALS

1. For many couples, the top priority is to provide for the needs of the surviving spouse.
2. Once the surviving spouse's needs are adequately met, it is typical to direct attention to children, grandchildren, and other family members to provide for their financial benefit.
3. Streamline the orderly and successful administration of an estate, while avoiding the cost, delay, and lack of privacy found in probate.
4. Minimize estate shrinkage from federal and state transfer taxes.

5. Plan for the possibility of physical or mental incapacity and prevent the cost and indignity of a guardianship hearing.
6. Consider the special needs of minor and spendthrift beneficiaries and those with disabilities, and include provisions for professional financial management.
7. Use a lifetime gifting program in order to thin an estate, and institute other tax planning strategies.
8. Arrange planned giving as a way to support favorite charities on a tax-advantaged basis.
9. Deal with health care issues by having written statements of intentions in place in accord with personal health decisions.
10. Attend to business matters, including succession, transfer, funding, charitable, and, especially, taxation issues.

Billionaire Howard Hughes died intestate in 1976. Like too many Americans without a will, his oversight proved to be a particularly thorny mess. "No one knew who owned the estate or where Hughes was domiciled," ruefully observed William Rice Lummis, a lawyer and distant relative of Hughes.

Once it became known there was no claim on file to Hughes' vast fortune, bogus wills appeared out of nowhere. For example, the tabloid press spent ink on the tale of a trucker who picked up a stranger stranded on a remote desert highway. To thank him for this act of kindness, the stranger, Hughes, purportedly made this Good Samaritan sole beneficiary of his wealth.

Hughes' estate consisted of a mishmash of holdings, much of it illiquid or not fully valued. There was an $80 million judgment against Hughes, and the IRS was demanding a heavy 77% piece of the pie. State revenue departments in California and Texas also eyed their tax bounty. Probably he was a resident of Nevada, which imposes no state death taxes, but Hughes didn't bother to declare Nevada his domicile.

Reportedly, it took a full 20 years to untangle this complicated estate—at a cost of some $100 million in legal fees.

Perhaps an eccentric recluse like Howard Hughes can be excused for not putting his affairs in order, but the same slack is not as likely to be accorded the former top lawyer of the land.

Retired Chief Supreme Court Justice Warren Burger passed away in

June 1996 at the age of 87. A widower, Justice Burger did leave a will, but not an estate plan appropriate for his $1.8 million estate. He apparently decided against outside expertise, instead drafting and probably typing a three-line document himself, complete with typographical errors. For whatever reason, he did not feel it worthwhile to seek more sophisticated estate planning counsel. Such counsel could have secured additional assets for his son and daughter and might have reduced or eliminated the $450,000 estate tax that was imposed.

Some people believe tax avoidance is unpatriotic. The fact is, the minimization and elimination of estate taxation is a prime objective of estate planning. Laws are on the books that allow for great savings.

Perhaps Justice Burger should have reviewed the 1945 U.S. Supreme Court ruling that upheld the "legal right of a taxpayer to decrease the amount of what otherwise would have been his (or her) taxes or to avoid them altogether, by means which the law permits."

Judge Learned Hand—a great moniker for a justice—elaborated: "Nobody owes any public duty to pay more than the law demands; taxes are enforced extractions, not voluntary contributions. To demand more in the name of mortals is mere cant."

When Elvis Presley died prematurely in 1977 at the age of 42, he left an estate in excess of $10 million. The king may have assumed he was immortal, because it appears he did little in the way of estate planning. How else can one explain why the government tax coffers ended up with 73% of his accumulated wealth, and his heirs got the short end?

We know this information from fully accessible probate records. "Don't Be Cruel" could serve well as the title of a song lamenting why substantial estates leave more money to Uncle Sam than to true relatives.

There is much to be learned from contrasting the lack of proper estate planning of these celebrities with the model estate plan of the late Jacqueline Kennedy Onassis. The famous twice-widowed spouse of a slain U.S. president and a Greek shipping tycoon left a detailed estate plan. Her will alone ran to 36 pages. It was so well done, it is now used as a case study in law schools.

> "In a world where supposedly nothing is inevitable except death and taxes, a good will and a sound estate plan are valuable gifts."
> —Susan E. Kuhn, *Fortune*, July 11, 1994

This very private public figure, mother, grandmother, and sister left an estate valued in the vicinity of $200 million when she died of cancer at age 64 in 1994.

Jackie Onassis, with the aid of a prestigious New York law firm's estate planning attorneys, matched her personal wishes with a carefully crafted estate plan. A byproduct of the plan was the effective minimization of taxes on the transfer of wealth at her death.

Her astute estate planning offers some valuable lessons.

- We can assume she paid heavy legal fees. However, sound estate planning pays for itself many times over in terms of lower taxes, less delay, fulfillment of wishes, and lack of confusion. Be willing to pay for solid professional advice.
- She specified precisely who was to receive each item of personal property. This was a wise move; as a senior trust officer told me, the thorniest disputes always occur over dividing personal property.
- When she made bequests it was in cash, with detailed instructions about how taxes should be paid.
- She utilized charitable lead trusts to shelter estate taxes, provide for her favorite tax-qualified charities, and bequeath generous sums for her grandchildren 24 years down the line.
- The last time she updated her will was just two months before her death. Update your will and estate plan regularly.
- It is surmised she made intelligent use of lifetime annual gifting strategies to transfer wealth to her children to escape taxation at her death.
- She named as executor and co-executor trusted, competent individuals outside her immediate family to carry out her wishes—a decision that maintains family harmony.

Planning dictates managing and adapting to change. All financial planning, especially estate planning, is conducted in a dynamic environment. We must be prepared to respond to changes in our personal and family situations, changes in our financial conditions, and the inevitable changes in tax legislation.

In our personal lives we experience marriage, divorce, remarriage, the birth of children and grandchildren, adoption, stepchildren, and death.

Your health and that of your spouse and beneficiaries eventually deteriorate. Employment changes may alter your income and result in possible relocation to other states with different tax laws. Or you may need to coordinate benefits packages from your old to your new job.

Your personal financial condition and net worth are constantly fluctuating. The bull market in the 1980s and 1990s resulted in substantial appreciation in stocks and bonds, just as the 1970s saw a boom in real estate values leading to substantially higher-valued estates. Additionally, the depletion of an estate through a lifetime gifting program or the sale of a business has a major impact on all financial and estate matters.

The tax arena continues to undergo a continuous transformation. The Taxpayer's Relief Act of 1997 contains more changes relative to estate planning than any other piece of legislation in 16 years.

Planning is essential if you are to benefit from the generally favorable provisions found in this law.

Estate plans need to be reviewed in light of:

- a gradual increase in the unified credit (exclusion from transfer taxes) from $600,000 to $1 million beginning in 2006
- the $10,000 annual gift tax exclusion, which is now set to rise slowly, indexed to inflation
- the repeal of the onerous excise taxes attached to outsized IRA balances
- the special estate tax treatment of up to $1.3 million for certain family-owned businesses
- the almost 30% reduction in capital gains taxes on profits from the sale of assets held at least 18 months
- the generous expansion in capital gains exclusion on the gain of the sale of a personal residence.

Estate planning is clouded in emotional issues and family relationships. Often, procrastination brought on by indecision or an unwillingness to make decisions is the major impediment to sound, effective estate planning. But for those who choose to ignore or delay planning, the result after death for their families is likely to be turmoil and disharmony.

Estate planning is technical, complex, and shrouded in legal jargon. It is also highly personal and confidential. My advice is that you consult with an attorney who specializes in estate planning. Many states certify attorneys as "estate planning specialists" if they pass an exam that tests their knowledge. Find someone with whom you feel comfortable and confident. Many people put off obtaining this professional service because they think it will be too expensive. Often I find that clients expect to pay more than the charges they actually incur. In my opinion, carefully drafted and properly executed estate planning documents represent a valuable investment.

You, as estate owner, have the responsibility to direct and orchestrate your plan. I recommend that you assemble a financial services team. In addition to an estate planning attorney, your team might include an insurance professional, tax counselor, investment advisor, financial planner, and trust officer.

Whoever said, "Anyone who acts as their own lawyer has a fool for a client"?

Harking back to the example of Justice Burger's simple will, obviously it was a step up from the complete disregard for this important planning matter exemplified by Howard Hughes. According to some statistics, 50% of *attorneys* have not had their wills drawn. However, I strongly advise against drafting your own will or using a fill-in-the-blanks will kit. Your will, first and foremost, is a legal document. It is just one part of a comprehensive estate plan. What may be saved in legal expenses today has the potential to develop into a costly disaster in the future.

In estate planning, each individual's situation is unique. Moreover, each state has its own technical requirements that must be dealt with.

By reaching for a cookie-cutter estate plan, you give up the valuable expertise of an estate planning attorney who can create a customized plan that will be recognized in the state and jurisdiction in which you reside.

Estate planning is a specialized field. Not just any attorney is qualified or trained to handle your estate plan. I have witnessed instances in which attorneys, because they are not knowledgeable or because they want to probate an estate and collect a hefty fee, fail to recommend living trusts, which bypass probate. Always be on guard that your self-interest and that of your heirs are being served.

Using the services of a competent estate planning attorney, you can expect to avoid potential conflicts and have your objectives met. For example, a poorly drafted estate plan is more likely to encourage a will contest, an increasingly common phenomenon, especially when children from a previous marriage are involved. Your estate planning attorney should keep abreast of changes in the tax and estate laws and notify you when it affects your personal situation so you can continue to avoid pitfalls in the future.

Understand that life insurance is likely to play a significant role in your estate planning. Life insurance is a unique product, capable of providing liquid cash to coincide with the time of death.

Life insurance needs change dramatically over a life span. In your preretirement accumulation stage, the priority is likely to be for insurance to provide an instant, sustainable estate for surviving dependents. Looking at the postretirement stage, life insurance might be used to leverage a charitable bequest, pay estate taxes, complement an illiquid portfolio, or perhaps keep a business in the family. As a result, your life insurance policy needs and objectives should be reviewed regularly by a life insurance specialist.

I have always been disturbed by parents who purchase insurance on their lives to protect the family, but do not draw up a will naming guardians for minor children or specifying investment management for these same insurance proceeds.

The seriousness of this lack of planning is exemplified by a tragic accident in which young parents were killed by a drunk driver who crossed the median and hit them head-on. Miraculously, this couple's two young children, a son aged two and a baby daughter just two months old, were buckled up in the back seat and survived this deadly crash with only minor injuries. Unfortunately, the tragedy for these orphaned children continues with a nasty legal guardianship fight. Sadly, part of the motivation for the suit may be attributable to funds made available from life insurance and settlement proceeds.

Had the parents drawn up a will to name a guardian for their minor children, this anguish could have been minimized.

On a personal note, my wife and I have named my sister to act and make decisions regarding the care and well-being of our children, should this nightmare ever befall our family. Because my brother-in-law has a financial and tax background, he would be responsible for the investment management of the financial assets of our estate.

Very importantly, before naming them in our documents, we asked each of these relatives if they would accept this responsibility.

ESTATE PLANNING TOOLS

In many fields, tools help you to get a job done, with different tools for different purposes and applications. Fortunately, various estate planning tools and documents exist to help you meet your identified goals and objectives. Among these tools are wills, joint ownership, durable power of attorney, living trusts, health care documents, and tax planning.

WILLS

When you plan for retirement, it is paramount you have a periodically updated will in place. Looking to the future implies putting your affairs in order for your inevitable demise. A properly drawn will is the cornerstone of even the simplest estate plan. I regularly urge clients to update this legal document to keep current with new family conditions and obligations, legislation, and tax laws.

A will allows for disposition of your property, nominates a guardian for minor children, facilitates the appointment of your executor (personal representative), and provides for creation of trusts and the appointment of trustees.

Basically, a will is a legal declaration of what you want done with the residue of your estate upon your death, and it dictates some control over the myriad details concerned with probate administration, fees, and expenses. Both spouses need a will. When one spouse dies, the survivor should update his or her will as soon as possible.

A word about probate. Probate is perhaps the most misunderstood component of estate planning. Probate refers to the court process of proving the will. The will determines only how probate assets will be distributed—it does not avoid the process of probate.

JOINT OWNERSHIP

Joint tenancy with right of survivorship (JTWROS) is the most common form of co-ownership and carries with it the right of survivorship. JTWROS means a joint tenant (owner) automatically and instantly assumes full ownership upon the death of the co-owner. An important task in an estate plan overview is to inventory all property and identify what form of ownership exists. No form of ownership by itself is desirable or undesirable. However, be aware that all forms have estate, gift, and income tax implications. If too much wealth is owned jointly with a spouse, death taxes could be increased when the surviving spouse dies.

The positive features of joint tenancy include simplicity, no cost, and an automatic transfer at death that avoids probate. On the other hand, joint tenancy should never be considered a substitute for a will. When transferring property from sole to joint ownership, expect to lose full control. Joint owners share equal rights to their common assets as soon as the designation becomes effective.

BENEFICIARY DESIGNATIONS

A common misconception is that a will dictates disposition of all of the deceased's property, and that in the absence of a will, assets go to one's spouse and then to any surviving children. The fact is, for many in the preretirement stage the bulk of our estates consists of assets that pass by contract outside the will to beneficiaries. Hence, the will may play a small role as to disposition.

My personal case is not unusual. Even though I have a will, almost all of my estate and net worth involves nonprobate assets. Included in the list dictated by beneficiary designation are my 401(k) retirement plans, IRAs, individual and group life insurance policies, and annuities. Our home, mutual fund portfolio, and liquid assets are titled in joint tenancy with my wife, so they, too, are not subject to probate.

The failure to coordinate beneficiary designations on 401(k)s, 403(b)s, SEPs, IRAs, and insurance and annuity contracts is one of the most common and potentially costly estate planning errors.

We can profit from the tragic case of a woman who endured a bitter divorce and soon after suffered a fatal heart attack. Her employer-sponsored retirement plan and group life insurance both listed her ex-husband as beneficiary, a designation she had made three years earlier. Her ex-husband is entitled legally to this money, even though that would not have been her wish. A word to the wise: keep your beneficiary designations up to date by periodic review.

It is a prudent and simple procedure to designate a contingent or secondary beneficiary on all your retirement plans in the event your primary beneficiary predeceases you. When making beneficiary designations, be sure you understand spousal rights and benefits available only to spouses.

DURABLE POWER OF ATTORNEY

Owing to increasing life expectancies, it is a distinct possibility that at some point, due to either mental or physical deterioration, you might be unable to manage your financial affairs. Think for a minute of the situation facing former president Ronald Reagan. Alzheimer's disease has felled this former world leader.

We might not want to contemplate our own disability, but it is a real possibility. In a worst-case scenario, you could be dragged through the indignity of a legal process to prove your competency to manage your own affairs. This could result in court supervision of your estate and the appointment of a guardian. Guardianships can be expensive, time consuming, and the cause of a rift or feud among family members. They also are legal maneuvers that can be avoided.

The durable power of attorney (DPOA) provides one solution. Another option is the revocable living trust, discussed below. With a durable power of attorney, you, as principal, appoint an agent to do certain things with the same authority as if you were doing them—handling primarily financial matters, since a separate power for health care also exists.

The holder of a DPOA typically is a trusted family member or friend. His or her selection should be based on trust, competency, capability, and willingness to serve. When needed, this person can act on your behalf to sell stock, sell your home, file tax returns, transfer assets, deposit checks, pay bills, and deal with the IRS and the Social Security Administration.

It is important to execute a power of attorney that is durable. There is a statutory form available to prepare this document, but don't grant this power without forethought to whom you choose.

REVOCABLE LIVING TRUSTS

Revocable means it can be changed, altered, terminated. *Living* means it is operating during one's lifetime (as opposed to testamentary, operating after death). *Living* also refers to the trust having its own life; i.e., it's a separate legal entity. *Trust* means a legal document. A revocable living trust can in many cases be the centerpiece of an estate plan.

A revocable living trust has many advantages. It:
- allows you complete control over your assets; only the form of ownership has changed
- allows for disposition of trust assets after death without probate
- allows for professional asset management during your lifetime and avoids legal guardianship in the event of incapacity
- can provide a mechanism, if properly drafted, for the minimization of transfer taxes
- reduces the risk of a will contest, avoiding family disputes
- protects trust assets from creditors
- becomes irrevocable (cannot be changed) at death, and functions like a will, thus providing continued management of trust assets after death

It should be noted that living trusts, even with their many advantages, are not for everyone. They have too often been oversold. Note below that probate does not have to be the challenge some make it out to be. A living trust does not negate the need for a will. A living trust does not by itself reduce estate taxes, and it has no impact on income taxes. There is a cost involved in drafting documents and possibly for maintaining the trust.

I urge you to use the services of a qualified estate attorney when drafting a sophisticated document such as a living trust. Remember, a living trust is not useful unless assets are retitled or directed into the trust.

The problems with probate and reasons to avoid probate include time delays, executor and legal costs of settling the estate, and lack of privacy. However, probate need not be the nightmare it is sometimes made out to be, nor a plague to be avoided at all cost. Granted, there are certain states and instances where probate deserves its bad name. Proper planning will avoid probate, or at the least minimize its negative aspects. Keep in mind that in addition to living trusts, assets held in joint tenancy escape probate, as do retirement plan and insurance beneficiary designations, because they are nonprobate transfers of assets.

When the subject of trusts is raised, some individuals assume they are unlikely candidates to use these mysterious documents. They visualize marble-columned financial institutions and think Rockefeller rich and stuffy. Trusts are really not mysterious, nor are they only for the rich. Trusts are highly valuable as estate planning tools.

A trust merely establishes a fiduciary relationship whereby a grantor (creator) transfers property (assets) to a trustee who agrees to hold, manage, and distribute property for the benefit of specified individuals (beneficiaries). The provisions of a trust are spelled out in a written agreement.

All trusts have three parties: the grantor who establishes the trust, the trustee who manages the trust, and those who benefit from the trust.

Trusts are very flexible planning documents. As an example, you could establish the trust, act as your own trustee, and also be its beneficiary. There are many types of trusts, which can be classified as follows:

- living—established during the grantor's lifetime
- testamentary—established under a will to begin at death
- funded—assets have been transferred into the trust
- unfunded—no assets are held by the trust
- revocable—can be amended until the death of the grantor
- irrevocable—cannot be amended

A single trust can have more than one of the above features; it can be, for example, a funded revocable living trust.

A trustee is responsible for managing the trust. You can be your own trustee or name a family member, friend, professional, or trust company to act on behalf of the beneficiaries. In selecting a trustee, take into account knowledge of investments and trust administration requirements.

HEALTH CARE DOCUMENTS

Advances in medical science have reached the point at which a once-imminent death can be postponed. Many individuals would like more control over these very personal and literally life-and-death matters.

A health care power of attorney is an important legal document that allows for decision making by an appointed representative. A living will, on the other hand, is a treatment directive. While you are fully capable, and after careful thought, you can indicate your intentions in writing and give directives for what you want done in the event of a terminal condition. Your decisions could involve the power to decline life-prolonging medical treatment, including the use of a respirator and tube feeding in cases of terminal illness, brain death, or irreversible coma.

The health care power of attorney is generally broader in scope than the living will and is not limited to terminally ill or vegetative conditions. Ideally, you may well want to employ both documents: a health care power of attorney for treatment decisions, and a living will for directions on when to pull the plug.

Statutory forms are available for each of these documents. For such documents to be useful, you should distribute multiple originals to your agent(s) and physicians. Request that such documents be included prominently in your medical chart, and ask family members to remind your physician of their existence if the occasion arises.

TAX PLANNING

Estate planning is often driven by the desire to minimize personal income taxes and estate and gift taxation. Through proper planning, tax-minimization strategies can be highly valuable and save hundreds of thousands of dollars. Minimizing taxes is a prime motivation for initiating planning efforts.

> "I feel very honored to pay taxes in America. The thing is, I could probably feel just as honored for about half the price."
> —Arthur Godfrey

There are three taxes—income, gift, and estate—that you must be aware of in all estate planning matters.

PERSONAL INCOME TAXES—CAPITAL GAINS

One of the first tasks to undertake in estate planning is a capital gain tax planning analysis. Inventory each asset, determine a current market value, and establish the original cost or basis. Armed with these two figures, you can use simple arithmetic to calculate the difference and arrive at paper (unrealized) capital gains and/or losses.

Market value minus cost (basis) = capital gain/loss

The following scenarios will familiarize you with some tax planning opportunities. For our purposes, assume you own 1,000 shares of XYZ stock. Today's current market value is $20 per share, for a total of $20,000.

The original cost (or basis) of these same 1,000 shares is $10 per share, for a total cost basis of $10,000. This translates into an unrealized long-term capital gain of $10,000.

If you elect to sell this stock and if the $10,000 gain is subject to a 20% capital gains tax rate, you pay $2,000 in federal taxes in addition to any state taxes. However, until you sell this security, the gain is on paper and unrealized. Your cost basis is fixed, but the market price will fluctuate, subjecting you to a greater or lesser stock value that determines the amount subject to tax when sold.

Let's assume you and your spouse elect to gift this stock to your favorite college-age nephew. Your basis becomes his basis. If he as new owner sells the stock and has little other income, his capital gains tax rate is likely to be at a lower 10% rate, making his actual tax substantially less than your tax would be. By making this gift, you have reduced your estate and shifted the tax to someone facing a smaller current tax bite.

Say you decide instead to gift this appreciated stock to a qualified charity. Your generosity allows you to take the full $20,000 charitable tax deduction. Your charity could sell this stock and realize, tax exempt, the full $20,000 proceeds. If you are inclined to make a charitable gift, highly appreciated assets are a good source of funds. Again, you have removed this asset from your taxable estate and from generating currently taxable dividend income.

Here's another example: A 90-year-old gentleman in poor health owns the same XYZ stock and desires to gift it to his two daughters. Since his life expectancy is short, his daughters might be better off, from a tax standpoint, to inherit this security rather than receive it as a gift, because they will be entitled to a stepped-up basis. Put another way, the cost basis for the daughters steps up to the market value at the date of his death (or, alternatively, six months later). If he passes away when the stock is worth $20 a share, each daughter's basis is $20, not the $10 basis of their father. If and when they decide to sell their XYZ stock, they will not be taxed on the first $20 in share value.

BEQUESTS

I was privileged to know philanthropist Warren P. Knowles as a mentor and a friend in the years preceding his death at age 83. Affectionately known as "the Governor" because of his position as leader of Wisconsin from 1965 to 1971, this white-haired gentleman was generous in life and at death.

After long service in public life, Governor Knowles dedicated the last 20 or so years of his life to his community through active involvement in causes related to education.

At his death, his generosity continued through bequests to support educational institutions, including, among others, the Medical College of Wisconsin, Mount Mary College, the Alcoholism & Drug Abuse Council of Milwaukee, Inc., and the Association for Retarded Citizens in Milwaukee.

Warren Knowles as an attorney, not-for-profit trustee, and astute financial administrator knew the value and importance of planning and planned gifts. His financial support and remembrance of these institutions and organizations will sustain them long after his passing. These generous gifts in posterity also reduced estate taxes that otherwise would have been due.

Billionaire James Stowers, founder of American Century Investments, says that at his and his wife's passing, "we're going to give everything we have" to charity for medical research.

> "We make a living by what we get, but we make a life by what we give."
> —Winston Churchill

A bequest is the most common form of bestowing a charitable gift. It is a popular, flexible, and relatively simple method of remembering a favorite charity. A bequest becomes valid at the donor's death, meaning the donor has full use of the asset during his or her lifetime.

Equally important, bequests made to qualified charities are fully deductible when calculating the taxable estate. Many people, if they take the time to reflect on it, would rather direct their wealth to charities than have a generous sum swallowed up by the government through federal and possibly state estate taxation.

ESTATE AND GIFT TAXES

It is important to understand that estate and gift taxes are *unified*. In other words, there is one tax schedule, and both taxes are combined on a cumulative basis during life and at death for tax computation.

The estate tax is levied on the right to transfer an estate to heirs at death. The gift tax is assigned on wealth given away during one's lifetime that exceeds the amount of the gift tax exclusion.

Many important planning implications revolve around estate and gift taxation. This tax rate is substantial, starting at 37% and rising to a steep 55%, as shown in Figure 7-1.

Unified Transfer Tax Rate Schedule

A Taxable Amount Over	B Taxable Amount Not Over	C Tax on Amount in Column A	D Rate of Tax on Excess Over Column A as a %
$ 0	$ 10,000	$ 0	18%
10,000	20,000	1,800	20%
20,000	40,000	3,800	22%
40,000	60,000	8,200	24%
60,000	80,000	13,000	26%
80,000	100,000	18,200	28%
100,000	150,000	23,800	30%
150,000	250,000	38,800	32%
250,000	500,000	70,800	34%
500,000	750,000	155,800	37%
750,000	1,000,000	248,300	39%
1,000,000	1,250,000	345,800	41%
1,250,000	1,500,000	448,300	43%
1,500,000	2,000,000	555,800	45%
2,000,000	2,500,000	780,800	49%
2,500,000	3,000,000	1,025,800	53%
3,000,000	--------	1,290,800	55%

Figure 7-1

Fortunately, three primary shelters from estate and gift taxes are available.

1. MARITAL DEDUCTION

An unlimited marital deduction exists for qualified transfers to a spouse. There is no dollar limit, and estate and gift taxes do not apply to transfers during lifetime or at death. Realize that although the marital deduction is easily and readily available, it should not be over used, since the spouse's assets will be subject to estate taxes at his or her ultimate demise.

2. EXEMPTION AMOUNT

Now called the *exemption amount* rather than a unified credit—a product of the Taxpayer Relief Act of 1997—this figure is scheduled to rise from $600,000 to $1 million by the year 2006. This amount can be applied during one's lifetime and/or at death from combined estate and/or gift taxes.

Individuals with total estates of less than the applicable exemption amount would owe no tax on estate transfers. Hence, for many estates, taxes may not be an issue. However, all other planning considerations remain necessary.

The Unified Credit Exemption Amount		
Decedent's Dying or Making Gifts In:	Exemption	Credit
1997	$600,000	$192,800
1998	$625,000	$202,050
1999	$650,000	$211,300
2000-2001	$675,000	$220,550
2002-2003	$700,000	$229,800
2004	$850,000	$287,300
2005	$950,000	$326,300
2006 and later	$1,000,000	$345,800

Figure 7-2

Due to this substantial credit, many people dismiss the need for engaging in estate planning tax strategies. But realize that all your property, assets, interests, and insurance proceeds are included in your estate. The $600,000 exemption figure remained frozen between 1987 and 1997. Had this $600,000 exemption been indexed for inflation over the past decade, it would now exceed $828,000, according to the calculations of the accounting firm Coopers & Lybrand. So in real terms, due to inflation, the value of the exemption has been steadily eroding. A modest estate can be expected to grow over the years, fueled by appreciation, retirement accounts, inheritances, increased home value, added savings, and life insurance proceeds, bumping up the total to or exceeding the $600,000 figure.

For example, an estate worth $750,000 today would be subject to $55,500 in estate taxes prior to transfer to a beneficiary:

$$\$750{,}000 - \$600{,}000 \text{ exemption} = \$150{,}000 \ @ \ 37\% = \$55{,}500$$

With proper planning, each spouse has the ability to take advantage of a full $600,000 exemption, making it possible to exempt a combined $1.2 million estate from estate taxation; and, when expansion is fully in place, a $2 million estate. Probably the number one costly mistake occurs when married couples underutilize their unified credits. Three factors are responsible:

1. Failure to correctly project the final value of their estates. There is a tendency for individuals later in life to understate the actual value of their holdings.
2. The notion that the unified credit is available automatically to each married individual, whereas they hold assets jointly; or, they passively fall back on the unlimited marital deduction.
3. Naming the spouse beneficiary of life insurance, IRAs, and other "nonprobate assets" that, as I mention earlier, often represent the bulk of the decedent's estate.

Planning Pointers

1. An individual has an estate projected to exceed $600,000. Planning is initiated to minimize transfer taxes.
2. A married couple with individual estates at the $600,000 exemption (or projected to exceed it) is directed to a qualified attorney to seek tax minimization.
3. A married couple or individual with a substantial estate is urged to benefit from the advanced and sophisticated planning techniques offered by highly specialized tax and legal counsel.

3. ANNUAL GIFT EXCLUSION

Every individual is currently allowed to gift up to $10,000 annually to an unlimited number of people free of a gift tax and without reducing the $600,000-plus unified exemption. No gift tax filings are required. This annual gift tax exclusion represents a valuable planning tool.

Married individuals each have a $10,000 gift allowance, for a total of $20,000 that can be given to any one individual. Take the example of a married couple with three married children and four grandchildren. If they so choose, this couple can gift a total of $200,000 ($20,000 to 10 recipients) each calendar year to their children, their children's spouses, and each grandchild. Over a period of 10 years, this couple could transfer a cool $2 million without incurring any gift taxes, and not having to even file gift tax returns. So you can see it is possible to gift away a lot of money before death to avoid estate taxes that would otherwise be due.

A number of misconceptions prevail involving the gift tax exclusion. Here are some *facts:*

- You can elect to gift to anyone. The exclusion is not limited to relatives.
- You may make as many gifts as you wish.
- As the donor, you cannot deduct the gift, as it is not to a qualified charity, but the recipient does not have to report it as income. You may, however, reduce taxes by gifting assets generating current taxable income. When the donee (recipient) of the gift invests the principal, any income is taxable.

Whereas the maximum individual gift is $10,000 in any one year, you may choose to give away any sum below that, and you are under no obligation to continue to make gifts or to retain a certain level of giving. Under current tax legislation, the $10,000 annual gift tax exclusion is scheduled to be indexed to inflation.

A planning caveat: A gift is irreversible and must have no strings attached. So don't make gifts without having the desire and the means to afford the gift. It is laudable to be generous, provided it does not deprive you of your own future financial security and dignity.

Use of a gifting strategy alone or in concert with other techniques has many planning implications:

- It reduces (thins) estate size.
- A reduced estate lowers transfer taxes.
- The strategy reduces the donor's current income taxes by shifting income-producing assets.
- Used in conjunction with the unified credit, a gift can effectively reduce or eliminate estate transfer taxation.
- Gifting makes it possible to transfer wealth for use now by the next generation.

ESTATE PLANNING PROMPTS

The following questionnaire is designed to stimulate thought and probe ideas regarding estate planning matters. It might prove helpful to use it as a checklist.

1. Do you have a will? Was it drawn in your current state of residence? Has a personal situation (marriage, birth, death, divorce, remarriage) changed since the will was drafted? Has your will been reviewed in the last five years?
2. If you have minor children, does your will name guardians and provide for financial management in the event of the death of both you and your spouse?
3. Are you still comfortable with and confident about the personal representative(s) and trustees you have selected?
4. Have you reviewed your beneficiary designations, and are they integrated with your overall estate plan and objectives?
5. Do you and your spouse have estate plans designed to take full advantage of the individual unified credit exemption?
6. Do you and your spouse each own sufficient assets to take full advantage of the maximum unified credit exemption?
7. Are you aware of the $10,000 annual gift tax exclusion? If appropriate, are you taking advantage of it?
8. Do you have or have you considered the advantages of a living trust? If you have a living trust, have you titled assets into the name of the trust?
9. Have you evaluated your life insurance policies and risk protection in light of your overall estate plan?
10. Have you and your spouse executed durable powers of attorney for financial purposes in the event of incapacity?
11. Have you and your spouse executed health care powers of attorney for personal health decisions?
12. If you are a business owner, have you undertaken comprehensive tax planning? Do you have a succession plan in place, and, if appropriate, a buy/sell agreement?
13. Have you reviewed your forms of ownership (titling), and are you confident they are structured to provide optimum control and strategic tax planning?

14. Have you identified the cost basis of all your assets and, if needed, consulted a tax advisor?
15. Have you reviewed your estate plan in light of changes brought about by the Taxpayer Relief Act of 1997?
16. If you have charitable intent, have you expressed your desires to the charity(ies) and pursued various tax-motivated, charitable planned-giving techniques?
17. Most important, have you mapped out what you would like to accomplish, acted on your goals, and assembled a team of financial services professionals to help carry out your plan?

ESTATE PLANNING RECAP

- Using the 10 estate planning goals at the beginning of this chapter as a guide, identify what you are looking to accomplish and what is important to you.
- Review the estate planning questionnaire and checklist to assist you in fine-tuning your estate planning objectives and initiatives.
- Inventory all your assets and property:
  - Identify forms of ownership.
  - Determine valuations.
  - Establish a tax-cost basis.
- Identify the beneficiary designations on all retirement accounts and annuities.
- Conduct a review of all life insurance policies: establish face values, cash values, and ownership, and review beneficiary designations.
- Construct a net worth statement and add life insurance in force to calculate a death estate.
- Select an estate planning attorney and assemble a financial services team.
- Be prepared to respond to changes in your personal and financial condition and to any tax legislation and legal revisions that affect you.
- Make a commitment and follow through to actively manage your estate.

CHAPTER 8

MUTUAL FUNDS: TOOLS FOR YOUR FINANCIAL PLANNING

"In the fullness of time, the mutual fund will come to be regarded among the greatest financial innovations of the modern era."
—SEC Chairman Arthur Levitt

Mutual funds have experienced two decades of phenomenal growth, becoming the investment of choice, reshaping how Americans save and invest, and advancing as the most dynamic element of the burgeoning financial services industry. Total assets in stock, bond, and money market funds exceeded $4 trillion in mid-1997, having surpassed the $1 trillion mark as recently as 1990.

The challenge going forward will be to effectively use mutual fund investing to meet specific financial objectives.

The problem is that the tremendous popularity of mutual funds has spawned roadblocks that complicate matters. Chief among these obstacles are the plethora of funds, the excessive performance emphasis and hype, and the fostering of unhealthy investor behavior. Couple these roadblocks with two additional problems inherent in mutual fund promotion: a dizzying distribution system and excessive costs.

The financial winners in the future will be those investors and planners who follow a common sense path, exploiting the advantages of mutual funds while avoiding the pitfalls.

The versatility of mutual funds offers opportunity and choice to today's intelligent investor and a solution to funding a secure retirement or an education.

The essence of successful investing is to devise the highest possible return commensurate with the lowest possible risk. Mutual funds by design offer professional money management to help maximize return, and broad-based diversification to help minimize risk. Their appeal is heightened by their familiarity and the amount of information available, an industry relatively free from abuses, a host of attractive features, a multitude of choices, versatility, flexibility, and public accountability.

In a fund, individuals pool their money and own shares of an investment company, most commonly referred to as a mutual fund. These monies are invested by professional money managers into a diversified portfolio of selected investment securities according to a specified investment objective.

A mutual fund is a security in which you purchase shares. In principle, this works the same way as stock ownership, where shareholders reap either the financial reward or the misfortune accompanying ownership. A mutual fund acts as a holding company for ownership positions in a multitude of stocks and/or bonds. Professional money managers are hired by a fund's board of directors to actively manage investments under the terms of an investment advisory contract.

The mutual fund industry is relatively free from the fraud and abuses that too frequently plague financial services. Funds are regulated by the Securities and Exchange Commission (SEC) and operate under rules set down in the Investment Advisors Act of 1940. Although such federal oversight does not in itself insulate investors, it has proven to be a good framework. I believe this investor confidence derives from the overall fund structure, which provides daily pricing, a public record of performance, and continuous marketability.

The popularity of mutual funds and the influences propelling their phenomenal growth help build a case for using mutual funds. Upon closer examination, we discover their popularity is due to a convergence of factors.

- ♦ A major impetus was the introduction of the money market fund in the early 1970s. For some time, money markets had existed to accommodate short-term cash needs of large borrowers and institutions. Only large institutional investors were able to participate in this relatively high-yield, short-term note marketplace, owing to prohibitively high investment minimums. In stepped opportunistic financial packagers who pooled investments from thousands of individuals. Their concept opened the door to individual participation. The money market mutual fund as an investment vehicle was born. It has since become a staple of investment offerings. Pooling individual money into a common (mutual) fund invested for a specific objective is the framework of mutual fund investing.

- The period of the late 1970s and early 1980s witnessed high levels of inflation, with correspondingly high double-digit interest rates. Investors came to recognize money funds with their higher yields, relative safety, and liquidity as attractive alternatives to fixed-rate passbook bank accounts. In the process, countless investors were introduced to the world of mutual fund investing.

- The bull market that emerged in August 1982 was a prime impetus for attracting money and adding substantial appreciation to mutual fund assets. It helped tremendously that the best-performing investments were stocks and bonds. In comparison, the place to be in the decade of the 1970s was clearly in real estate, precious metals, energy issues, and limited partnerships. Investors were clamoring for the current hot financial asset. The mutual fund industry responded by introducing hundreds of new funds, including popular new choices such as GNMA, international, small-cap, and sector funds.

- Retirement plans were a major reason for the growth in mutual fund assets. In the early 1980s, funds were a major recipient of IRA investments. Individuals are now receiving substantial lump-sum distributions from retirement plans. One area certain to continue growing is the expanded use of mutual funds as investment options for 401(k) plans. Individuals are increasingly responsible for making their own investment elections within a retirement plan. The investment of choice is likely to be mutual funds; hence, the necessity to more fully understand these investment instruments.

- The precipitous drop in interest rates during late 1991 and continuing into 1992 and 1993 only added to the exodus from traditional financial institutions. Owing to a 20-year low in bank yields, even reluctant savers started to take the plunge into funds. Adding to the allure, new mutual fund offerings appeared, such as adjustable rate mortgage (ARM) funds and short-term bond funds.
- Today's investor is increasingly sophisticated. The baby boom generation grew conditioned to using toll-free 800 numbers and placing money in any geographic area that offered a healthy return. Two-income couples and the women's movement added to the boom in mutual funds among a population demanding convenience. All in all, the timing was right for an explosion in funds.

ADVANTAGES OF MUTUAL FUNDS

Perhaps the best way to illustrate the advantages of mutual fund investing is to contrast this method to that of constructing a portfolio through individual stock and bond selection.

Let's explore the procedure, or rather the dilemma, of stock investing. When investing in the stock market, one is faced with difficult decisions, starting with the choice of what to buy. There are more than 1,500 stocks listed on the New York Stock Exchange, and thousands more on the smaller exchanges. The potential universe is immense.

Once a stock is purchased, an even more perplexing decision arises: when to sell. An abundance of sources, including brokers, investment services, newsletters, acquaintances, and even strangers, suggest tantalizing stocks to buy. Ask almost anyone, and I believe you will find plenty of hot stock tips. It is generally accepted that sell decisions are equally important, but few of those same people can tell you when to sell. A successful investment is as much a product of a timely sell determination as it is of a solid stock selection.

The decision to continue to hold a given stock investment is also important, yet it receives too little emphasis in investment decision making.

The decision as to when to stand pat and hold should be a deliberate action, arrived at as a result of a conscious, periodic, objective evaluation. Often this is not the case for individuals managing their own portfolios. A given security is most often held because to do otherwise involves making a decision and instituting action. Investors should realize that not making a choice is also a decision.

The entire stock investing procedure involves a constant buy/sell/hold decision-making process. Unfortunately, individuals often are ill-equipped to successfully direct any of these tasks. Once a stock is sold, or a dividend is received, or a bond is called or matures, the whole arduous process begins anew.

The solution is to employ professional money management. Every mutual fund investor receives the benefit of such professional money management. A professional is making the admittedly difficult buy/sell/hold decisions for you. Professional money managers possess the time, talent, resources, and incentive to effectively manage your money. The entire fund portfolio is scrutinized on a continual basis. Active deletions, allocations, additions, and substitutions are executed in an ongoing attempt to improve performance. Prior to the widespread acceptance of mutual funds, only the wealthy could afford to purchase this level of expertise. Through a fund, investors can avail themselves of top-flight money managers. Invest like a pro by investing with the pros.

Academic studies suggest that one needs a minimum of 10 individual stocks to build an effectively diversified portfolio. Further, a minimum investment of $50,000 in stocks is necessary to assemble an adequate portfolio. The latest study I have seen asserts the need for 30 stocks and $100,000. This requirement acts as an obstacle to individuals pursuing investment success.

Look at it this way—whenever people purchase a stock, they do so because they are convinced they have picked a winner. But the fact is, in the stock market, for every winner there is an accompanying loser. We could hold a stock-picking contest, asking a field of renowned experts to choose 10 stocks. I submit that if we look at performance after, say, three years, the results would look like this: Three of our experts' top 10 stock picks would turn out to be turkeys, four could be expected to be average performers, and three would have soared like eagles. Even if you polled the experts for their absolute favorite stock—and this has been done—you are as likely to end up with a turkey as you are an eagle.

Even the top stock pickers in the world pick losers and make mistakes—plenty of them. In an individual portfolio, the risk of having a turkey is magnified.

Perhaps the greatest benefit of mutual fund investing is that all investors obtain instant and continuous diversification. Diversification is inherent in all mutual funds by their very makeup. It is typical for a stock mutual fund to contain 50, 75, even 100 holdings. The investor receives two levels of diversification: first from the quantity of individual stocks, and second from a variety of industry groupings. Scan a stock mutual fund portfolio (always a good idea), and you will find a breakdown by industry groups (sectors). For example, a fund might have investments in these sectors: capital goods, consumer durables, consumer nondurables, energy, financial, raw materials, utilities, and more. Through economic sector diversification you receive some counter-cyclical protection. Put another way, auto stocks could be up while drug stocks are down, or vice versa. Diversification is valued in investing for its effectiveness in reducing risk. In Chapter 6 we learned how we can use mutual funds to add a third level of diversification, by using multiple funds with different objectives and investment styles.

A mutual fund bond portfolio might hold 50 different debt securities. Diversification protection takes the form of the quantity, industry, geography, and maturity levels. If a default occurs with one issue, the portfolio would be fortified by the remaining 49 debt issues. Remember, when a bond defaults, you can lose all your money. Distressingly, defaults can and do occur. In a diversified bond mutual fund, an individual bad apple will not spoil the whole bushel. If your money is concentrated in just one debt obligation, one bad apple spells hurt. A reminder: even professional bond managers make mistakes. Individuals make errors routinely.

Junk bonds offer a good example of the wisdom of diversified mutual fund investing. Some statistical studies show that one in every 10 junk bonds could default. Because defaults occur regularly, you simply cannot afford the risk of an individual high-yield bond. For this reason, if you are inclined to invest in high-risk, high-yield bonds, add a degree of protection by purchasing them through mutual funds.

The stock purchaser pays a commission going in. The seller pays a commission going out. Costs are appreciably greater for those who trade in small volumes. You pay the same commission whether you are a winner or a loser. There is an old saying on Wall Street: "Well, the broker made money, the brokerage house made money, and two out of three ain't bad."

Excessive transaction costs, indecision, poor timing, overwhelming choices, and inadequate diversification all serve to frustrate investors. Against this backdrop, mutual fund investing stands out as a logical, common sense solution.

It is worth repeating: mutual funds offer professional money management, thereby improving the odds of a successful investment performance. Two levels of diversification offer a proven means of reducing risk; in essence, the possibility of higher returns along with a method of lowering risk.

A valid explanation for the popularity of fund investing is that these twin advantages are delivered from the very first day and first dollar invested. Low barriers to entry (reasonable minimum initial investment) allow accessibility by masses of investors. Mutual funds have gained converts from the rank of novice to the most sophisticated investors. A widely held misperception is that truly great investment opportunities and top investment minds are the secret and exclusive preserve of the wealthy. Mutual funds should dispel this myth. They are available, affordable, and comprehensive.

Neuberger & Berman Management Company profiled the long-term performance record of its Guardian Fund through a dramatic advertising campaign that I found of interest, and, I suspect, was also effective. The campaign was really a tribute to Roy Neuberger, who started the Guardian Fund. He still retains a semi-active management role despite the fact that he is in his nineties, and a few years back he was run down by an aggressive bicycle messenger while walking to his Manhattan office.

The Guardian Fund had an inception date of June 1, 1950, which closely corresponds to my own conception. If my parents or grandparents had had the means and inclination to invest $10,000 in my name at that time, the value as of December 31, 1996, some 45½ years later, would have been an astounding $2,669,371. Today I'd be a multimillionaire. I am aware that $10,000 was a lot of money in 1950, as it is today. But even if $1,000 had been invested back then, it would have grown 25-fold to $266,937.

A lesson can be learned from this example. Over the past 45 years, close to a 13% average annual total return was achieved—far from a straight line, and subject to and influenced by numerous recessions, bear and bull markets, market crashes, a series of wars, assassinations, and tumultuous global, political, and economic upheavals.

The Guardian Fund, typical of a garden-variety growth and income fund, owed its success most of all to the long-term nature of the investment, competent professional management, diversification, and consistent dividend and capital gains reinvestment. These advantages are available to every patient mutual fund investor.

TOOLS FOR YOUR FINANCIAL PLANNING

Mutual funds are flexible enough to allow us to respond to our changing financial conditions. We can readily elect to transfer to alternative funds, change investment objectives, and add or redeem funds among a myriad of fund choices to meet our immediate needs. We have features available to provide automatic investing or fixed, systematic withdrawal. Ownership (registration) can be changed, and you can elect to take distributions as income or in additional shares through dividend and capital gain reinvestment.

A TOOL FOR CASH MANAGEMENT

Virtually anyone serious about money should have a money market fund at his or her disposal. The only decision in my mind is what type of money fund to have. You can choose among taxable, tax-exempt, and government varieties. Money market funds provide an investor with instant liquidity, including convenient check writing capability. Since money market funds seek to maintain a stable share price, usually $1.00, sales or redemptions do not trigger capital gain tax consequences. You also have a high degree of confidence that your principal is not exposed to risk. No mutual fund, including money market funds, is FDIC insured or guaranteed in any fashion.

However, money market funds are considered safe, conservative investments.

A money market fund, as an investment staple, can be used as a parking place, a cash reservoir, or a liquid emergency fund. A standard financial planning piece of advice is to maintain three to six months' income needs readily accessible in a vehicle such as a money market fund.

There are all sorts of reasons why you need to access cash quickly — for emergency expenses, home or car down payment, tuition, judgments, bail, wedding expenses, taxes, funeral arrangements, margin calls, or urgent investment opportunities.

A money market fund is referred to as a cash investment, owing to its liquidity and the absence of value fluctuation. When you don't know what to do with a sum of money, you can always safely park it in a money market until the smoke clears and you decide to redeploy. As a conservative investment, it is also a refuge in times of financial market turmoil. Sometimes you hear investors saying they are going to the sidelines, which means they are taking money out of stocks and bonds (off the playing field) and putting it into a cash equivalent; namely, money markets.

A TOOL FOR A HOUSE DOWN PAYMENT

Newlyweds Tom and Sheila are excited about building a life together, which includes fulfilling the American dream of owning their own home. They target the purchase of a starter home in about three years, calculating they will need a down payment of $20,000. They are fortunate to have $5,000 in cash wedding gifts to begin saving.

They choose a short-term bond fund to fuel their goal. This vehicle will provide a higher yield than a money market yet has greater price stability than is found in longer term bond funds.

As a young two-income couple, Tom and Sheila mutually agree to live solely on Tom's income and invest Sheila's net pay, less a car note, toward their home down payment.

To fulfill this plan, they utilize a valuable feature found in all mutual funds: automatic monthly investing. They arrange to have $500 automatically deducted directly from their joint checking account the 15th of each month.

After two years, they are blessed with the arrival of Tommy Jr. As was their plan, Sheila elects to stay home to care for their son. They reduce their systematic investment plan to $100 a month, but continue to automatically reinvest dividends to help their account grow. At the end of three years they meet their goal of $20,000 and accelerate their house hunting.

The happy story continues as they find a house. It needs work, but with Tom and Sheila's sweat equity, they go about making their house a home.

A TOOL FOR EDUCATION FUNDING

Grandma Kay is thrilled with the news that her only child, Ann, after considerable anguish and dashed hopes, has delivered healthy bouncing baby girls. Girls, plural—as in triplets! Martha, Maggie, and Mary Nell (Nellie) are named after their great-aunts.

Grandma is a believer in education, having graduated from college in an era when few women received advanced degrees. Her goal is to invest in these girls' futures through their education. Kay is recently widowed and in the enviable position of being able to follow through on her goal. She decides to make a gift of $10,000 to each of her darling grandchildren, the maximum currently allowed as an annual gift tax exclusion. She can afford this generosity, and she correctly reasons that at her stage in life it won't harm her lifestyle to lower her taxable estate a little.

Kay opens three separate custodial accounts in a mutual fund, registering (titling) each with the Social Security number of one of the girls as a gift under the Uniform Gifts to Minors Act (UGMA), which in some states is a transfer rather than a gift, or a UTMA. Since her granddaughters are all newborns, it is reasonable to assume an 18-year period before tuition bills begin.

She wisely chooses a growth fund to provide maximum appreciation potential because the girls have a long-term horizon in which the fund can even out its inherent volatility. She signs up for reinvestment of all dividends and capital gain distributions, reasoning correctly that these options will provide the most fuel to finance her granddaughters' educational needs.

Grandma's thinking is to add $1,000 to each account for the girls' birthdays, easy to remember as it's the same date each year. If this fund vehicle grows at an 11% annual compounded rate, the educational stake could grow to a cool $100,000 for each child. Grandma Kay is proud to be endowing her own scholarship fund, leaving a lasting legacy for her grandchildren.

A TOOL TO CREATE A TAX-ADVANTAGED RETIREMENT PLAN

Nancy is single, successful, and self-employed, and she admits to being concerned for her future financial security. She would like to reduce her substantial tax burden, heightened by the fact that she has no dependents and chooses to rent an apartment over the responsibilities of home ownership.

Nancy calls herself a corporate-world dropout, having opted for a severance package after the last round of corporate downsizing and restructuring. She is part of a new trend, working out of her home, being her own boss, and loving it. One thing she does miss in comparison to her corporate friends is a 401(k) and profit-sharing retirement plan. Determined not to lose ground, she decides to build her own retirement plan.

Nancy establishes a Simplified Employee Plan (SEP), placing 15% of her net income into it. The mechanics are quite simple, which suits Nancy because she abhors complicated filing requirements and administrative headaches. She uses mutual funds to set up her account with a simple two-page application. With no family dependent on her, Nancy names her favorite charity as beneficiary for this account. She gains a sense of satisfaction as she sees the twin benefits of a dollar-for-dollar reduction in her taxable income for her contributions and the tax-deferred growth of investment earnings.

Basically, Nancy has developed a self-directed, tax-advantaged, diversified, simple financial security blanket and investment program. Being middle-of-the-road on the risk scale, Nancy opts to use a balanced mutual fund, sometimes referred to as an asset allocation fund. This way, in one package, she receives instant diversification from a mix of stocks, bonds, and cash holdings. She funds the SEP quarterly, adjusting the last quarter to be in line with her total annual income.

Nancy, who admits to being 30-something, calculates she can place $12,000 each year into this plan. If she realizes a 9% average return, in 25 years she could build a nest egg in excess of $1 million. Her own contribution would be $300,000, with the balance of $700,000 provided by compound growth. Additionally, assuming she is in a combined federal and state tax bracket of 33%, Nancy would reduce her total taxable income by $100,000 and delay taxation on the $700,000 in earnings. Who needs a 401(k)?

TROUBLE ON THE MUTUAL FUND FRONT

I have been an early and vocal advocate for mutual fund investing, believing mutual funds offer a common sense investment opportunity capable of helping individuals achieve financial objectives.

Yet I feel compelled to sound an alarm, warning that formidable obstacles now stand in the way of successful mutual fund investment implementation. The irony is that the mutual fund success story is proving problematic and a major distraction sidetracking mutual fund investors. Veteran investment pros have described the increasing tendency of too many fund investors to follow a "suicide investing" course. One industry leader never hesitant to raise his voice and share his strong opinions is John C. Bogle, author of *Bogle on Mutual Funds* and chairman of the Vanguard Group, the nation's second largest fund family. With the conviction of a man with a new lease on life after a successful heart transplant, Bogle has lashed out at his own industry, where he claims "distribution is becoming more important than money management and asset gathering is superseding trusteeship." These are serious accusations, yet I am afraid he is on to something.

In recent communications he has railed against fast-trading mutual fund companies that encourage short-term investing, a practice he has derisively labeled "casino capitalism." It is no secret that he holds his arch rival and industry leader, Fidelty, in disdain for promoting "two countervailing principles: switch and get rich, and pick hot managers."

There is trouble on the mutual fund front, but much of it has been masked by the euphoria and good times accompanying the current bull market. I am identifying such obstacles in the hope that, forewarned, you may steer clear and focus on properly using these valuable financial planning tools.

Here are 10 obstacles that represent trouble:

1. WAY TOO MANY FUNDS

Forbes magazine in a 1988 cover story referred to "the maddening multiplicity of funds." At the time of this madness, there were some 2,000 fund choices, a number that by 1997 had mushroomed to 8,000 and is continuing to multiply. Investors are drowning in a sea of choices, overwhelmed by confusion and complexity.

We now have many more funds than there are stocks listed on the New York Stock Exchange (NYSE). A strong case can be made for needing a universe of only 500 funds. This tremendous overcapacity lies at the root of the problem.

2. HEAVY EMPHASIS ON SHORT-TERM PERFORMANCE

Owing to the overcrowded field, fund investment managers are under extreme pressure to put up superior short-term performance numbers. The quarter-to-quarter performance derby makes fund managers more willing to push the envelope and take irresponsible risks in hopes of hitting a home run. This is why some supposedly conservative bond funds were loaded with derivatives in 1993 and 1994, and stock portfolios were heavy in junk bonds in 1989 and were making outsized bets in hot sectors, IPOs (initial public offerings), and emerging markets. This gunslinger approach has caused excessive turnover and other costs while raising the stakes on fund investing to a speculative game.

You can't entirely blame the aggressive nature of fund managers in this overhyped environment. You're either hot or you're nothing. Unless fund managers catch each and every wave, fickle investors quickly brand them as incompetent and flee.

Fund managers are flaming out, burning up, and jumping ship. Jeff Vinik departed as helmsman of the industry flagship fund Fidelty Magellan when its performance numbers slipped for one year. Vinik had misjudged the staying power of a bull market, opting instead to conservatively hold cash and bonds. His fall from grace is a textbook case of "what have you done for me lately."

One of his predecessors in this visible post, superstar manager Peter Lynch, abruptly retired at age 44, telling anyone who would listen that his superior performance results were unsustainable.

3. TOO MUCH MARKETING HYPE

Contrary to public perception, I am convinced that marketing prowess, not investment skill, is the most important attribute of today's financially successful investment companies (mutual fund families).

Fund companies loudly promote what's hot and keep silent on what's not, even going so far as to merge laggard funds with more attractive mates and change fund names to camouflage poor performers. A fund company hides behind its winners while putting its losers in the closet.

Investment sage Philip Carret speaks with the wisdom appropriate to an 1896 birth year. He suspects part of the reason for fund proliferation is a basic marketing ploy to "have enough funds that at least one of them always looks good."

Too many investment shops no longer adhere to an overall investment philosophy. Instead they make sure they have all their bases covered. In their lineup they play a numbers game, spotlighting players who have just hit a home run, even though they know statistically high flyers are more likely to strike out next time up.

In truth, all mutual fund families have winners and losers in their stable of offerings. No mutual fund family can rightly claim consistently superior investment success across their entire menu. Overall measurement is likely to produce a mixed bag and fall within an average range.

Yet fund companies spend millions to tout their superior investment capabilities and condition you to believe they are the ticket to riches. These expenditures drive up fund costs but have no effect on performance. Their express purpose is to gain or hold on to lucrative market share and never to reveal they are at best just average.

4. UNHEALTHY INVESTMENT BEHAVIOR

Too many gullible fund investors practice market timing in a futile attempt to ride the rocket of hot performers to spectacular gains. The cold reality is that investments often perform better than investors. A study done by mutual fund tracker *Morningstar* unearthed a startling revelation: the average annual investment return on growth stock funds over the five-year period from 1989 to 1994 was a healthy 12%, yet investors realized a paltry 2% return. How can that be, you might ask? It seems the average holding period over the five-year time frame was only 21 months for investors. This impatience cost investors dearly, for they committed a cardinal error of purchasing at the top (too late) and selling out at the bottom (too early).

Speaking of unhealthy investment behavior, I found reinforcement in a *Forbes* column by Kenneth Fisher in which he profiles a 1997 book by James Dines entitled *Mass Psychology*.

> "Yes, no-load funds beat load funds, but investors in load funds beat investors in no-loads. A paradox? No, but it took academics more than 30 years to figure out that people who pay loads are less likely to engage in costly in-and-out trading. Sometimes how tools are used is more important than the tools themselves."
>
> —James Dines, *Mass Psychology*

5. BETTING ON LAST YEAR'S WINNERS

The following caption is required by law to appear in fine print at the bottom of every mutual fund ad and promotion piece:

"PAST PERFORMANCE IS NO INDICATION OF FUTURE RESULTS AND ALL RETURNS ARE HISTORICAL"

Mutual fund investors would be wise to heed this warning rather than routinely ignore it. Perhaps it should be in bold print at the very top, for its message is that important.

Investors want to believe a fund's impressive track record is a precursor of future performance and that the upward pattern will continue. Not only is the past not indicative of the future, but in the case of fund performance, ample evidence suggests just the opposite.

Investors too often time their fund purchases using a rearview mirror selection process. They choose last year's performance winner or the manager whose picture most recently graced the cover of *Money* magazine.

CGM Capital Development Fund was the top-performing mutual fund in 1991, up an astounding 99%, more than three times the returns posted by the average stock fund that year. But in 1994 this high flyer shot to the very bottom of the barrel in its category, down 23%. Investor behavior in this example is easy to chronicle. Money gushed in during 1992 and made for the door after the disappointment of 1994, resulting in a sorry investment experience.

Charles Jaffe writes a syndicated mutual fund column, "Mutual Interest," in which he shares common sense advice and dispels common performance misconceptions. For example, he noted that three of the very top performing funds in 1995—Perkins Opportunity, Govett Smaller Companies, and Wasatch Mid-Cap—were in the bottom 1% of funds tracked in 1996 by Lipper. How quickly a fund can go from treasure to trash!

Top-ranking mutual funds have no lock on success, and attempting to hold winners is an exercise in futility. Personal finance author and columnist JaneBryant Quinn observes, "The personal finance magazines help drive this perpetual fund envy. In every issue, new funds are highlighted, stunning performances praised, hot managers worshipped. Your own fund always seems second-best." The elusive effort to own the best funds is as frustrating—and successful—as a dog chasing its tail.

6. THE CULT OF PERFORMANCE

Performance is overrated. We suffer from informational overload, much of it conflicting.

Just how many funds can claim a #1 ranking, anyway? Apparently, hundreds can and do. I have an ad in front of me proclaiming a #1 ranking for a one-year period as of March 31, 1995, in the multi-asset global fund category. The game is to find an obscure category, match it to a favorable time period, and trumpet that you are the best.

Chicago-based *Morningstar* is a respected mutual fund information source and very much a product of the phenomenal growth in the mutual fund industry. Intended or not, they are most known for their star ranking system. Funds are awarded stars from 1 to 5 (lowest to highest) depending on their risk-adjusted returns compared to peers. This system has serious flaws even the company admits to, and they are moving to amend the system. However, their top 4-star and 5-star rankings are highly coveted by mutual fund marketers and are found prominently in ad pieces.

The influence of the *Morningstar* system is so pervasive that a recent study indicated a full 65% of all new stock fund money flowed into funds sporting 4 or 5 stars, representing the top 32.5% of funds in *Morningstar*'s rating system. This is a troubling statistic, because *Morningstar* has presented its own study showing that funds ranking in the bottom third over a three-year period outperform the top third over the next three years. This should not be surprising, because investment styles and themes go in and out of favor, and performance levels inevitably gravitate to the middle over time.

Reinforcing this view is Mark Hulbert, the editor of a service that monitors the performance of investment advisory letters, and the contributor of a regular piece for *Forbes* magazine.

In a December 12, 1997, column he puts *Morningstar* under a bright light and states unequivocally that their top rankings (four and five stars) are a poor indicator of future above-average performers; indeed they represent a contrary indicator.

His firm's *Hulbert Financial Digest* has tracked *Morningstar*'s performance since the beginning of 1991 and discovered:

"*Morningstar*'s top-ranked no-load equity funds have lagged the stock market by an average of nearly three percentage points per year."

He goes on to point out that rival mutual fund ranker *Value Line Mutual Fund Survey* did no better. Its top-ranked general equity funds fell short of the market average by nearly four percentage points per year over a four-year measuring period.

What is troubling is that fund companies routinely tout their top-ranked fund offerings, and yet compelling evidence suggests that anyone following this marketing allure is purchasing a fund that will likely underperform going forward.

7. DIZZY DISTRIBUTION AND DELIVERY SYSTEMS

As if the load/no-load debate were not confusing enough, perplexed mutual fund investors must deal with an alphabet soup of fund classes: A, B, C, D ... M, and so on. Each class carries a distinct cost structure consisting of internal operating and management expenses, 12b(1) fees, and one form or another of load—front, back end, and level, to name a few.

Remember that a load is a sales commission that goes to reimburse a salesperson or broker. No-load funds are marketed directly to the public. The major advantage of a no-load is that all your investment dollars go immediately to work. A load must be justified by the value the broker adds to the investment process.

Investors may wonder how a no-load fund makes a profit. Brokers and sales forces of load products play on this perception, suggesting there is no free lunch. The fact is that all funds, no-load as well as load, charge an annual management fee and pass on fund operating expenses. These fees are separate from any load fees, which are strictly sales compensation. Other fees, known as 12b(1) fees and ranging from .15% to 2.5%, are subtracted from fund assets as part of the daily pricing of net asset value (NAV). As a good fund consumer, pay attention to these expense ratios. They have a direct bearing on your return.

The 12b(1) fee is sometimes referred to as a hidden load because it is imposed not at the time of purchase, but continually over the life of the holding. A fund purchaser could, in the long run, be better off by paying a steep up-front load than by incurring 12b(1) fees and high annual expenses.

The emergence of classes of shares is a calculated response to the resistance to paying up-front sales loads. These options allow a load mutual fund to compete effectively with direct-marketed no-load funds. Front-end loads have gradually been reduced and could well disappear over time.

A popular trend is the fund supermarket, where individuals can conduct one-stop (source) fund shopping and execution. The appeal is that investors can select from among hundreds of fund choices of dozens of fund families and do so without a load. All this, and a convenient and valuable consolidated monthly statement, as well.

The downside to this method is that fund complexes (interesting industry jargon for fund families) have increased their fund costs in disguised fashions to cover the costs associated with the supermarket concept and to compensate the selling agents.

Today's mutual fund investor has to be alert and cost conscious to operate in this complex web of choices and classes.

8. UNREALISTICALLY HIGH RETURNS

Fostered by the prolonged bull market since August 1982, investors have been lulled into a false sense of permanent prosperity. Too many investors naively have come to believe a stock mutual fund is really a CD carrying a 15% coupon rate. A major concern are those investors, and especially investment managers, who have never been tested by a major bear market like the one of 1973–1974.

Too strong a bull market was the case for both stocks and bonds in 1995. Everyone posted superior returns and some gained overconfidence bordering on invincibility. Too often, investors operate in a rearview mirror mode, dangerously believing the terrain ahead is similar to the one recently traversed.

The long-term historical returns from large-cap stocks since 1926 is in the 10-11% range, which suggests that returns can be expected to regress to the mean—or, in lay language, come back to earth.

9. DANGERS OF PERFORMANCE COMPARISONS

Be wary of brokers offering to conduct free mutual fund performance evaluations. Armed with hundreds of fund choices and backed up by reams of historical data, any commission-driven salesperson, I guarantee, can readily show that they have "better" funds than your current holdings. The selling argument is that the past data holds the truth, and by switching to their suggested alternatives you will be richly rewarded. This evaluation is likely to lack objectivity and result in increased costs and possibly tax consequences. A more valuable service is an asset allocation analysis, for which you do not need performance data.

Comparison shopping is a difficult undertaking for a would-be investor. You have to slice up a huge market that is differentiated by objectives, styles, stock-holding size, up-and-down market grades, beta (risk) measurement, and the quality and maturity of bond holdings. The time spent in this exercise is better placed on matching a selection to your investment objective and tailoring a portfolio with an asset allocation mix that fits you.

As previously suggested, standard common sense advice includes not chasing last year's winners, not following the allure of highly rated funds, and not believing a particular fund family possesses superior investment prowess. Finally, do your homework first, be conscious of all costs involved, be a patient, long-term investor, and plan to hold good quality mutual funds through at least a five-year economic cycle for best results.

10. SUBPAR PERFORMANCE FOR VALUE

Every mutual fund is required to establish a benchmark index that metaphorically represents what is "par for the course," against which its performance can be tracked and graphed. It is required to also publish this information in its annual report to shareholders. The sad fact is, the majority of funds fall distressingly short of matching their chosen benchmark. Fund investors are hoping to shoot birdies (beat par), but frequently end up scoring bogies.

Too many fund investors are blind to this underachievement, especially during up markets. Typical is the woman who is enthusiastic over a stock fund holding because it was up 20% in 1995, even though its benchmark was up 35%. Over the three-year measuring period, her fund badly trailed its index. But she feels good because she has seen the market value on her statements appreciate. She is inclined to add more money to a fund because it has "done well for me" and is a "good" fund. The same individual is attracted to bond funds with the highest distribution yields, oblivious to the decline on a total return basis.

In addition, fund investors incur high costs, loads, and fees that in many instances are actually accelerating.

Another problem is that heavy portfolio turnover (its manager's frequent selling and buying) within a fund results in capital gain distributions that outside of tax-deferred accounts translate into immediate taxable consequences.

Tax inefficiency, the burden of costs, and subpar performance cumulatively mean mutual fund investors are not receiving the value they deserve and expect.

A STRONG STORY

The Strong family of mutual funds based in Menomonee Falls, Wisconsin, is illustrative of the phenomenal growth of the fund industry. I have closely observed this well-regarded fund family over the past 15 years, both as an early shareholder and while recommending and monitoring these funds in my capacity as an investment advisor.

I have witnessed this hometown fund grow from 11 employees and three funds—when I first visited its headquarters in 1983—to a current crop of 35 funds and $30 billion in assets serviced by employees housed in an impressive Frank Lloyd Wright prairie-style headquarters.

The Strong funds' timing in entering the mutual fund business coincided with the boom in mutual funds. Chairman and founder Richard Strong lent his last name to the fund family, connoting strength and solidity to prospective investors.

The no-load fund complex has a full spectrum of investment offerings and provides an exemplary level of shareholder servicing and communications.

From my perspective, its success is due to superb marketing more than to investment management. It is not alone in this regard but operates in a vein similar to its industry peers.

It aspires to be the "Fidelity of the Midwest," and it appears to have patterned itself—for good or bad—after the Boston-based giant.

HEAVILY PROMOTE WHATEVER FUND STYLE IS HOT

Strong is quick to bring to market the fund style currently in vogue, be it international, small-cap, value, municipal, Asian, emerging market, or asset allocation. It heavily promotes new introductions and clearly offers the marketplace what they are clamoring for. Investor dollars flock to these hot new funds, which, unfortunately, tend to cool relatively soon.

STRONG IS JUST PLAIN AVERAGE IN PERFORMANCE

To support this bold claim, I refer to the stock mutual fund performance ratings supplied by Lipper Analytical Services for the period ending December 31, 1997.

Under the Strong Funds' grouping, a total of 19 stock funds were listed. Of this number, 12, or 63%, had not been around long enough to carry a five-year track record.

Fund tracker Lipper assigns five levels, 1 to 5, to its ranking of performance. A fund that finishes in the top 20% of all funds in its category earns a 1, the bottom 20% of funds rate a 5.

Of the seven Strong funds qualifying for a five-year track record, the same number of funds earned the top ranking as did the bottom: two funds. Average the rankings, and it comes out to a middle-of-the-road overall rating of 3.

Strong's performance is typical of other fund families. Look closely, as I do, at any fund family performance rankings in a newspaper listing. None owns top rankings or is immune from laggards. Note how many new funds exist that do not merit a track record.

American Funds is renowned for having top-flight investment managers, yet the same quick analysis reveals that American Funds falls short of Strong with an overall average ranking from Lipper of less than 3.

EXPENSE RATIOS ARE RELATIVELY HIGH

The Strong fund family prominently informs the investment public it is a pure no-load fund family. Fund expenses tend to be along the high average range, while operating expenses are high to cover a large and expensive overhead. Both management and operating internal expenses are inconspicuous enough to allow Strong to maintain a marketing advantage.

Strong is a major player in the fund supermarketplace. Its high expense levels allow it a margin to pay the required fees to the fund's network organization, be it Schwab or Fidelity.

EMPLOY A GREAT PR MACHINE

Similar to other large national advertisers, Strong receives attendant high levels of exposure and generally favorable media attention, thus effectively leveraging its substantial marketing investment. There should be no surprise if a direct correlation appears between the public perception of the worthiness of a given fund family and the size of its ad budget.

As an example of its marketing savvy, information has been released that the Strong Funds has set up college education IRAs for each of the McCaughey septuplets of Carlisle, Iowa.

REACH FOR HIGHER YIELDS ON BOND FUNDS

Like many funds, the Strong fixed-income funds rely on attractive yields to entice investors. In doing so, those funds push the envelope by going long with durations (length of bonds), as well as by accepting lower-credit (higher-risk) quality bonds. During periods of falling interest rates, this leverage propels them to the top of performers; yet, when rates rise, conservative, income-oriented investors suffer loss of principal. Strong also seems somewhat open to bet the market direction, a fine idea—until you suffer a wrong call.

TEASER RATES ATTRACT MONEY FUND ASSETS

The only real difference between money market yields is attributable to expense ratios. The lower the expenses, the higher the yield. Strong's advertising blitz heralds its #1-yielding money market fund. The reason for this honor is revealed in an accompanying footnote stating that the fund gained this distinction by temporarily absorbing (waiving) fund expenses of .55%. Hundreds of millions of dollars are attracted to this teaser yield, which will return to an average-yield money fund when fund expenses are turned back on.

Strong is not alone in exercising this marketing ploy. In front of me is an ad from Zurich, formerly Kemper funds, touting its #1-yielding money market fund. Reading the fine print, I find that a total of .63% of expenses is being temporarily waived. Otherwise, the yield would have been that much lower and less attractive.

DISGUISE YOUR POOR PERFORMERS

When I started following the Strong funds in the early 80s, it had but three fund offerings. Following the histories of the Strong Total Return, Investment, and Income funds proves illuminating.

Strong Total Return was the flagship fund of this fledgling fleet, and it pulled in substantial assets based on solid performance until it ran aground in September 1989. The downfall occurred the day its largest single holding, United Airlines (UAL), plummeted when a leveraged buyout deal fell through. Holdings of lower-quality junk bonds soured once the United deal was off the table. These events precipitated a decline in share value and, subsequently, assets.

Until that time, Strong had enhanced return by employing market timing. In the watershed fall of 1989, Strong made one bad move after another. It sold its illiquid junk bond funds at distressed prices and moved into high-quality government bonds just as rates were rising, losing even more capital.

To its credit, Strong survived this dark chapter, recruited a slew of new managers, and accelerated fresh fund offerings. Cochair William Corneliuson abruptly left the firm. Total Return began its long road back to acceptable performance.

Strong Investment, another inaugural fund, ran in tandem with Total Return, suffering the same fate in the 1989 debacle. Its name was changed to Asset Allocation a couple of years later after that theme became popular.

The Strong Income Fund is now forgotten, having been renamed the Corporate Bond Fund. All three of these initial funds remain in the Strong family, their former prominence overshadowed by newer offerings.

Like Fidelity and others, Strong has experienced a turnover of investment managers. It is similar to free agency in baseball. Strong continues to actively recruit big-name star investment talent to add to its roster and protect its niche in the mutual fund market.

CHAPTER 9
INVESTING IN STOCKS FOR GROWTH

Success in reaching your long-term financial planning goals dictates ownership in stocks. Sensible investing in stocks is your best ally in your pursuit of financial independence. This is easier said than done, as stock investing is clouded by the human foibles of fear, greed, and ignorance.

The most admired stock investor of this era undoubtedly is Warren Buffett. Andrew Kilpatrick is among a handful of authors who have written books attempting to decipher what makes this legendary billionaire tick. In *Permanent Value,* Kilpatrick suggests the answer lies in Buffett's application of common sense.

> "Common sense may be the most important factor helping Buffett to make more money in the stock market than anyone; he is the only person on the *Forbes* 400 richest Americans list—and number one, at that—who got there entirely by investing."
>
> —Andrew Kilpatrick

Each share of common stock represents a proportionate share of ownership in a publicly traded corporation. Stocks often are referred to as *equities* to describe the equal value of a share of ownership. When you purchase a stock, you become a shareholder, and as a shareholder, you are entitled to the financial reward or misfortune that accompanies ownership.

Unlike bonds, stocks are purchased primarily for their growth or appreciation potential. Dividend income is considered, if at all, secondarily, with the exception of utility stocks and equity income funds. Stocks are often referred to as *variable investments* because the nature of the return changes from year to year. Investors purchase equities with the expectation that their shares will appreciate in value, rewarding them with a capital gain.

Over the long term, stocks have clearly proven to be the best performing asset class, easily outpacing both bonds and cash. In fact, since 1926 the total return from stocks approaches 11% per annum, almost double the return of corporate bonds and triple that of treasury bills. Better yet, the average annual return of stocks in the postwar years 1946–1996 is an impressive 12.2%. As an added bonus, stocks have proven to be the best tonic in the fight against inflation, capable of producing real rates of return.

> "The mantra for the long-term investor should be: STOCKS-STOCKS-STOCKS."
> —*Kiplinger's Personal Finance Magazine*

The downside of these returns is that stock investors must cope with higher levels of risk and volatility.

To benefit from these superior investment vehicles, you as an individual must develop the ability to withstand risk.

Stock performance conforms to the classic risk/reward equation. Learning how to enjoy the sweetness of the bull markets without suffering unduly from the bitterness of bear markets is the task at hand. Although stocks trend up about 85% of the time, the pain of the down years can outweigh that pleasure. It is a typical pattern for stocks to rise slowly and gradually but fall quickly and sharply, as was the case in October 1987 and October 1997. But investors with a long-term view have been rewarded amply by the stock market's overall appreciation.

Year-to-year volatility in the equity markets tests the mettle of the average investor. Sensible investors should never lose sight of the dark side (risk and volatility) inherent in stock ownership. Too many naive investors believe a typical stock fund is a sure-bet, double-digit performer.

The risk found in stocks is market risk. The stock marketplace reacts to dynamic supply and demand forces that don't lend themselves to easy predictions or rational analyses. On bad news, the market can assign a lower value to shares in an individual corporation or punish the whole market.

For example, the share price of IBM's stock reached $175 in August 1987. This one-time glamour stock then suffered through a tumultuous period and finally hit rock bottom at $43 a share in 1993. It took almost a full decade, to May 13, 1997, for it to return to $175. This long grind proved unbearable for suffering shareholders. Particularly galling to holders of IBM stock was the fact that the Dow Jones Industrials Average bulled ahead from 2800 to 7200 during this same 10-year span.

No discussion of stock market risk would be complete without revisiting the debacle of the 1973–1974 bear market. From top to bottom, the market coughed up losses amounting to 45%. A stagnating economy, accelerating inflation, the Watergate scandal, and the Arab oil embargo served collectively to depress stock prices. This was one of the biggest losses ever for the Dow and the most recent lesson on the dark side of stock ownership.

In the 1987 crash, by contrast, the stock market declined a gut-wrenching 21% in the month of October alone, much of that on one day, October 19, 1987. But within one year it recouped its losses as the bull market regained momentum and surged ahead.

Common sense investors can benefit by being alert to historical perspectives on stock volatility as well as by recognizing realistic expectations about return potential. Figure 9-1 shows returns for a quarter century, a good illustration of the ups and downs of investing.

Veteran mutual fund manager Ab Nicholas claims to have learned hard lessons in the bracing bear market of 1973–1974 and readily admits it tempered his thinking. Chief among the lessons was how far you have to bounce back to get even when a stock falls a certain percentage.

Twentieth Century Investors, now American Century, used to use an advertisement graphically depicting the relative bounce-back capability of an egg and a tennis ball. If a stock falls 15%, it must rise a full 18% to get back to even. A 25% drop needs 33%, and a 50% downdraft needs an astounding 100% gain to recover. Such investment mathematics instilled Nicholas with an affinity for more value-based stocks with better price-earnings ratios (P/E). He cautiously hopes this was a once-in-a-lifetime occurrence.

Stock Returns Standard & Poor's 500 Index	
Year	Total Return
1970	4.0%
1971	14.3%
1972	19.0%
1973	−14.7%
1974	−26.5%
1975	37.2%
1976	23.8%
1977	−7.2%
1978	6.6%
1979	18.4%
1980	32.4%
1981	−4.9%
1982	21.4%
1983	22.5%
1984	6.3%
1985	32.2%
1986	18.5%
1987	5.2%
1988	16.8%
1989	31.5%
1990	−3.2%
1991	30.6%
1992	7.7%
1993	10.0%
1994	1.3%
1995	37.5%
1996	23.0%

Figure 9-1

Although the average annual return from stocks since 1926 is closing in on 11%, the worst performance year occurred in the heart of the Depression, when stock prices collapsed by 43.3% in 1931. The best year was a short two years later, when the market recovered and ended up 53.9%.

Recent stock performance has been extraordinarily good. Note, per Figure 9-1, that since 1978, only two down years have occurred, and they were modest losers at that, a minus 4.9% in 1981 and minus 3.1% 10 years later in 1990. There were sharp and scary declines in 1989, as well as during the well-publicized crash of 1987, yet the market in both cases ended the year in positive territory. Extreme volatility is the chief drawback of investing in common stocks.

The up years, on the other hand, have seen banner years of 30%-plus returns handsomely reward stock investors in 1980, 1985, 1989, 1991, and 1995.

This top-shelf performance has been too good, perhaps disorienting novice investors and supposedly sophisticated professional money managers alike. Market observers cite statistics to remind us that stocks inevitably regress back to the mean; in other words, come back to more normal performance levels.

The Standard & Poor's 500 index averaged an incredible 17.5% compound total return for the 1980s. But realize that such outsized returns are typical every third decade, as the annual return was just 5.9% in the 1970s, 7.8% in the 1960s, and a robust 19.4% during the 1950s.

It is enlightening to note that the 25-year compound annual return from 1968 to 1992 was a more normal 10.56%.

Historically, buy and hold investors have never lost money in stocks over a 15-year period. But this needs to come with a warning, as there have been 20-year periods in which annual returns were less than the 5% that a money market account currently yields.

One element of risk is how much you stand to lose by not being in the stock market when it is stampeding on a bull run. Such is the case, as of this writing, in these examples: 1995 was a superb year, up 37.5%, followed by a 23% performance in 1996, and, as some would say, an incredible 30% rise as of September 30, 1997.

At this juncture, stocks seem to be at serious risk for a fall. There is a chorus in some quarters that things are different this time—that stocks can continue to break record highs. However, the history of the market proves it can turn on the unsuspecting. There was no warning in the sharp, painful trapdoor declines in 1962, 1966, and 1987.

Laura Tyson, former chief financial adviser to President Clinton and now a professor at the University of California at Berkeley, warns:

> "Investors' expectations were built up in one kind of market.
> It would be a mistake to predict it would be the same market forever in the future."
>
> —Laura Tyson

A common sense investor would be wise to prepare for a bear market, psychologically, mentally, and financially. As an exercise, ask yourself what would be your state of mind and reaction to a 1000-point, or 1500-point, or 2000-point freefall of 15%–20%. Would you be inclined to panic and sell at a loss, wake up in a cold sweat, or, tragically, jump off a building, which was done in the crash of 1929?

Do you find yourself spending paper gains as if they were bankable, realized gains? Are you perhaps seduced by paper profits and over-leveraging through the use of margin loans? Has your portfolio's asset allocation gotten out of alignment, too often disarming your risk temperament, caught up in the euphoria of the toppy market? Are you keeping some cash in reserve, dry ammunition available to fire should bargain values become available?

Make no mistake about it, investing is a tough, challenging pursuit, made all the more frustrating and ineffective unless pursued with basic investment sense. First and foremost, stock ownership should be a patient, eyes-open, long-term proposition. This has proven to be the best response to the risk of volatility.

I wholeheartedly agree with Bill Gross, who uses the following analogy in his new book, *Everything You've Heard About Investing is Wrong!*

> "Investing is a long-distance race, and because it is, investors should pattern their behavior after a marathon runner's—not a sprinter's. Marathoners pace themselves, plan ahead, and run within their physical limits. Investors must do the same."
>
> —Bill Gross

RALPH WANGER OF THE ACORN FUNDS

My interest in Ralph Wanger, president of the Acorn Funds, was piqued when he and his investment strategies were profiled in *The New Money Masters*, a 1989 book. Author John Train takes an intriguing look at the winning strategies of an elite group of eight investors that includes Wanger. Since then, as an Acorn Funds shareholder and Morningstar Conference participant, I have observed Wanger. Recently, I caught up with him while he was conducting a promotional tour for his book, *A Zebra in Lion Country*. From this encounter, I came away with further insights—as well as an autographed copy of his book.

So, in a way, I have come to know this esteemed mutual fund manager and money master. Wanger differentiates his investor reports from the usual dull and uninspiring reports by spicing his communications to shareholders with wit and wisdom. His dry humor comes through when he admits to being drawn to the investment business because the pay is good and no heavy lifting is required.

The subtitle of his book, *Investment Survival Guide,* builds upon a jungle theme. To him, the most important survival skill for stock investors is to stay levelheaded. He also warns that deceptions lurk, and that statistics and performance claims can be very misleading.

Wanger says the most important advice he can give stock investors is to "have a strategy, a way of looking at the world of stocks." Most investors do not. Consequently, their portfolios end up as a "haphazard collection of stories," all because they have no plan or discipline, chasing whatever is the latest fad, buying at the top.

According to Wanger, good investors are those who have a vision and stick with it. By all performance measures, the Acorn Fund is managed by a very good investment manager.

In keeping true to his philosophy of investing, Wanger's fund concentrates on small company stocks. He finds these stocks more attractive than large-caps. Candidates to his liking are companies he understands, that enjoy a dominant market position, that are financially healthy, and that have increasingly a worldwide demand for their products or services.

Historically, small stocks have enjoyed an edge in performance, surpassing their larger-cap cousins by averaging a substantial 2% better showing, at 14% per year since 1946. Wanger observes, "Investing in small companies is a little like baseball. Whenever you come up to bat, you always hope for a grand slam."

According to Wanger, all it takes is patience to capture solid returns from small-cap stocks. Their return premium has been earned in spurts when the small-cap effect plays out. Wanger wants to purchase his stocks at good value, what he and others now refer to as GARP, or growth at a reasonable price.

PRICE/EARNINGS RATIOS

A key valuation measure is the P/E ratio; a piece of information so important it is listed in stock tables. A sensible investor should at least have a grasp of the P/E if he or she is considering purchasing or already owns stocks. Peter Lynch said it succinctly: "Spend at least as much time researching a stock as you would to choose a refrigerator."

The P/E ratio quickly tells us how the market values *price* (P) in relationship to a given dollar of *earnings* (E) on a per-share basis. It is calculated by dividing a company's market capitalization by the earnings allocated to its stock. For example, if an entire company is valued at $1 billion with earnings of $100 million, its P/E ratio is 10. Often referred to as a multiple, P/E provides a clear measure of how the market accords value for each dollar a share earns.

VALUE VERSUS GROWTH INVESTMENT STYLE

Low P/E stocks relative to an average market multiple fall into the value-style camp. Stocks with faster growing earnings tend to be favored as growth stocks, sporting higher multiples to earnings and a higher stock price.

Rigorous academic studies conclude that P/Es do matter. Studies support an edge for value investing, finding that low P/E stocks perform better in most, but not all, market conditions.

William Nasgovitz, chair of Milwaukee's Heartland Funds, has positioned his firm into a niche as America's Value Investors. I attended an industry conference at which Nasgovitz laid out his case for the superiority of a value approach over a growth investment style, saying, "In every segment of the stock market, value investing has outperformed growth investing over time. Moreover, it has done so with less volatility." He preempted arguments by stating that any difference of opinion results from slanted measurements and interpretations. If value is clearly superior, Nasgovitz wondered aloud, why does the growth style in practice dominate investment.

One answer is that growth stocks provide more sizzle, a better story, more sex appeal. In a raging bull market, growth investors in the momentum of a hot sector are guaranteed to be at the pinnacle of short-term performance rankings, and it is these managers of growth funds who adorn the covers of popular personal finance magazines.

In tandem with Nasgovitz, Ralph Wanger asserts that in the long run, value works. He surmises that there is a tendency to overpay for growth. Temporary outperformance appears to be a result of investor exuberance. Wanger starts his stock selection process by applying a value template.

Growth stock managers, who represent the majority opinion, want to dispel the notion that growth is not value. None of the multitude of growth managers would ever want to be characterized as specializing in purchasing overvalued securities. They would argue convincingly that high valuations and P/Es are supported by the equally fast-growing earnings of their holdings.

Value investors counter that these extreme pricing valuations will get shot down during times of market turmoil or when earnings of individual stocks disappoint. The growth faction retorts that value stocks are priced low because they deserve to be priced low.

Value disciples sincerely believe that although their holdings are undervalued and underappreciated by the market, eventually their attractiveness will be recognized. They suggest that growth stocks are too volatile and that value stocks provide a smoother ride.

What is not in doubt is that growth and value stocks tend to cycle in and out of favor, reinforcing the wisdom of style diversification.

Veteran stock fund managers Nicholas and Wanger have each been called, alternately, value and growth investors. When they are pressed to make a choice of style, the nod goes to value. Consequently, they admit to being very comfortable with the GARP label to describe their investment philosophy.

STOCKS VERSUS FUNDS

> "Considering the time, discipline, skills, knowledge, resources, and personality that investing demands, mutual funds are the sensible course for 95 percent of the public. All things considered, then, mutual funds make sense for most people."
> —Ralph Wanger, *A Zebra in Lion Country*

A main argument favoring funds includes the desirability of broad-based diversification to effectively reduce risk. Investing in foreign stock markets, for instance, is difficult to do as an individual, and it is an area in which mutual funds unquestionably offer the best avenue for participating.

Additionally, you employ the services of a full-time investment professional, one who has lived through both up and down markets and has, one hopes, learned from both.

Wagner quips that one good reason for hiring a pro is you will have someone to blame other than yourself if the results are sour. On a more serious note, he cautions that you can be too diversified with mutual funds and end up constructing nothing more than a high-cost, tax-inefficient index fund.

To add a semblance of balance in favor of individual stocks over pooled investments, stock ownership provides more control, especially in terms of tax management. There also is the possibility of style drift by some investment managers; in other words, going away from what you understood to be their investment boundaries.

Ab Nicholas talks of the value of a fund manager who maintains consistency in a world of change by steadfastly sticking with a disciplined investment philosophy rather than riding the latest winds of the market.

Mutual fund ownership loses its edge if you select among funds burdened by excessively high costs or rapid turnover, or with the disadvantage of having neither a proven long-term success formula nor a well-defined investment philosophy.

THE MA BELL STORY

A major reason I do not offer advice or make individual stock recommendations concerns my experience with AT&T stock. It goes back to early 1995 when I was adding an investment advisory service to my financial planning practice. At about this same time I became enamored of AT&T's prospects, convinced it was the best stock to own in America. You might be familiar with the practice of asking investment people what stock they would own if they had only one choice. My quick answer then would have been AT&T.

I found the stock so enticing I seriously considered breaking my mutual-fund-only policy to include it as a core holding when constructing portfolios. It possessed a recognizable brand name, held a dominant market position in a high-tech growth industry, and enjoyed seemingly limitless global growth potential. If that were not enough, it also carried an above-market dividend and valuation that suggested a growth at reasonable price play. Clearly, this was a winner I could promote and ride.

Fortunately, I decided not to include this or any individual stocks, primarily for mechanical, procedural, and compliance reasons. It was fortunate I did not spotlight AT&T as my star and sole recruit, because it plummeted some 18% in 1996 while the market as a whole went up 23.5%. The first half of 1997 also saw lackluster performance for this most widely held blue chip stock. No sooner had I and others given up on the prospects for AT&T stock than its fortunes turned around dramatically. The catalyst was Michael Armstrong's assuming the CEO post, which propelled this stock to a phenomenal gain of 70.4% over the final two quarters of 1997.

Clearly, the lesson to be learned is that I am not an infallible stock picker. I should have remembered this from my previous foray into individual stocks, a list that includes such nonstellar performers as Sears, IBM, Allis Chalmers, AMC, Burroughs, and Honeywell.

AT&T, better known as Ma Bell, was forced by government regulators to break up in January 1984 to avoid being branded a monopoly. As a result, Ma Bell gave birth to and spun off seven regional local operating carriers, dubbed Baby Bells. For every 10 shares of AT&T stock, holders received a proportionate share of the seven Baby Bells, such as Ameritech and Bell Atlantic. The big question became which of these eight new stocks commanded the best growth prospects and merited holding, additional purchase, or sale.

As of this writing, some $13\frac{1}{2}$ years after the breakup of AT&T, the telecommunications industry is once again in the midst of massive movement, consolidation, and realignment. Renewed interest is triggered by every rumored alliance or merger of AT&T with the other carriers.

It is interesting to look back at the growth history of AT&T owners at the end of 1983, when each share of AT&T was valued at $12. This amounted to $1,200 in ownership valuation for those with a round lot (100 shares). The combined value of those original 100 shares of AT&T, along with the spin-offs, was worth some $28,000 in June 1997. The almost 24-fold appreciation over this time period doesn't include reinvestment of dividends.

As the Baby Bells grew they enriched shareholders by regular stock splits. In the ensuing years, AT&T also spun off telecommunication equipment-maker Lucent Technologies, and NCR, its once-promising computer business.

AT&T's story continues to be written, but its previous chapters reveal the hazards and rewards of the dynamic telecommunications industry, as well as the growth potential offered by long-term equity ownership.

THE WISDOM OF INDEXING

Indexing describes an investment approach that seeks to match closely the returns of a specified benchmark or index established by the industry. The most popular index attempts to duplicate the makeup and hence the outcome of the Standard & Poor's (S&P) 500, an index representing the

500 largest U.S. stocks as measured in terms of market valuation.

About 1995, a debate began heating up over the wisdom of taking a passive approach to selecting stock funds by using stock index funds. The major reason for heavy media and investor attention is that indexed stock funds beat actively managed stock funds in the up markets of 1995, 1996, and the first half of 1997.

This substantial performance advantage is best exemplified by charting the recent fortunes of fund giant Fidelity Magellan Fund and Vanguard's flagship Index Trust 500 Portfolio. For more than a decade, Fidelity Magellan was held up as champion of an active management approach. But now its star is tarnished by a period of underperformance that has led to a dwindling asset base and the possibility of its losing its position as the largest mutual fund.

Coincidental to Fidelity Magellan's decline has been the emergence of the Vanguard 500 Index. Because of its superior investment performance over actively managed funds, the popularity and consequent asset growth of the 500 Index Trust has been phenomenal.

Don Phillips, president of Morningstar, predicts it is only a matter of time before there is a leadership change. "I would expect that in the not-too-distant future the Vanguard Index 500 fund will become the biggest fund in America and stay like that for a long time."

Vanguard clearly has triumphed in this round. For proof, look no further than to Fidelity, the champion of active management, nodding to change with its decision to offer and heavily promote its own version of a passively managed index fund.

AMONG THE CONCLUSIONS

- Index mutual funds outperform actively managed mutual funds about 70% of the time.
- Only a handful of actively managed funds consistently beat the market index over the years.
- Index funds average only 20% of the average annual expenses of managed funds.
- An indexed fund has the potential to outperform an actively managed fund by 1.5% to 2% a year, compounding to a substantial difference over a sustained period.

- Index funds have extremely low turnover, 2% as compared to 80% for the average fund, keeping transaction costs down.
- Lower turnover minimizes capital gain distributions, an important advantage when comparing results on an after-tax basis.
- Indexing is simple, holds few surprises, and offers broad diversification to go along with relative predictability.

WHAT IS INDEXING?

Indexing takes a passive approach to investment management, in contrast to actively managed mutual funds in which an investment manager makes "bets" on the stock market with frequent buy-and-sell decisions. Active management results in turnover expenses, transaction costs, and tax consequences. Ample evidence demonstrates that the majority of active managers fall short of their category benchmarks and index funds.

The popularity of index funds is an acknowledgment that many investors are content to reap passive stock market returns rather than to rely on a fund manager's attempts to better the market. As *The Wall Street Journal* opined, "Beating the market by a few percentage points every year would certainly be nice, but many of us will be fairly happy and we will reach our investment goals, just so long as we get returns that aren't too different from the stock market averages."

A legitimate question can be raised: Why, if index investing is convincingly superior, does active management continue to receive the bulk of assets and attention? I suggest the answer is due to many factors. For one thing, actively managed funds are extensively promoted, while no-load, low-expense index funds are not. A highly lucrative industry is built on the little-challenged assumption that active management provides the most value.

I recently attended a gathering of financial planners at which the respective merits of active versus passive management were hotly debated. I was caught off guard when the conference audience was polled and overwhelmingly disregarded the compelling evidence for index funds, holding firm on their belief in the advantages of active management.

A neutral observer would have noticed that the vast majority of those in attendance were broker-dealer, commission-driven representatives. To affirm a place for index funds was to threaten their livelihood.

But I take comfort that plenty of respected investment professionals recognize a place for index funds in the average investor's portfolio. Included in this impressive list are the previously highlighted investment masters Peter Lynch, Bill Gross, Warren Buffett, Ab Nicholas, Ralph Wanger, and, of course, John Bogle.

Also weighing in are the astute institutional investors responsible for the prudent management of millions of dollars in pension assets. They are clearly capable of hiring top investment managers, but have opted to go the passive route for more than one-third of their core assets, a figure that continues to rise.

I contend that the simplicity found in indexing seems to work against its general acceptance. Unsophisticated investors get caught up in the excitement of investing with a superstar manager and hitting the occasional investment equivalent of a home run. The trouble is, home-run hitters also strike out. In the investment field, unlike baseball, past performance is a weak indicator of future returns.

Defenders of active management and the status quo like to say you shouldn't be satisfied with the averages accompanying market returns. One could counter that an investment approach that consistently landed you in the top third in performance is above average. A better argument is to think of market returns as par, where passive investing effectively meets investment goals.

In a baseball game, the ultimate measure of a team's success is winning, not hitting home runs. If you hit six home runs and still lose 7-6, you are not successful in reaching your goal.

Like any investment approach benefiting from a strong tailwind, the favored status of the S&P 500 index won't last forever. Vanguard's index manager, George Sauter, warns refreshingly:

> "The market environment we've had in the past decade has greatly favored large-cap stocks over small-cap stocks and therefore has greatly favored S&P 500 indexing. That environment won't persist indefinitely."
>
> —George Sauter

Sure enough, in the third quarter of 1997, actively managed funds have tested the market as small- and mid-cap stocks have shone. Sauter's chief at Vanguard, John Bogle, is so concerned he issued the following caution about index funds: "We are concerned ... that a number of investors may simply be focusing on the (Vanguard Index) Trust's portfolio performance—the wrong reason to invest in the Trust. Investors attracted by recent short-term results may well be disappointed by shifting market conditions."

One should be aware that large-cap stocks seem to be a more appropriate vehicle for indexing. Small-cap index funds have not been as successful in mirroring the performance of their benchmark index. It would appear that an astute small- to mid-cap manager can enhance the returns of a managed portfolio.

With their many complexities, international markets and emerging markets represent other areas in which a talented portfolio manager can earn his or her keep by helping investors navigate the maze of the global landscape.

In summary, index funds are not a panacea. They will not protect you in a bear market. To the contrary, you are guaranteed to lose as much as the market does.

Perhaps the best avenue is to consider passively managed index funds for a portion of the large-cap allocation. The best place for such a holding might be in a nonretirement portfolio so you could benefit from tax efficiency.

CHAPTER 10

PRERETIREMENT PLANNING: THE CLIMB TO FINANCIAL INDEPENDENCE

Close your eyes and imagine your life without a paycheck. Does the thought make your blood pressure shoot up, or do you experience a feeling of calm? Are you able to be unemployed, retired on your terms?

For most individuals, a financially secure retirement is the highest financial goal.

There is no area within the financial planning framework where effective planning is as important and as rewarding as in the preretirement years. Preretirement planning focuses on the accumulation stage, putting you on track to financial independence. In these crucial, wealth-building years, the aim is to put in place your power over tomorrow. You want to grow a nest egg sufficient to provide an income adequate to lead a lifestyle of your choice. The financial side of retirement should provide the resources to fully enjoy life. A financially secure retirement describes a period of life with all new opportunities and freedom from money concerns.

FINANCIAL INDEPENDENCE—PRERETIREMENT

Many individuals in the start or middle of their earning years are turned off by the term *retirement* in any context. I have found it difficult to attract 30- or 40-somethings to any seminar that has retirement in the title.

Perhaps they think it is too distant or connotes a phase of life not pertinent to them. Financial independence means you can choose not to work for a living but still enjoy a comfortable lifestyle, a status sought after by this group that seems to eschew discussions about retirement. So I now use the equivalent theme, *quest for financial independence,* instead of planning for a secure retirement.

Retirement planning is a relatively new phenomenon. Earlier generations had shorter life spans and expected to expire at their desks or die with their boots on. Today the picture has changed dramatically. Increased longevity and changing employment patterns have created a retirement life cycle. Recognize that you are likely to be retired and without an earned income for a quarter to a third of your life. It is a financial necessity to provide for this period of life, which could amount to 15 years or as much as 40 years—the equivalent of an entire career.

PREPARING FOR RETIREMENT IN THE 21ST CENTURY

When it comes to retirement issues, most Americans are in a state of denial. Baby boomers need a loud wake-up call if they want to meet their expectation of a comfortably secure retirement. Boomers who have been surveyed fully expect to retire early, at an average age of 61, while maintaining an equivalent or indeed enhanced standard of living. In this regard, there appears to be a gap between perception and reality.

Part of this perception problem stems from attitudes shaped by looking at the financial status of current retirees. Their parents' generation, whether or not they acknowledge it, has been very fortunate in regard to retirement. This World War II demographic group has witnessed a huge run-up in housing values since the 1970s, stable lifetime employment patterns, healthy private pensions, and generous Social Security benefits. Add in highly appreciating financial assets during the 80s and 90s, coupled with correspondingly tamer inflation rates, and you have a formula for a secure retirement.

Baby boomers who count on similar scenarios are likely to be disappointed. The challenge of funding a secure retirement will be much greater in the coming decades. What is particularly alarming is that according to a recent study prepared by Merrill Lynch, boomers are saving at only one-third of the rate they need to if they expect to retire at age 65 without a reduced standard of living.

THE REALITY OF RETIREMENT

Those planning for retirement must open their eyes and take a good look at the cold, hard truth of financial reality. To get the message means addressing the following:

PLAN NOW OR YOU MAY LIVE TO REGRET IT

Are you prepared to live until age 90? Do you realize you or your spouse could well live to 100?

We are witnessing steadily increasing life expectancies. For example, the average man at 65 today can expect to live close to another 15 years. A woman of 65 has a life expectancy of close to 20 additional years. These are just the averages. Many men and women will lead much longer lives. Retirement planning is especially crucial for women because of their longer life expectancies and generally lower income at retirement.

A long-term retirement means that much more money will be required to meet monthly living expenditures, pay increased medical bills, and protect against the ravages of inflation.

SOCIAL SECURITY CONCERNS

There is a well-founded erosion of confidence concerning the future of Social Security. Jim Getz, president of Federated Investors, drew a laugh at an industry conference when he remarked that more boomers believe in UFOs than in the future solvency of the Social Security system. The uncertainty of Social Security increases the urgency of taking charge of our own future financial security.

THE SPECTER OF INFLATION STILL LOOMS

Inflation is public enemy number one for retirees and potential retirees alike. Inflation erodes purchasing power, shrinking the value of tomorrow's dollar, over time, into a quarter.

If there are any black clouds on the retirement planning horizon, they arise from fear of renewed high rates of inflation. Inflation is a measure of the increase in the cost of living. In the decade of the 1970s and early 1980s the Consumer Price Index (CPI) rose an average of 6% each year before cooling to a more tolerable 2% to 4% in the 1990s. In 1980, cautious, conservative financial planners were suggesting we use 8% as the future projected inflation rate.

Assuming just 5% inflation, the loaf of bread that costs $1.00 today will cost $1.05 next year. In 14 years, that same loaf will cost twice as much, or $2.00. Your $1.00 would be worth only 50 cents in goods and services in 14 years.

If your current income requirement is a multiple of $1,000 per month at inflation rates of 3%, 5%, and 6% per annum, you would require the following inflation-adjusted income just to stay ahead.

	Inflation Rate Per Year		
$1,000	3%	5%	6%
5 Years	$1,159	$1,276	$1,338
10 Years	$1,344	$1,629	$1,792
20 Years	$1,806	$2,653	$3,207
25 Years	$2,094	$3,386	$4,292

Figure 10-1

YOU ARE SOLELY RESPONSIBLE FOR MANAGING YOUR OWN RETIREMENT

Although still found in the public service sector, the traditional defined benefit pension plan has gone out of style. Defined benefit plans, though not without their faults, do not require sophistication on the part of employees. Participation is usually compulsory, and investment decision making is handled by the employer or professionals.

Contrast this with the now-popular 401(k) defined contribution plan, where control has been shifted to the individual. You, the employee, must decide whether to participate, how much to contribute, what to invest in, whether to make early withdrawals, and how to take distributions when leaving the plan. You are the boss, and the stakes are enormous. Any missteps could well doom the future of your financial security.

Chapter 10

LOOKING AHEAD TO THE FUTURE

When you gaze into your crystal ball, is a financially secure retirement attainable with a specific course of action, or is it merely an elusive goal?

Think of financial independence as a quest to reach the summit of a distant mountain peak. The goal is challenging, but reachable with determination and an appropriate strategy. Think of retirement security as a similar quest, with *preparation* the key to reaching the summit of financial independence. Retirement planning becomes the task necessary to reach the top, to turn the dream into reality.

We can't just admire our mountain peak. We must start climbing upward to our goal.

> "The secret of getting ahead is getting started. The secret of getting started is breaking your complex overwhelming tasks into small manageable tasks, and then starting on the first one."
> —Mark Twain

HOW MUCH MONEY WILL YOU NEED FOR RETIREMENT?

A while back, I participated in a retirement planning panel for a local TV channel's evening news call-in. After being met and briefed by the news anchor, the assembled group of experts sat behind phone banks, ready to field calls from viewers.

At precisely 5:05 p.m., the anchor invited viewers to call in with their questions while the station flashed the phone number and panned across the dozen retirement planners. As we had been warned, the first few callers were from bored kids, who'd shout something silly into the receiver, then hang up laughing. After that, I settled in for an exhausting two-hour session of nonstop retirement planning queries. From this experience, I gained further appreciation of this topic's popularity, as well as insight into the minds of the many callers.

The number one question came straight to the heart of the retirement dilemma: *How much money do I (we) need to be able to retire?* An anonymous stranger seemed to expect, in 90 seconds, a specific dollar answer to this heavy-duty retirement question. Imagine my position!

This question, however, is basic to preretirement planning. The answer is complex, individual in nature, and dependent on four primary factors.

1. WHEN ARE YOU PLANNING TO RETIRE?

In other words, when do you wish to be non–wage-dependent and financially independent? You will require substantially more retirement income should you elect to retire at an early age (prior to age 60). On the other hand, if you plan to work to the so-called normal retirement age of 65 years or later, your total retirement income needs will be significantly reduced.

2. HOW LONG ARE YOU PLANNING TO LIVE?

Take this as a serious inquiry. Combined with your projected age of retirement, the figure suggests how many years of retirement you must finance. In essence, how long will you be retired and in need of creating a retirement check?

3. WHAT INITIAL ANNUAL RETIREMENT INCOME IS SUFFICIENT?

What is your retirement lifestyle going to cost you? What sort of spending budget do you desire? Will you enter retirement carrying debt, desiring to do a lot of travel, maintaining two residences, staggering under the burden of a heavy tax load, or being responsible for one or more other individuals?

A related question to ponder is, what percentage of your current income will you require at retirement? One general rule of thumb is that you can maintain an equivalent retirement lifestyle with 50% to 90% of your last year of preretirement income; 67% is a standard.

4. WHAT WILL THE RATE OF INFLATION BE?

Inflation will have a significant impact on the previous three factors. Down the line, retiring will mean a higher initial retirement cost of living. A more expensive lifestyle will be adversely affected by increases in inflation. A longer life expectancy would see inflation play a larger role in total income requirements.

Change any of these variables—length, cost, and inflation rate—and the total needs are significantly altered.

Chapter 10

THE CLIMB TO FINANCIAL INDEPENDENCE

Fortunately, computer software programs have been developed to do the number crunching and quantify the effect of planning variables. The math comes down to calculating various time-value-of-money tables.

You input some basic assumptions and estimates from a worksheet to yield a ballpark estimate of your retirement planning needs.

Once armed with the projected results, you are in a better position to determine whether you are on track toward retirement security, what gap exists in the amount of your retirement savings, and whether it is even practical to consider the dream of early retirement.

These retirement planning modeling programs are inexpensive and readily available from numerous sources. I have used programs from fund companies T. Rowe Price and Vanguard, as well as personal financial software from Quicken. I suspect a score of similar formats exists, including the capability to harness the interactive ability of a home page on the Internet for this same purpose. Numerous financial services providers also have geared up to help you interpret and analyze your retirement needs and to then offer you products and solutions to help push you over the top.

There is no valid reason to put off this important planning task.

The primary benefit from running the numbers is the clearer picture that develops of where you stand in the quest for financial independence so you can take appropriate action.

The speed and computational ability of the personal computer is an invaluable planning aid that allows us the ability to play "what if" scenarios and receive an instant reading of the results.

Retirement planning software has been enhanced with features such as graphing capability to aid you in understanding your road map to success. Use the power of the computer to get a readout on your future.

To reach the summit of financial independence we must prepare ourselves and start the climb.

What follows are 14 steps, which I like to think of as a stairway providing the best route to the peak of financial retirement security.

> "The journey of a thousand miles begins with one step."
> —Lao-Tzu

STEP 1. START YOUR ENGINE

Successful retirement planning is not the product of some magic formula; it requires a commitment. The critical first step in the retirement planning process is to make a promise to yourself and get started. A common lament of many retirees is that they did not work harder to get their financial affairs in order for retirement.

If you want to jolt yourself into action, just think of retirement as permanent unemployment. Are you prepared to have your payroll income abruptly cut off? How will you survive?

HOW MANY YEARS TO YOUR PLANNED RETIREMENT?

The first part of any plan is setting a goal, in this case a target date. Is it 1, 5, 10, 20, or 30 years away? A common question put to me is, "When should someone start to plan for retirement?" Obviously, the more time available until your planned retirement, the more beneficial the planning you can do. I believe age 35 is a good age at which to seriously begin providing for your financial future. Twenty-five years of planning and saving seem appropriate when you consider you are preparing for 25-plus years of actual retirement.

If your planned retirement is within 10 years, or you have reached age 55, you are in "crunch time." Your planning takes on a heightened sense of importance. You must make a concerted effort to plan your financial affairs.

Make a commitment now to actively plan for your retirement. Sit down with your partner, set a target retirement date, and initiate the steps.

The number of years to your target retirement date becomes the planning horizon on your march to financial independence.

STEP 2. EMPLOY RIGOROUS SAVING HABITS

Think of retirement security as life's biggest purchase, something bought through monthly installments. Rigorous saving is synonymous with planning for retirement. Realize that you are attempting to build a nest egg capable of providing you with sufficient retirement income when your earned income stops.

The Millionaire Next Door reveals that millionaires routinely save

Chapter 10

14 Steps To Planning A Financially Secure Retirement

14. Stay on top to get on top.
13. Get your act together.
12. Protect your backside.
11. Nurture your nest egg.
10. Put the power of tax-advantaged accumulation to work.
9. Zero in on your retirement income gap.
8. Match your needs with income sources.
7. Check out your retirement cost of living.
6. To retire well—first invest well.
5. Learn about social insecurity—learn your Social Security entitlements.
4. Get out from under debt—make efforts to reach retirement relatively debt-free.
3. Don't delay—the benefits of starting early.
2. Employ rigorous saving habits.
1. Start your engine.

Figure 10-2

15% to 20% of their current income. Preretirees need to squirrel away as much of their current income as feasible. From a financial security standpoint, you can't oversave. In most cases, the ability to enjoy a secure retirement is directly related to allocating a significant portion of every dollar to building a healthy nest egg. Failure to take this essential step will doom most retirement planning efforts.

> "If putting money away is something you have been putting off, just think how quickly one year goes into the next."
>
> —Bill Berger, Berger Funds

STEP 3. DON'T DELAY — THE BENEFITS OF STARTING EARLY

Time is your best investment ally; it brings your goal of reaching the financial security summit closer. Having time on your side makes an uphill climb seem like a gentle slope.

To emphasize my point, learn from the example of "Early Byrd" and his pal "Eyle Waite." These two good fishing buddies do everything together, with the exception of practicing their respective retirement saving habits. Both at age 30 talk about making $2,000 annual IRA contributions. Each talks about using an equivalent investment vehicle with a 10% per year return. However, only Early takes the bait and decides to start right away. At age 30 and for the next 11 years, Early Byrd dutifully invests his $2,000 annual sum and then elects to stop further contributions, allowing his IRA account to grow until age 65. Eyle Waite has a different strategy, putting off his IRA retirement contributions until his 40th birthday, rationalizing that he will continue to contribute for 26 years until age 65.

Early boasts that his jump start will make him richer, while Eyle counters that he is putting away $52,000 to Early's $22,000, and that will put him ahead.

As it turns out, the early bird catches the worm and, hence, a more bountiful feast. Early Byrd's account at age 65 is worth $401,560. Eyle Waite's higher contributions yield $218,364, a costly delay of $183,196.

Make time work *for* you, not against you. The sooner you start accumulating your retirement goal, the easier it is to meet. Say the goal is to amass a nest egg of a cool million dollars. A 35-year-old, with a lead-time of 30 years to a targeted age of 65, would need to sock away $710 monthly, assuming a reasonable 8% return. If the same retirement planner procrastinates 15 years until age 50, he or she would have to ante up over four times that sum, $2,970 monthly, to reach the seven-figure goal.

Monthly Investment Needed to Build Nest Eggs of $500,000 and $1,000,000 by Age 65

Age When You Start	Monthly Investment at 8% Return		Monthly Investment at 10% Return	
	$500,000	$1,000,000	$500,000	$1,000,000
35	$355	$710	$242	$484
36	387	774	268	536
37	422	844	297	594
38	461	922	329	658
39	503	1,006	365	730
40	551	1,102	406	812
41	603	1,206	457	914
42	661	1,322	502	1,004
43	726	1,452	559	1,118
44	799	1,598	624	1,248
45	880	1,760	697	1,394
46	972	1,944	781	1,562
47	1,076	2,152	876	1,752
48	1,194	2,388	985	1,970
49	1,330	2,660	1,112	2,224
50	1,485	2,970	1,258	2,516
51	1,666	3,332	1,429	2,858
52	1,878	3,756	1,631	3,262
53	2,128	4,256	1,871	3,742
54	2,428	4,856	2,161	4,322
55	2,791	5,582	2,514	5,028
56	3,241	6,482	2,953	5,906
57	3,809	7,618	3,511	7,022
58	4,548	9,096	4,238	8,476
59	5,542	11,084	5,221	10,442
60	6,950	13,900	6,617	13,234
61	9,086	18,172	8,741	17,482
62	12,701	25,402	12,343	24,686
63	20,111	40,222	19,735	39,470
64	43,730	87,460	43,325	86,650

Figure 10-3

STEP 4. GET OUT FROM UNDER DEBT—MAKE EFFORTS TO REACH RETIREMENT RELATIVELY DEBT-FREE

Remember that debt represents a cost and a burden, and it raises the bar on your cost-of-living expenses. Just think how helpful it would be to have your mortgage completely paid off by the time you retire. Eliminating a monthly $1,000 mortgage payment would make for an equivalent reduction in postretirement expenses. In pursuit of financial independence, you would be wise to opt for a shorter duration mortgage (10, 12, or 15 years) to coincide with your targeted independence year.

It is not absolutely necessary to have your mortgage completely paid down, but it is critical to not be carrying nondeductible car notes or installment or credit card debt. It also is a good idea to get major expenditures such as a car purchase or kitchen remodeling completed prior to retirement, so as not to carry unnecessary debts into retirement.

Entering retirement with a clean balance sheet on the debt side makes for a healthier financial condition.

STEP 5. LEARN ABOUT SOCIAL INSECURITY— LEARN YOUR SOCIAL SECURITY ENTITLEMENTS

It is important to get a handle on the amount of Social Security retirement income you and your spouse, if married, can expect at retirement. The Social Security Administration has now made this step easy. Simply call 1-800-772-1213 and ask for a "Request for Earnings and Benefit Estimate Statement." If you prefer, you can pick up the form at a Social Security office, or download a form from http://www.ssa.gov, the Social Security Administration's Internet site.

After submitting the completed form, you will be mailed a Personal Earnings and Benefit Estimate Statement. The PEBS provides valuable information, including an estimate of benefits at retirement or in the event of disability, and survivorship benefits to your family in the case of death. You'll want to verify your earnings record as shown on the statement and immediately report any discrepancies.

Former Social Security Chief Dorcas Hardy calls this statement a "financial planning tool" and a useful check-off in your march to retirement.

You should be aware of trends affecting Social Security and retirement planning in the 21st century, including:
- uncertainty over the capacity of the system to pay benefits after the year 2020
- the possibility of a "means test" as to who receives benefits
- a continued trend toward taxing Social Security benefits
- the continued pushing back to a later age the start of eligibility for full benefits

STEP 6. TO RETIRE WELL—FIRST INVEST WELL

Form your investment strategy. Performance in the investment arena is where you can make great gains in achieving a financially secure retirement.

> "Common sense is worth more than cunning."
> —a retirement planning maxim, Neuberger & Berger Management

To gain a healthy nest egg, follow a well-conceived investment strategy that includes:
- defining precisely what it is you are looking to accomplish
- recognizing that retirement planning represents a long-term proposition; invest for the balance of your life
- answering honestly what kind of investor you are by defining your own risk temperament and timeline
- evaluating your current investment portfolio and working toward maximizing your return on investment while employing methods to minimize risk
- targeting a rate of return on your investment consistent with your attitude toward risk (the higher the risk, the greater the potential gain or loss)
- determining if your current investment portfolio meets a realistic target
- shifting and repositioning your investment portfolio if necessary to align it with your expectations, your risk tolerance, and the guidelines capable of producing your targeted results

Three factors determine the size of your retirement nest egg:
1. How soon you start—length of investment measured in years
2. How much you save, your fodder
3. How well your chosen investments perform

STEP 7. CHECK OUT YOUR RETIREMENT COST OF LIVING

If you were to bail out of the employment and income-producing world today, what would you need to budget in order to maintain your desired lifestyle?

The truth is, most people are not aware of how much it costs them to live *now*. I find it best to think in terms of monthly needs and to start with a cost infrastructure. Obviously, this understanding of your personal cost-of-living weight is an important piece of information. Some retirement counselors go so far as to suggest that preretirees practice retirement reality by trying to live on what they plan to retire with.

What percent of your current income is necessary at retirement? Retirement does bring significant changes in the makeup of the expenditure component of the income statement. On the one hand, you can subtract certain work-related preretirement expenses such as commuting, wardrobe, or union or professional dues. Then again, there may well be added expenses such as a higher cost for health insurance or the loss of a company car or company-paid club dues. Start the process by estimating housing costs, fixed expenses, insurance premiums, and budgeted living expenses.

One rule of thumb: you can maintain an equivalent retirement lifestyle with 50% to 90% of your preretirement income. Some of this is dependent on debt reduction, as outlined in Step 4. It is likely that once retired, you will see your taxes go down because wage income faces the stiffest tax burden, and you will no longer be paying employment taxes (FICA) as in the preretirement years.

I'd like to have you think of your annual savings as a budgeted cost item. Once you retire, the amount you are accumulating in savings from your income is finished.

If you are saving 20% of your preretirement income now, your postretirement budget can be reduced by that amount.

STEP 8. MATCH YOUR NEEDS WITH INCOME SOURCES

Retirement planning boils down to identifying how much income you need to carry on, then matching that need with adequate income sources.

Remember, at retirement—or upon reaching financial independence, if you prefer—the revenue portion of your income statement is no longer driven by employment income. Rather, you must look to alternative income streams to provide retirement spending needs.

In retirement, your income is derived from three to four primary sources: Social Security, pension, investment, and, perhaps, miscellaneous supplemental income. In retirement planning, it is common to visualize these sources as the legs of a stool, with the implication that three sources are needed to support the weight of retirement years.

Note that of these sources, you may be able to exert control over the investment leg only. Hence, building up this asset pool to an amount capable of generating an adequate income stream is a critical step in the preretirement planning process.

This is especially true of those of us entering retirement well into the 21st century. As I discussed, we are deemphasizing reliance on Social Security and are witnessing the virtual disappearance of the once-universal defined benefit plans. In fact, your retirement investment source is largely due to the influence of defined contribution plans such as 401(k) plans. In this view, we will be the farmers and clergy of half a century ago who lived out their final years without pensions or much of anything in Social Security.

Another accelerating trend is the appearance of an increasingly common income leg; namely, some form of supplemental income. This could take the form of rental or lease income, or perhaps a form of business income continuation agreement. But the most frequent income source is from part-time or seasonal employment. The new economy has a strong demand for recent retirees who can bring their talent, skills, and work ethic to fill a variety of positions.

So what will your income sources be once your earned income ceases? Planning involves identifying those retirement income sources. Put together a postretirement income statement, listing estimated sources of expected pension, Social Security, investment, and supplemental income.

Once you identify your postretirement income sources, a useful planning exercise is to analyze what percentage of income you can expect from each source.

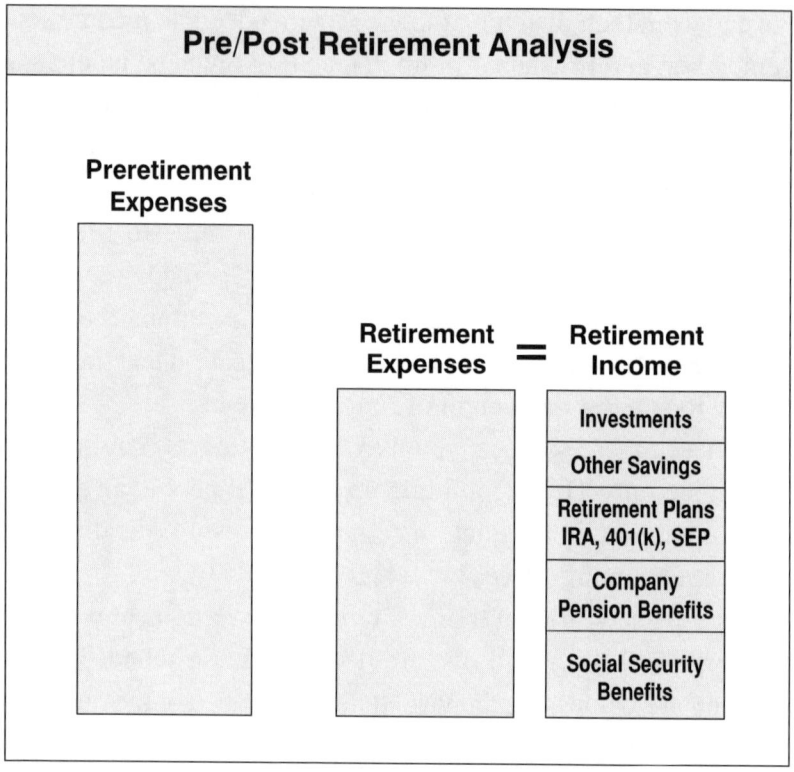

Figure 10-4

STEP 9. ZERO IN ON YOUR RETIREMENT INCOME GAP

If you peel back the concerns on the minds of preretirees, what is revealed is the big question: Am I (are we) on track to be able to live and lead a financially secure retirement?

In the new millennium, even a modest retirement lifestyle will require a million dollars of income passing through your checking account to finance your retirement.

Therefore, an important step in the preretirement planning process is to determine if you are on the mark. Does a shortfall exist in your accumulation progress report? If a deficit exists, how much in additional savings will be necessary to close the gap?

As discussed at the start of this chapter, the power of the computer can help you calculate your retirement income gap. The moment of truth comes when a surplus or deficit figure based on your estimates is calculated. You receive an instant diagnosis of where you stand. If a shortfall exists, this exercise should prod you to remedy the inadequacy of your saving efforts. On the other hand, a surplus confirms that you are headed in the right direction, leaving you with a sense of satisfaction and relief.

STEP 10. PUT THE POWER OF TAX-ADVANTAGED ACCUMULATION TO WORK

The very best way to accumulate wealth and attain financial independence is to contribute to plans expressly designed for retirement savings.

This vital step dictates that your number one priority is to fully maximize your contributions to such plans as 401(k), 403(b), SEPs, and deductible IRAs. These plans, with their powerful twin tax advantages of pretax deductibility and tax deferral, can be described as super-retirement savings vehicles as well as fantastic tax shelters. Participation in these plans is the best ticket to financial security.

The systematic, automatic payroll contribution available with many plans provides the perfect means for paying yourself first, with dollar-cost averaging an added bonus. Future retirees will derive much of their financial security from the increasingly popular 401(k) plan. Many 401(k) plans make themselves even more attractive by adding a matching provision to your voluntary contribution. For example, if you sign up to contribute 6% of your gross pay and your employer matches 50 cents on each dollar, or 3%, this amounts to an immediate 50% return on your investment before any other investment return.

If your plan has a matching provision, it would be foolish not to participate to the maximum level that is matched. I recall the daughter of a client who was reluctant to contribute 4% of her income, even though the employer generously matched 25 cents on the first 4%, or a total of 1%. She was led to believe by a know-nothing ex-boyfriend there were better investment opportunities elsewhere. Her father told her in no uncertain words that *a tax-deductible, tax-deferred, automatic, disciplined opportunity with a no-risk, legal, 25% return kicker did not exist for her outside of this retirement plan.*

LARRY AND MAUREEN

Larry and Maureen are a hardworking two-income couple, both 35 years old, who want to build future financial independence.

Larry's employer offers a 401(k) plan. Larry will contribute $4,000 a year off the top of his pay to get a 25% employer match of $1,000, for a total retirement fodder of $5,000.

Maureen is employed by a nonprofit organization, and her plan is a 403(b). She is allowed to contribute a greater percentage of her paycheck than her husband's corporate plan allows, but there is no matching provision. She, too, places $5,000 pretax into her qualified plan.

Both Larry and Maureen are targeting a 10% average return on investment, building on a 25-year span until age 60. They are subject to a 28% marginal income tax bracket.

Retirement plan sponsors and providers are making great strides in communicating the benefits and educating participants in these super-retirement plans. They offer their efforts to you in the form of education sessions, written communication pieces, on-line updates and information, telephone hotlines, and kiosks, which include interactive programs that print out growth projections and tax savings.

	Larry 401(k)	Maureen 403(b)	Total	25 Years
	$4,000 Yr.	$5,000 Yr.	$9,000	$225,000
Co. Match	$1,000 Yr.	------------	$1,000	$ 25,000
	$5,000 Yr.	**$5,000 Yr.**	**$10,000**	**$250,000**

Pre-tax Savings	**@ 28% MTB**		
$ 9,000	@ 28%	=	$ 2,520 per year
$225,000	@ 28%	=	$63,000 25-year total

Projected Growth	**@ 10% ROI**	=	**$1,081,818**
$1,081,818 minus $250,000		=	$831,818 Tax-deferred buildup

STEP 11. NURTURE YOUR NEST EGG

Effective management of your retirement plan is your most important task in pursuing a financially secure retirement. Nurturing this nest egg will move you a long way toward your goal of financial independence.

As alluded to earlier, a major trend has taken place in retirement plans. Defined contribution plans have eclipsed the traditional defined benefit (fixed pension) plans that dominated choices just a few short years ago.

The most popular type of defined contribution plan today is the 401(k), which continues to experience explosive growth. An advantage of a defined contribution plan such as a 401(k) is that you can readily identify the value of your individual account—daily if desired; and you can literally take it with you in a lump sum when you switch jobs or retire. This portability feature in our transient employment market allows you to build a healthy retirement sum.

Retirement plans continue to evolve by offering more flexibility, from the number of investment options and voice-response systems to the frequency of allowing changing elections, changing contribution levels, and reallocating balances.

Mutual funds have emerged as the primary investments due to daily valuation and switching capability. Investment choices now cover a wide spectrum, from stable money funds and Guaranteed Investment Contracts (GICs) to aggressive growth and international fund offerings. Their increased flexibility and menu of choices is a two-edged sword, adding complexity and individual responsibility.

Informed retirement planners welcome the opportunity and accept the responsibility of piloting their own ship. On the other hand, the passive and ill-informed are likely to suffer under the burden of self-direction, with unsatisfactory results.

The following advice is offered to help you avoid possible mistakes and navigate around the pitfalls. The aim is to invest responsibly and achieve independence. Think of 401(k)s and 403(b)s, IRAs and SEP plans as the engine, contributions the fuel, and investments the horsepower to propel you to financial independence. The key: careful management of your total retirement program and careful investment decision making.

KEY—PARTICIPATE TO THE MAXIMUM

A typical plan now offers anywhere from 6 to 15 distinct investment offerings, ranging from stable and safe to volatile and aggressive. A multitude of choices is good, but it could result in more confusion and increase the odds to compound errors.

As in all investment matters, it is important to educate yourself about the relative risk and return expectations of each choice and about the ways to vary the menu of investment offerings. This risk/return comprehension is essential to plan management and will prove valuable over a lifetime of investment decision making.

Do not be misled by the year-to-year performance turned in by various investment categories. Over the long term (10 to 15 years) they will fall into line on the risk/return scale.

DON'T CHASE LAST YEAR'S WINNER!

Doing so is the number one mistake in investment decision making inside retirement plans.

The plan sponsor or investment agent distributes a report or memo detailing the performance returns for each fund for the preceding calendar year. For example:

        Fund A   -10%
        Fund B   + 5%
        Fund C   +10%
        Fund D   +20%

Now, guess which fund is likely to attract a whole slew of contribution dollars? Surprise—the top performer for the most recent period. The logic goes that since it performed best, it must *be* the best, and you want only a winner for your hard-earned retirement investment. The reality is that this high flyer is likely to be shot down on your watch. You then sidle up to a new winner. This commonly followed investment "strategy" is like a dog's chasing its tail; you get nowhere and end up dizzy.

There is a better strategy—one capable of producing superior returns at a lower risk. Warning—if you share this strategy with fellow employees, be prepared for ridicule. Consider betting on the loser and channel 100% of your new contribution sums into the slow boat. Actually, this method of going against the herd is practiced by intelligent investors and is called *contrarian investing*. As a by-product, you minimize risk by buying low, rather than high.

As evidence, I turn to mutual fund tracker Susan Paluch of *Morningstar*, who pointed out that this year's top-performing funds are likely to come from last year's least popular fund types. She observes:

> "Funds in categories that grew the least on a percentage basis in one year outperformed the average fund over the next one, two, and three year periods 79% of the time. They outperformed the most popular funds 92% of the time."
>
> —Susan Paluch, *Morningstar*

THINK LONG TERM

Retirement planning is a long-term proposition. Patience is definitely a virtue and a sound ally in your investment approach. Retirement does not constitute an end to your life, or to the management of your nest egg. A 60-year-old plan participant could likely have a life expectancy of 25 years, a full quarter of a century. Remember, you are not required to take any distributions from your retirement plans until age 70½. Even then, it can be a minimum amount. As a result, this money can be growing for many years to come.

SET AN ASSET ALLOCATION STRATEGY

Your retirement money has the strong potential to grow to a sizable investment pot. It is becoming increasingly common to see retirement accounts of $500,000, $750,000, and even $1 million. To ensure this prosperity requires that an investment plan be in place to guide you.

The primary investment issue to define is your asset allocation strategy. In my opinion this centers on how you wish to carve up your portfolio between stocks and basically everything else (bonds, fixed, cash equivalents).

Increasingly, retirement plans are offering so-called asset allocation funds as investment elections. Sometimes referred to generically as "life cycle" funds, they can provide a welcome solution to the asset allocation dilemma. Basically, these are mutual funds composed of a strategic mix of asset categories designed to correspond to a given risk/return profile.

The appeal is a professionally designed and managed off-the-shelf asset allocation plan in a single package. There could be four packages, differentiated by objective, each appealing to different segments and their risk-bearing capability. On one end would be an income-oriented security, conservatively weighted 20% in stocks and 80% in bonds; at the other end of the spectrum, an aggressive growth choice with the reverse mix: 80% allocated to stocks and 20% to bonds.

DON'T BE TOO CONSERVATIVE

The plain fact is, many employees are too conservative with their investment direction. Studies show that the greatest amount of money in retirement plans is in guaranteed investment contracts or fixed accounts. Obviously, many retirement investors find comfort in the concept of guarantees and fixed returns.

A myth deserving to be dispelled is that retirement investing must be conservative. There is evidence that many feel it should be ultraconservative, meaning exposing no principal to risk. The truth is, guaranteed investments are guaranteed to produce a more modest nest egg than a long-term position that accepts reasonable risk. A better investment stance is to set your portfolio in line with your time horizon as well as your risk temperament.

DON'T NEGLECT GROWTH

The antidote to being too conservative is being able to tolerate a dose of risk. By growth, I mean stocks or stock funds. Stocks (equities) add balance to your overall portfolio and are the only asset category with the potential to average double-digit returns. Retirement investing should be synonymous with long-term investing consistent with successful stock investing. In an asset class (stock funds) that is capable of averaging 10%, a $1 investment doubles in value every seven years. The same dollar in a fixed guaranteed account at 7% takes about 10 years before it is worth $2. Over a 25-year accumulation period, the $1 in a stock index fund could be expected to be worth $10.83, whereas the fixed rate option would be worth just $5.43, half as much.

> "Behold the turtle. He makes progress only when he stick his neck out."
> —James B. Conant

If you want to power up your portfolio, add some octane. Place as much in the growth category as your investment temperament permits. Then exercise patience and let compounding do its work.

PRACTICE OVERALL INVESTMENT PORTFOLIO MANAGEMENT

It is useful for planning purposes to segregate your total investment portfolio into two pots, retirement and nonretirement sums. This is because each pot receives different tax treatment.

For whatever reason, many investors pay little attention to their retirement money. Your retirement funds should be actively managed to complement your overall (global) investment plan.

First measure your current asset allocation and then determine a desired strategic allocation. If you discover you are heavy in stocks, perhaps your retirement plan additions should be placed into bonds. This is especially appealing to high-bracket taxpayers, who can shelter income generated from bonds under the umbrella of a tax-deferred account.

An advantage of managing a retirement portfolio is that you can lock in and protect gains without triggering a taxable gain consequence. If your targeted asset allocation gets out of alignment, you can easily rebalance without a tax effect.

A disadvantage is that capital losses incurred inside a retirement account are wasted. This is a good argument against using your IRA for highly aggressive speculative investments. Also bear in mind that any capital gain generated will be taxed as ordinary income when distributed.

An oversight I see is the emphasis on current investment allocation, while scant attention is given to the allocation that is represented by the current principal balance—which is likely to be far more substantial.

Take the example of Joe, who contributes $200 each paycheck to his retirement plan. Joe agonized over the investment allocation, finally settling on 40% ($80) into fixed, 40% ($80) into bonds, and 20% ($40) into the equity fund. Yet ask Joe how the $50,000 balance in his plan is allocated and he doesn't have a clue. Determine and direct how a current balance is mixed by doing simple division.

REALIZE YOU ARE DOLLAR-COST AVERAGING

Perhaps the best feature of retirement plan participation, on a par with tax advantages, is the discipline derived from automatic, systematic payroll deductions. If you don't add fuel, the fire doesn't happen.

The effect of the pattern of regular additions means you are practicing dollar-cost averaging—a proven technique to reduce the risk of entering the market at an inopportune time. When you invest in the volatile stock market, your fixed payroll purchase buys more shares when the market is depressed and fewer during periods of high valuations. Think of it as entering a pool by taking gradual steps as opposed to diving in. The dollar-cost-averaging method of investing involves consistency, regardless of changing price levels. Over time, averaging means that investment ups and downs work in your favor.

Dollar-cost averaging, coupled with a long-term outlook and the choice of a growth vehicle, can put you in a position to succeed.

DON'T LOAD UP ON COMPANY STOCK

In larger plans, a company's own stock could well be one of the available investment options. Your employer's matching contribution or profit-sharing addition is likely to be paid in shares of company stock. I believe it is a positive on many levels to have an ownership in your employer. However, I discovered that many plan participants make the mistake of loading up too heavily on this single issue.

There is high risk whenever a single holding accounts for a too-heavy concentration of one's portfolio. Look at the case in which XYZ stock is held in a plan and an individual stockholder also receives stock options, participates in an employee stock purchase plan, and possibly even inherits some of the same stock.

This single security risk could seriously erode the nest egg should a fickle market devalue ownership. In a worst-case scenario, the same economic forces having an impact on the stock price could also affect your personal employment situation. The XYZ Company, in an effort to prop up its stock price, could follow the lead of others and initiate a massive restructuring, spin off divisions, institute layoffs, or decide to outsource certain operations. Thousands of employees of giant corporations have experienced a double whammy of net worth decline coupled with the loss of employment income.

Diversify away some of this risk and constantly be on guard so that you are adding balance to your retirement portfolio.

AGAIN—LEAVE PLAN BALANCES ALONE

- Borrowing from your retirement nest egg should be an extreme measure. I am against liberalizing of plans for any other than a long-term retirement purpose.
- When you change jobs or leave your employer, do not look at your retirement account as a windfall. Rather, have the foresight to roll it over into your new employer's plan or a retirement rollover IRA so you keep your retirement dream alive.
- In dipping into your retirement fund, you steal retirement capital and lose the tremendous lift that compound growth gives to your goal of future financial security.

STEP 12. PROTECT YOUR BACKSIDE

With all the emphasis on taking the offensive and building a nest egg, it is also necessary to have a defensive plan in place. Don't overlook the risk management component of your preretirement planning strategy.

As an employee, your benefits—including a retirement plan, half of Social Security taxes, and group life, health, and long-term disability—form a valuable part of your overall compensation package. In some employment situations this could account for 30% to 40% of gross pay. You quickly gain an appreciation for how much these fringe benefits are worth if you take the plunge and become self-employed.

Evaluate the defensive component of your overall strategy. Investigate your insurance protection, including the costs and coverages in the areas of life, disability, and especially health.

When weighing a job offer, consider employee benefits. Dual-income couples should analyze the makeup of their respective packages and coordinate plans for maximum benefit. The proliferation of flexible spending accounts and cafeteria plans makes intelligent planning beneficial.

When you approach retirement, your most important insurance protection is adequate health insurance. Even the wealthiest individuals can be bankrupted quickly without adequate protection. Health care costs are accelerating at rates much higher than the general level of inflation. A fact of life is that the aging process leads inevitably to more health-related problems and associated greater expenditures.

One of the first questions I ask people planning on retiring or leaving a job is the nature of their health insurance plan. The primary objective in the preretirement years is to stay in some type of group insurance plan because group coverage is the most economical choice.

For many people planning retirement, health insurance coverage plays a major role in determining when they retire. At age 65, one becomes eligible for Medicare coverage. This health insurance program, administered by the Social Security Administration, is designed for people 65 or over, regardless of health or financial capability.

STEP 13. GET YOUR ACT TOGETHER

Planning for retirement and financial independence is serious business. Following is some common sense medicine intended to keep you healthy and your dream alive.

CHECK WHETHER YOU ARE ON THE MARK

The start of the New Year is a time for reflection and for making resolutions. It is also an ideal time to put pencil to paper and construct a net worth statement. This simple exercise allows you to quickly assess your financial condition. As a good personal finance manager, you want to see assets growing, debt declining, and wealth increasing. Comparing your net worth summary with last year's informs you of how far you've come. See Chapter 2 to recall details on preparing a net worth statement.

You should set a realistic net worth number to try to reach by a target date. You then can plot your progress toward your goal.

DO A QUICK INVESTMENT ANALYSIS

In conjunction with your constructing your net worth statement, I advise you to conduct an investment inventory and quick portfolio analysis. This simple procedure yields a revealing look behind the numbers.

Often, I see overemphasis on how well or how poorly individual investments are performing. The tendency is to dump the laggards and reward the winners with more money—an arrangement that makes for poor music. If you believe in asset allocation, listen to how well the orchestra is playing and how effectively individual sections are working in concert.

ARE YOU SAVING ENOUGH?

Recheck your saving strategy, charting what percentage and dollar amount of your employment income you are salting away. Formulate a plan for how best to place this seed money to grow your nest egg.

What do you estimate your capital to be worth at retirement? What is your targeted number? Project your current investment and new annual savings with the help of a number-crunching financial program. Are you on track?

BE SURE YOUR ESTATE PLAN IS IN ORDER

As you grow your estate and make progress toward financial independence, it is only logical to have an estate plan in place consistent with your financial condition and personal desires.

STEP 14. STAY ON TOP TO GET ON TOP

The greatest obstacle in reaching the summit comes from being uninformed and ill-prepared. Developing a financial independence security plan involves becoming a better-informed consumer in matters affecting your financial health and future.

Work to educate yourself on important planning considerations, investment choices, tax effects, pension options, estate matters, inflation, tax deferral and so on.

The forces affecting financial planning are as dynamic as weather on the proverbial mountaintop. Stay abreast of changes. The best approach is to focus energy on a lifetime planning and learning process.

CHAPTER 11

INVESTING IN BONDS FOR INCOME

Bill was a sales manager in his late fifties when he suffered a debilitating stroke that left him unable to work. When he came to my office, he was looking to generate regular monthly income from the proceeds of a piece of property he had just sold. Assume the amount he was investing for this purpose to be an even $100,000.

Basically, Bill wanted to accomplish two goals with this money:

1. To generate the highest possible regular monthly income to supplement his pension and disability pay.
2. To maintain the $100,000 principal amount relatively intact so his wife and sons would have use of this money should his failing health lead to his premature death.

Since his objectives were clear-cut, it became apparent that high quality bond funds were most appropriate to meet his objectives. I spent a considerable amount of time educating Bill on the various investment options suitable for him and suggested we focus on a combination of high-grade corporate and government bond mutual funds and bank CDs as right for him.

The yield on such a portfolio during that time averaged about 8%. In effect, the plan called for realizing about $8,000 in annual income with monthly distributions in the amount of $667. There was a high expectation that the $100,000 principal would fluctuate only mildly. I thought we had agreed on a workable plan.

That weekend Bill saw an advertisement in his local newspaper sporting an outsized 12% return. Thrilled, he tore out the ad, believing he had found an incredible opportunity for a yield 50% greater than my proposal. Bill's arithmetic was easy: 12% on $100,000 is $12,000 a year, or $1,000 monthly.

First thing Monday morning Bill called the brokerage firm sponsoring this high-yield debt offering. A broker suggested he would be wise to invest the whole $100,000. Inclined to do just that, Bill agreed to meet with him later that day.

He contacted his wife at work and proudly informed her he had discovered a great deal. His wife, as the voice of reason, suggested Bill had better get my opinion.

Bill did phone me, but the only part of the conversation I could understand was 12%. The stroke had affected Bill's speech, making him difficult to understand, especially on the telephone, so I suggested we meet in person. He drove to my office, visions of a 12% return dancing in his head.

I informed him this offering was high risk, and such a speculative investment was unsuitable in his situation. He questioned how I was so certain it was high risk. My reply was simple; the high yield of 12% and comparative market returns of 8% on quality high-grade debt told me so.

Bill and I were on two different wavelengths. He continued to fixate on the potential of a 12% return, while I was worried about the substantial risk to his principal of $100,000.

Since he was still not convinced, I pointed out how he as a homeowner could borrow money at a 10% rate, the federal government could do so at 7.5%, and financially sound corporations could borrow at 8%. I then queried him about what type of borrower (bond issuer) would be forced to pay 12% to attract investors to this debt issue.

The answer was, someone who did not engender in investors a high degree of confidence that the IOU could be paid back and in a timely manner.

Bill reluctantly followed my advice, prodded by his concerned wife. I did not know that Revco, the holder of this particular debt (borrower), would eventually file for bankruptcy. Yet I was concerned that the financial risk of this single-issue, high-yield security was too great to accept.

Bill passed away about a year later, but at least his widow didn't have to face the loss of income and a principal balance that was paid back at just 35 cents on the dollar some five years later.

> "In investing money, the amount of interest you want should depend on whether you want to eat well or sleep well."
> —J. Kenfield Morley, 1937

THE PETER LYNCH OF BONDS

Newsweek magazine labeled Pimco's mutual fund founder and chief investment officer Bill Gross "The Peter Lynch of bonds." Duly recommended, his common sense wisdom is distilled in his book, provocatively entitled, *Everything You've Heard about Investing is Wrong!*

The exclamation point is alarming, considering that hundreds of billions of dollars have flowed into bonds and bond funds, and hundreds of new bond funds have been spawned. In itself this is not a negative; however, I am concerned that this influx of investment is driven by the low-rate environment found in traditional savings investments and not by a move to a more sophisticated investment posture.

Surveys of potential bond fund investors found the majority mistakenly believing the best time to buy and own bond funds is when interest rates are rising. This is alarming, but I am convinced it represents an accurate reading.

I have no doubt that more confusion and misconceptions surround bond investing than any other investment area. This is why it is essential for your financial well-being to become grounded in the basics of bond investing, especially the risk and reward parameters.

Bonds and bond funds play an integral role in financial and investment planning. They offer:
1. a steady stream of income by design
2. potentially greater returns than cash equivalents and traditional savings products
3. generally lower risk and volatility than stock investments
4. an element of diversification from stock investments

Bill Gross, while making a case for bonds, reminds us that stocks don't always outperform bonds.

> "Although stocks are definitely the best bet for the long haul, there
> have been periods as recently as the early 1970s when bonds and
> even money market funds did better over a ten-year time frame.
> It would be a mistake to structure your personal portfolio with
> 100 percent stocks, especially considering the
> income advantage offered by bonds."
>
> —Bill Gross

I have learned from wise sources that a basic measure of understanding and comprehension comes from knowing what questions to ask.

With this in mind, to help you grasp the basics of bond investing, the following pages use a question-and-answer approach along with intelligence garnered from top-flight bond experts.

ARE YOU SATISFIED WITH 3% YIELDS?

The above query was contemplated frequently during the Fall of 1991. Yields on short-term investments and money market instruments were at their lowest levels in 20 years. Frustrated savers and investors had grown accustomed to "fatter" returns. As a result, many investors opted for higher-yielding bonds and bond mutual funds. This move often was undertaken without a true understanding of the risks, crippling the primary motive of securing a higher overall investment return while maintaining principal.

The search for higher-yielding investments leads one to bonds. Let's revisit an elementary piece of common sense investment advice: Never purchase anything you don't understand. The fundamentals of bond (fixed income) investing are not too difficult, if you take the time to grasp the basics.

WHAT ARE YOU ACTUALLY PURCHASING WHEN YOU BUY A BOND?

A bond can be thought of as an IOU. In many cases, a bond is referred to as a *promissory note*. You become a lender to the government, corporations, or municipalities by purchasing the bonds they offer. Each type of bond possesses distinctive characteristics. A government bond is an issue backed by the U.S. Treasury. Treasury (T) debt nomenclature relates to the length of time to maturity: T-bills (short term), T-notes (intermediate), and T-bonds (long term). Treasury securities are issued to finance the national deficit. These debts are rated highest in quality and safety. As direct obligations of the U.S. Treasury, government issues do not have the risk of default as other debt offerings do.

Corporate debt is used to finance the diverse borrowing needs of corporations. This debt is subject to financial (credit) risk. The quality of issues varies greatly and is graded according to the financial condition of the borrower. Because of the risk of default (not paying back in full and on a timely basis), corporate bondholders (investors) demand the highest returns.

Municipalities have borrowing needs to fund public works projects. The prime characteristic of this type of debt is that the income is usually exempt (free) from federal income taxation. This is appealing to high-bracket taxpayers who will realize a higher after-tax return on "munis" (municipal bonds) when compared to a taxable equivalent.

Bonds can be purchased individually, in a package, or pooled through a mutual fund. Bonds provide an income stream. Investors in search of current income without capital appreciation should be looking at bonds or bond funds. Fixed income investments get their name because of the stability of return they provide. Contrast this with variable investments, such as stocks, in which the return varies and is inherently uncertain, but offers potential for capital growth.

The mechanics of bond investing call for an understanding of principal (P) and interest (I). An investor purchases a new issue bond for $1,000 (face value or principal). Assuming a 10% stated yield (coupon rate), the investor expects a fixed $100 return each year (typically $50 every six months) over the course of the bond term. When the bond matures in 10 years, the principal (initial $1,000) is returned to the investor by the borrower. Over that time period, $1,000 total interest has been generated.

SOUNDS SIMPLE ENOUGH—WHERE ARE THE PITFALLS?

In a host of areas, bond principal is subject to fluctuations in market value prior to maturity. Some bonds may be subject to *call* (paid off prior to the scheduled maturity). Also, there exists a wide spectrum of bond offerings, each with different risk/reward characteristics. Bonds are interest-rate sensitive. As the general level of interest rates changes, the market value of bonds reacts accordingly. Interest rate risk, in my opinion, is the most misunderstood risk investors face.

Changes in the direction of interest rates directly affect the principal value of outstanding bonds, with the lone exception of U.S. Savings Bonds. Such risk kicks in when general (market) interest rates rise. The principal value of an existing bond, whose coupon (yield) is below the market rate, is reduced.

The danger with supposedly safe, conservative investments such as 30-year treasury bonds or zero-coupon bonds arises during periods of rapidly rising interest rates. Many people are shocked to discover that if interest rises by 2 percentage points in a year, the effect on a 30-year, 8% coupon, $10,000 bond is its revaluation at just $8,107—the zero coupon loses an alarming $4,368, or 43%. Novice and some experienced investors overlook or fail to appreciate their exposure to interest rate risk.

WHY DOES PRINCIPAL FLUCTUATE SO MUCH?

Say, for example, you hold a bond yielding 10%, and a comparable (same type, quality, and maturity) bond is now yielding 12%. No reasonable investor will pay you face value ($1,000) for your 10% coupon. If you sell, it will be at a discount (less than $1,000). You will suffer a loss of capital in the $100, $200, or $300 range, depending on the bond's length to maturity. The longer to maturity, the greater your loss.

In response to this threat, certain individuals counter they will avoid risk because they will hold the bond to maturity. The error in this financial logic is that in the interim to maturity they lose the opportunity potential found in the higher-yielding alternatives. And, of course, in a mutual fund, active management (buying and selling) is taking place, and changes in bond pricing are reflected immediately with a change in the NAV (net asset value). In either case, the market value of your bond or fund declines.

Investors can lessen interest rate risk by choosing bonds or bond funds with shorter maturities (3 to 10 years versus 15 to 30 years). The shorter the maturity, the less dramatic the fluctuation in principal. In the decade of the 1980s, bonds exhibited extreme volatility (movements in price up and down) as a result of interest rate swings.

WHAT HAPPENS WHEN INTEREST RATES GO DOWN?

A lowering of interest rates (the cost of money or capital) is good news for current bondholders. Higher-yielding bonds become worth more (sell at a premium). If you do elect to sell, you are rewarded with a capital gain. The problem is no one can predict consistently the future direction of interest rates.

ARE BONDS SAFE INVESTMENTS?

Bonds, with the marked exception of junk (high-yield) bonds, are considered conservative, relatively safe investments. This is because they provide an identifiable income source (return) and are more predictable than stocks. But it is very important to realize that all bonds and bond funds expose your principal to risk and possible loss. Investors moving out of money markets and federally insured CDs must realize they are taking a step up the risk ladder in pursuit of a potentially greater return. Bond alternatives should not be thought of as high-yielding substitutes for a money fund or insured CD. A drop in share price could quickly offset the benefit of the higher yield, and a loss of principal is possible.

The most recent example of risk to principal in bonds occurred during 1994, when interest rates turned up sharply. That year total returns on long-term treasury bonds tumbled 7.6%, the worst performance in over 50 years.

The five-year period of 1977–1981 had high interest rates to go along with surging inflation, producing the worst environment possible for bond investors and very sorry returns. However, patient investors were richly rewarded in 1982 when the long-term treasury index advanced an amazing 41.8% in a single year.

WHAT IS MEANT BY TOTAL RETURN, AND WHY DO I NEED TO BE CONCERNED WITH IT?

All too often, uninformed investors focus their attention on current yield (payout expressed as a percentage on an annual basis). Total return is a difficult concept to comprehend for many investors. It is more encompassing and includes both interest earnings and any gain or loss in principal. It provides a complete measure of past performance.

To illustrate, let us use an example of a $1,000 bond with a 10% yield. Over the course of one year, this yield computes to $100 in interest on the bond. If this same bond declines in value to $950 ($50 or 5%) as a result of rising interest rates, the cumulative effect is a total return of just 5%:

+ $100 - $50 = +$50; 5% of $1,000

On the other hand, if interest rates decline during our annual measuring period, the bond appreciates in value to, say, $1,050 ($50 or 5%), for a total return of 15%:

$100 or 10% coupon + $50 or 5% capital gain = $150 or 15% total return

Note that total return computations are historical and should not be used to predict future performance.

In 1990, junk bond funds were yielding 16.3% in interest. Yet the total return on average was a negative 11%. The lesson to be learned is that current yield should not be the sole determination for evaluating bonds.

WHY NOT SIMPLY CHOOSE THE BOND WITH THE HIGHEST YIELD?

You could well be choosing the most popular course of action. Many individuals believe—erroneously—that the highest-yielding alternative is the best. Using this measure as your selection criterion means any financial success is more likely a product of luck than of insight. Remember one point: The higher the anticipated return, the higher the associated risk. The risk/return trade-off is basic to bond fund investing. You cannot have it both ways when it comes to bond investing.

Very simply, if you are faced with a choice between two bonds, each with equivalent maturities, you can judge quickly the higher-risk alternative by looking at the bond carrying the higher yield. As an example, show me a 10-year corporate bond yielding 9% and another 10-year coupon at 8%, and the risk/reward trade-off test quickly and accurately informs me the higher-yielding bond holds higher risk. In fact, show me two bond funds, one yielding 6.5% and another 6%, and this law tells me the differential is due to risk. Too many investors, when faced with a choice between 6% and 8% yields, casually jump for the higher return.

Determining the higher number is grade school math; evaluating the associated risk is just as easily determined.

HOW DO YOU PROTECT AGAINST RISK?

In summation, bond investors need to be conscious of two elements of risk. There is the risk that the IOU will not be paid back on time and in full. The issuing corporation or municipality could run into extreme financial distress or bankruptcy, precluding fulfillment of its obligation. You can minimize this risk by concentrating on quality issues—those judged as having the best capability for meeting their debt service. Included in this group are direct government treasury obligations, government agencies, and the highest-rated (investment-grade) corporate and municipal borrowers.

The second risk is interest rate risk, which, as discussed, can be minimized by staying with lower volatility short-term to intermediate-term bonds.

AREN'T BONDHOLDERS AT THE MERCY OF INFLATION?

True enough, especially for those dealing in long-term bonds. Bond manager Bill Gross views inflation as a disguised form of tax, devaluing a stream of future interest payments.

However, he is bullish (favorably inclined) toward the Treasury Department's recently introduced "inflation indexed" bonds. These bonds are designed to be reset in line with increases in the Consumer Price Index.

Bonds should be an integral part of your portfolio. By understanding the basics, you are more likely to eat well and sleep well.

LISTEN TO 30 YEARS OF EXPERIENCE

Tim Bultman is president and founder of Bultman Investment Management in Milwaukee. His 30 years of experience mark him as a respected fixed-income specialist.

In interviewing Bultman for this book, I found him to be a strong advocate for common sense bond investing. He, too, is outspoken in his belief that most investors go down the wrong path, and he was eager to offer advice on the correct course.

- He claims the packagers and sponsors of bond funds and unit investment trusts do great for themselves but at the expense (literally) of the investors in their products. This is especially the case for anyone purchasing loaded products or owning high-expense funds.
- He believes many bond fund investors would be better off staying with the safety and predictability of CDs. The disadvantages of bond funds include risk to principal, no set maturities, high expenses, and unwanted capital gain distributions.
- Although an advocate of individual bonds over bond funds, he currently disdains corporate bonds altogether, favoring government issues. In this view he concurs with money manager and *Forbes* columnist David Goldman, who says he advises his clients to stick with treasuries because of how tough it is to produce superior returns from corporates compared with treasuries, which have no credit or quality risk and are state-tax exempt. Addressing mutual fund investors, he says, "There's little point owning a mutual fund that invests in high-grade corporates right now because there is little the manager can do to earn his keep."
- Bultman is in complete agreement with the other bond money managers chronicled in this chapter, who say that the way to reduce interest rate volatility is by concentrating solely in high quality, short- and intermediate-term maturity bonds.
- He sees many investors so repulsed by paying taxes on their investment earnings that they foolishly accept lower after-tax tax-exempt returns. The appeal of tax-free income is so strong that many tax-sensitive investors too readily leap at lower-quality issues or those with unattractive call features. Bultman says that unless investors are in at least the 31% tax bracket, they should turn instead to lower-risk treasuries that are exempt from state tax.
- He claims individual investors would be wise to avoid purchasing or trading corporate bonds because of excessive

spreads. The *spread* is the difference between bid (buy) and ask (sell) pricing.

Marilyn Cohen, president of a fixed-income money management firm, refers to "killer spreads" and warns that individual bond investors will be clipped at every turn. She counsels investors to avoid trading (selling before maturity). Bultman, recalling his brokerage days, admits that individual investors trading corporate bonds should expect the short end of the stick.

He sees too much evidence of supposedly intelligent (he prefers not to use the term *sophisticated*) investors not placing their financial self-interest first. He was perturbed by the unsound argument of a broker who persuaded a mature client to suffer a $5,000 surrender penalty to move away from a Fidelity annuity purchased just a month before to go with the broker's annuity choice. The client was persuaded to take this nonsensical action because of Fidelity's supposed investment problems. Fidelity is a premier investment management firm, and the only logical reason to make this transfer was so the broker could generate a healthy commission. Unfortunately, this is not an isolated incident. Bultman queried the client about his justification for leaving $5,000 in blood on the table for no apparent reason. He feebly offered that he had to trust the broker and build a relationship. Bultman questioned what kind of trusting relationship a client could expect from one built on a foundation of self-serving, non-objective advice.

- To summarize Tim Bultman's bond investment philosophy, he favors individual bonds over bond funds, currently disdains corporate bonds altogether, concentrates on short- to intermediate-maturity treasury notes to reduce risks and costs, prefers taxable treasuries over tax-exempts for all but the very highest-bracket taxpayers, and sees no merit in the appeal of international bonds.

One strategy Bultman thinks he might employ would be to use treasury notes of varying short- to intermediate-maturities to construct a laddered bond portfolio.

> **Laddering**
>
> Here's an example of laddering. If you are working with a sum of $100,000, for example, break it equally into five pieces and place it in investments that will come due at five different times:
>
> | | | |
> |---:|---:|:---|
> | | $ 20,000 | 2-year T-note |
> | | 20,000 | 3-year T-note |
> | | 20,000 | 4-year T-note |
> | | 20,000 | 5-year T-note |
> | | 20,000 | 6-year T-note |
> | TOTAL | $100,000 | |

The features of a bond portfolio as described by Bultman include these:

1. It is low risk, no credit-quality risk, because the bonds are direct obligations of the U.S. Treasury. Interest rate risk is side-stepped by the intention to hold these bonds to full maturity.
2. Operating within the maturity range of 2–6 years, you historically expect to capture 90% of the return of the long-term treasury bonds, but without the volatility of long-term bonds.
3. This portfolio is characterized by low costs to put into place and low minimums ($10,000 per bond) to participate.
4. Income generated from treasury securities is exempt by law from state taxation.
5. You gain relative predictability, because treasury issues, unlike corporate and municipal bonds, are not callable—or subject to call.
6. Flexibility is maintained in that all or parts of the portfolio are quickly and readily marketable at reasonable cost and do not have the stiff surrender or early withdrawal charges found with annuities or CDs.
7. The timing issue is addressed in that you have the opportunity to reinvest 20% of your portfolio every year, with complete return of principal.
8. This portfolio is capable of providing a regular source of dependable income.

The beauty of such a common sense portfolio is that it contains no surprises, is easy to comprehend and implement, and accomplishes a stated objective.

BOND FUND UPDATE: ANOTHER POINT OF VIEW

David W. Schulz is a Chartered Financial Analyst and president of M&I Investment Management Corporation. Previously he headed M&I's fixed income group and managed high-quality bond funds. *Worth* magazine, in its October 1992 issue, named Schulz one of the best bond portfolio managers in the country. Here, he shares his perspective on bond fund investing.

Q: WHEN PROSPECTIVE INVESTORS CHECK OUT A BOND MUTUAL FUND, WHAT QUESTIONS SHOULD THEY ASK?

A. First, they should note the quality of the bonds purchased by the fund. Pay particular attention to the minimum- or lowest-quality bonds that may be held in the portfolio. In addition, look at the mix and grades among government, agency, and corporate debt.

Second, inquire about the average weighted maturity of bonds held in the portfolio, a figure designated in years. Ask the authorized range of maturities. No matter what the current weighted maturity, you could find some funds with a range of zero to 30 years.

I would take a close look at a listing of the bonds held currently to get a sense of the fund's philosophy. I find that the prospectuses, although important, all sound too broad, with similar boilerplate language. A quick look at the actual portfolio proves more valuable.

Q: YOU NEGLECTED TO MENTION CURRENT YIELD. ISN'T THAT THE MOST IMPORTANT MEASUREMENT?

A: Current yield is important to the extent it generates a desired cash flow from an investment. However, you also need to know whether that income flow represents strictly interest or interest along with principal. Basically, current yield can be manipulated or targeted at virtually any level.

Current yield is overemphasized in the mind and decision process of the typical investor. By definition, as you boost current income, you are sacrificing future principal. Knowledgeable bond investors can discern fairly closely the current yield if they know the fund's makeup and average maturity level.

This is not to imply that the average investor should be able to estimate yield. After checking the quality and determining the average maturity of the bond fund, inquire about current yield. Keep in mind, it bears a direct relationship to the quality and maturity of a fund's holdings.

Q: DO YOU HAVE ANY ADVICE FOR INVESTORS LOOKING TO MOVE UP THE YIELD CURVE TO INCREASE INCOME? JUST WHAT IS THE YIELD CURVE?

A: In short, proceed with caution. Historically, the yield pickup from money markets to bond funds is greater when bond interest rates are at the bottom or near bottoming out. You can lose a portion of your principal in a bond fund if the market doesn't go your way, and the risk of that happening is greatest when rates are low. Consumers inevitably go the wrong way on this matter, and poor timing disrupts their initial intent to protect principal and maximize income.

As for the yield curve, it involves the relationship between the length of a bond's maturity and the yield that the bond carries currently. This relationship is best depicted graphically and is a guide to basic bond analysis. It constitutes a trade-off between the willingness to make a commitment and the return that commitment may bring.

Q: DO SALES LOADS MAKE MUCH OF A DIFFERENCE IN BOND FUNDS?

A: I am very definite on this point. You never make up the initial load in a bond fund. Even the best and most able bond fund managers would be hard-pressed to start out with a 4% to 5% deficit to overcome. On a related matter, the annual costs incurred by funds directly influence bond fund performance.

EDITOR'S NOTE: On this matter, there is no disagreement among professional investment managers, although some marketing departments could be expected to take exception. A noted mutual fund industry figure has stated on numerous occasions: "There are few certainties in mutual fund investing, but 'never pay a sales load on a bond fund' is one of them." Informed investors not only are limiting their bond fund choices to no-load funds, but also are increasingly paying close attention to expense ratios. Bill Gross concurs: "In the long run, fees become a heavy load." Over a relatively short time period, lower-expense bond funds inevitably demonstrate superior performance.

Q: WITH 30-YEAR TREASURY BONDS NOW YIELDING CLOSE TO 8%, WHY DO YOU CONTINUE TO STRUCTURE YOUR PORTFOLIO WITH SHORT- TO INTERMEDIATE-TERM BONDS?

A: Academic studies support the fact that intermediate-term bonds historically have provided near-equivalent returns to long-term bonds and at a fraction of the risk. Generally speaking, an intermediate-term portfolio offers you 90% of the yield at only one-third the risk. Over the past 35 years, short- to intermediate-term U.S. government securities have generally provided yields of 85% to 95% of those provided by 30-year U.S. government bonds. In our opinion, this strategy provides the best risk/reward trade-off. It has been adopted by many astute bond managers.

EDITOR'S NOTE: This would include Ian MacKinnon, who, as head of Vanguard's fixed income group, manages more billions in bonds than any other fund family. "Intermediate securities seem to provide competitive returns to long bonds without the extra risk. Evidence suggests that we probably shouldn't own long treasury bonds in whole or in combination with other asset classes. They ought to be a lot less volatile or we ought to earn a higher yield on them."

Q: A HIGH-QUALITY, SHORT- TO INTERMEDIATE-TERM BOND FUND CARRIES LESS RISK, BUT IT ALSO POSTS LOWER CURRENT YIELDS. DOESN'T THIS HURT THE ALLURE IN MARKETING THE FUND TO YIELD-CONSCIOUS INVESTORS?

A: The answer is a definite yes. It is much easier to attract money with higher yields. However, as a manager I am after the highest total return with the least amount of risk. Bond fund managers bang their heads against this challenge every day.

Q: WHAT IS YOUR OPINION OF HIGH-YIELD—ALIAS "JUNK"—BONDS?

A: They do not belong in this discussion of a high-quality bond fund, because they are so far apart. I view junk bonds on a par with an aggressive stock fund. Also, I believe junk bonds are inappropriate for most people considering a bond fund.

EDITOR'S NOTE: Once again, many industry observers would agree. Individual junk bonds are analyzed more like a stock than a bond.

There is support for categorizing junk bond funds along with the higher-risk stock funds. The concern is that to group and compare high-yield bond funds with other bond funds tends to mask the full impact of their inherent risk.

A Case in Point

When Harrah's Jazz Company defaulted on its 14.25% bonds issued to build a New Orleans casino, two Fidelity junk bond funds fell 1.9% in a single day because they held this issue. This big one-day hit is similar to what might be expected from a small-cap growth fund.

Other lessons can be drawn from this example. Fidelity had no special insight into this situation, mistakenly believing that parent Harrah's would stand behind Harrah's Jazz. I suspect this same logic was dispensed by bond salesmen anxious to promote these bonds. Anyone holding the individual bonds saw their value fall 64% in one day. At least individuals owning the bonds through fund holdings lessen their risk because of diversification.

Q: WHAT IS YOUR THINKING ON AN INVESTOR'S PROJECTED HOLDING PERIOD WITH A FUND?

A: I would say three to five years as a minimum. This is arbitrary, yet the tendency for investors as a whole is to be too short-term oriented.

Q: WHY WOULD ONE CHOOSE A BOND MUTUAL FUND OVER INDIVIDUAL BONDS?

A: The most obvious answer is diversification, the protection afforded by a fund holding a quantity of individual bonds. Additionally, if I might be outspoken on this, I believe that the individual retail bond customer gets the short end of the stick. First of all, bonds suffer from a serious problem of liquidity. It is very difficult to sell bonds other than U.S. government securities without a substantial price concession on the secondary market.

Furthermore, the retail customer is unlikely to enjoy purchasing efficiencies. Most often, the individual investor is left with the least desirable securities because the best products have been taken by institutions. Callable bonds are another example of where the consumer frequently gets stung. I feel that the mechanics of fixed income investing being what they are, professional management in the surveillance, management, and selection of bonds is warranted.

EDITOR'S NOTE: Bond fund manager Bill Gross agrees. "Bonds are still too hard to buy in small quantities for any investor with less than $500,000 in his or her portfolio." Again the exception to this observation, as Schulz, Bultman, and Gross agree, is the purchase of treasury securities.

Mutual funds offer avenues to reduce risk. Diversification found in all funds provides protection by offering a quantity of bonds of varying quality (ratings) in the portfolio. If an individual bond defaults, the balance of the portfolio helps cushion its effect.

Professional management provides continuing credit surveillance, which may help minimize the negative effects of bond defaults and downgrades.

Q: GLOBAL BOND FUNDS ARE CURRENTLY POPULAR. DO YOU CARE TO COMMENT ON THEIR SUITABILITY TO THE AVERAGE INVESTOR?

A: Tell me which direction the dollar is going in relation to other currencies. Currency risk adds another dimension and even more uncertainty to fixed income investing.

Q: DO INVESTORS NEED TO BE CAUTIOUS IN THE MUNICIPAL BOND MARKET? IS THERE SUCH A THING AS MUNICIPAL JUNK?

A: This is an area of concern, and we are witnessing an increasing number of defaults. Poor reporting also makes it difficult to assess adequately the credit standing of these issuers.

If an investor is considering municipals, I would think a high-quality, professionally managed, tax-exempt fund would be worthy of consideration.

CHAPTER 12

POSTRETIREMENT PLANNING: SECURING THE GOLDEN YEARS

The postretirement phase of life ranges anywhere from five to forty years. These so-called golden years can be comfortable, exciting, and enriching for those who operate with a plan.

> "Retirement planning doesn't stop at retirement."
> —Craig Hoostra, AARP

Successful postretirement years are built on a foundation of financial security. For the most part, the accumulation process is complete and attention turns to income generation and the consumption, distribution, and preservation of capital.

When I was interviewed by the *Milwaukee Sentinel* to profile my first book in 1989, the young reporter asked my profession. I could have legitimately answered, *financial planner,* or *retirement planner,* or *financial services educator.* Instead I opted for something quotable and proclaimed that I was in the "anxiety removal business." Sure enough, this unconventional self-description appeared in the article.

Postretirees tend to be especially security conscious, possibly due to the lingering effects of being children of the Great Depression. Unlike the younger generation, this group realizes that the capacity to earn employment income is not guaranteed. There hovers the legitimate fear that the cost of a catastrophic illness or financial reversal could rob them of their security, because they don't have the time to recover.

Without a doubt, the cause of major anxiety among those already retired is of running out of money before they run out of breath. I have noticed this fear especially prevalent among women, a logical concern influenced by longer life spans. Just visit any retirement or nursing home and notice the gender imbalance.

The sad fact is, many living under this cloud of fear do so needlessly, negatively affecting their quality of life. Many retirees yearn to travel, be generous to family and/or charities, and generally enjoy these last chapters in their book of life. But many are reluctant to spend any of their nest egg. If only they could be sure their spending budget and gifting actions would not jeopardize their security blanket.

Prosperous retirees are not immune to this basic level of security anxiety. I have witnessed well-off senior citizens opt for a one-bedroom apartment when a two-bedroom is their strong preference. They drop club memberships and turn down that dream overseas trip, all because of a guarded financial condition. Retirees have been known to scale back their charitable giving and are hesitant even to purchase airfare to visit cherished grandchildren in distant locales.

This sense of unease about financial solvency is grounded in life experiences. Retirees are highly conscious of the burden imposed on their wealth from both income and estate taxation. Health concerns and related costs constantly shadow them. Their cost of living continues to spiral upwards. They might not appreciate the fact that they have amassed a sizable net worth, but instead continue to deny their comfortable financial status. Retirees have daily reminders that the prices of a gallon of milk, pound of bacon, and loaf of bread have risen dramatically over their lifetimes. This generation remembers that stock markets do crash and that much of their wealth is on paper, which can suddenly and dramatically be knocked down in value.

Mature individuals as a group appear to be more pessimistic in their financial outlook than is warranted by an objective assessment of their financial condition. The under-35 generation possesses no such reserve, routinely inflating their financial health and hyping their prospects.

Juniors act as though their ship will come in by their winning a lottery or inheriting a bundle. Beyond that, they possess earning years in which to produce income they are confident will convert to sustainable wealth.

Seniors have no such illusions and are reconciled to the fact that their financial lot has been cast.

The World War II set probably can afford a higher level of consumption, whereas baby boomers would be better served by adopting some of their predecessors' thrift and frugality.

Postretirees struggle with the balance between consumption and asset transfer versus long-term financial security. The financial plan must demonstrate a confident prediction that their money will survive them. Developing a plan counters anxiety and can offer comfort, satisfaction, and optimism to the golden years.

HOW LONG WILL MY MONEY LAST?

This is the big question in postretirement planning. To address this basic query, I like to have preretirees draw an hourglass. For illustration purposes, let's place an investment sum of $100,000 inside it. The round

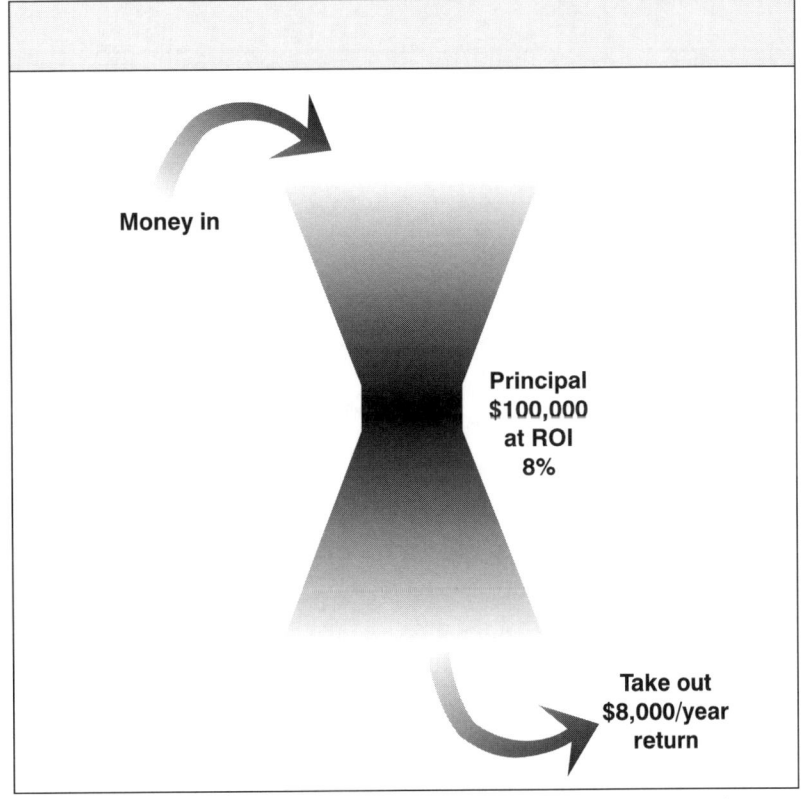

Figure 12-1

number makes for simple arithmetic and is easily computed on a percentage basis. Investment income flows through the bottom of the hourglass. The amount of income flow and the size of the investment balance depend on the return on investment and the annual rate of withdrawal.

Assuming an 8% return on investment (ROI), income would flow out at the rate of $8,000 per year from an investment nest egg of $100,000.

This cash flow can be consumed to meet retirement living expenses. You could crank out $8,000 each and every year forever without ever touching the $100,000 principal. In effect you have created your own annuity.

If you take out more than the average annual return, say 10% or $10,000 each year, you would be deflating principal. How long your money would last when outgo exceeds income is dependent upon the return on investment and the amount of excess pulled out each year.

Figure 12-2 illustrates how long your money will last, given a variety of expected returns on investment (shown as percentages) and a fixed level of withdrawal.

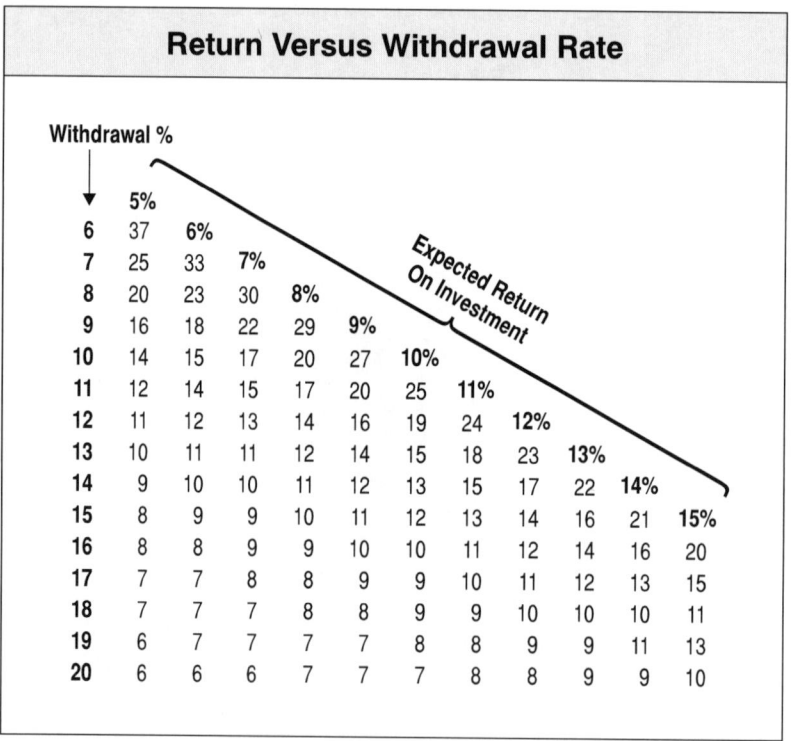

Figure 12-2

Follow the example of a 10% withdrawal rate of $10,000 per year and an 8% investment return. As you can see, there is a 20-year supply of retirement income at the table's intersection of 10% withdrawal and an 8% return.

If your anticipated rate of return is equal to or greater than your withdrawal rate, the retirement fund will hold in value and—in case of a positive spread between return and withdrawal flows—actually grow.

The ability to have the nest egg gain in value during the first phase of retirement portends a positive trend for a financially secure retirement.

A concern commonly voiced by postretirees is their hesitancy to dip into principal, which is viewed as sacred for retirement security.

In other words, they want to use just the interest income and maintain the principal intact. In periods of low fixed-income yields, this thinking can pose hardships on maintaining a level standard of living. Retirees should instead learn to think of the total return on the investment supply.

A further problem is that inflation forces the need for rising income flows rather than level withdrawals.

Figure 12-3 on the next page shows the effects on a $100,000 investment pot over a 20-year postretirement income span, assuming an initial $500 monthly expenditure, or $6,000 annually, which rises at a 4% inflation rate. Each column shows the balances you could expect after you consume your inflation-paced spending if you were to have investment returns of 5%, 6%, 7%, and 8%.

Obviously, a withdrawal strategy of 5% and an inflation level of 4% runs your investment kitty down to empty. At a 5% return, the money well runs dry after 18 years and the cumulative deficit comes to $22,438. Even a 6% return and 6% withdrawal rate fall short, the result of increases in inflation of 4% annually. In our example, this shortfall is $1,716.

Only with return levels of 7% or 8% does the nest egg provide enough cash for the 20-year period.

Retirement, as we have stressed, is a long-term proposition. It is advantageous if your principal can remain untouched or even grow for as long as possible.

The fear is, if you invade principal, the sum will disappear too quickly.

This fear can be addressed by estimating how long your money lasts under certain conditions.

$100,000 Sum

Year	Withdrawal 6% Plus 4% Inflation		Net Year-End Value			
			@ 5% ROI	@ 6% ROI	@ 7% ROI	@ 8% ROI
1	$500 mo.	$6,000 yr.	$98,700	$99,640	$100,580	$101,520
2	520 mo.	6,240 yr.	97,083	99,004	100,944	102,902
3	541 mo.	6,492 yr.	95,877	98,063	101,064	104,123
4	562 mo.	6,744 yr.	93,590	96,798	100,922	105,169
5	585 mo.	7,020 yr.	90,899	95,165	100,475	106,001
6	608 mo.	7,296 yr.	87,783	93,141	99,702	106,601
7	633 mo.	7,596 yr.	84,196	90,678	98,553	106,925
8	658 mo.	7,896 yr.	80,115	87,749	97,003	106,951
9	685 mo.	8,220 yr.	75,490	84,301	94,998	106,629
10	712 mo.	8,544 yr.	70,293	80,302	92,506	105,932
11	741 mo.	8,892 yr.	64,471	75,695	89,467	104,803
12	770 mo.	9,240 yr.	57,993	70,442	85,843	103,208
13	800 mo.	9,600 yr.	50,813	64,493	81,580	101,097
14	833 mo.	9,996 yr.	42,858	57,767	76,595	98,389
15	866 mo.	10,392 yr.	34,089	50,218	70,837	95,037
16	901 mo.	10,812 yr.	24,441	41,770	64,227	90,963
17	937 mo.	11,244 yr.	13,857	32,358	56,692	86,097
18	975 mo.	11,700 yr.	2,265	21,897	48,141	80,349
19	1014 mo.	12,168 yr.	-9,790	10,313	38,491	73,635
20	1054 mo.	12,648 yr.	-22,438	-1,716	27,652	65,866
Totals		$178,740				

Figure 12-3

Figure 12-4 examines this area and provides a graphic example of choices that can be made. It shows how much income can be withdrawn over a given number of years before the nest egg is reduced to zero. This particular table is based upon a reasonable 7% annual rate of return.

Look at the case of a $100,000 nest egg and a retirement span of 25 years. As you can see from Figure 12-4, you can withdraw $704 each month, or $8,448 annually, for 25 years before your $100,000 is fully depleted. Over the course of the 25-year period, your initial $100,000 in retirement seed money will have yielded $211,200 ($704 x 12 x 25) in retirement income distributions. If your goal is to keep your principal intact, the last column on the right shows that you can spend 7% of your pot ($585 x 12 = $7,020 a year).

Returning to the big question, how can retirees be assured they won't run out of money? After all, this group faces a spend-down that can span 25 to 30 years or longer, along with the threat of a major market pullback

How Long Will Your Money Last?

Starting with a lump sum of...	...you can withdraw this much each month for the stated number of years, reducing the nest egg to zero					...OR you can withdraw this much each month and always have the original nest egg intact.
	10 yrs.	15 yrs.	20 yrs.	25 yrs.	30 yrs.	
$50,000	$580	$4 48	$386	$352	$332	$285
100,000	1,160	896	772	704	668	585
200,000	2,320	1,792	1,544	1,408	1,336	1,170
250,000	2,900	2,240	1,930	1,760	1,670	1,460
350,000	4,060	3,136	2,702	2,464	2,338	2,050
500,000	5,800	4,480	3,860	3,520	3,340	2,925

Assumes a 7% return on investment

Figure 12-4

such as occurred in the wrenching 1973–1974 bear market. Add to this the constant fact of escalating prices, which drive up the cost of living.

Many financial planners counsel concerned retirees that it is safe to withdraw 5% annually of the investment pile, assuming there is an investment allocation balanced equally between stocks and bonds.

However, as financial planner William Bengen discovered in his own research, published in the *Journal of Financial Planning,* this 5% yearly withdrawal rate rule of thumb might be excessive and the assumption too rich to ensure retirement security under all circumstances.

To support Bengen's contention, look at the outcome of a retirement starting in 1966, whose 5% drawdown would fully extinguish a portfolio by 1984. That particular 18-year period marked a lousy retirement investment span. The bear market of 1973 and 1974 mauled stock prices and, coupled with a dismal bond market in the late 70s and early 80s, pulled down portfolio values. The retirement portfolio would have been almost depleted and unable to benefit from the robust market in stocks and bonds that emerged in 1982. This period of investment malaise was accompanied also by a decade of a rapidly escalating cost of living, pumped up by heavyweight inflation. The two big threats to ultimate retirement security came together; namely, brutal inflation and declining values on financial assets.

According to Mr. Bengen's calculations, the safe withdrawal rate to ensure a 30-year retirement span is 4.1%, almost 20% less than the assumed 5% rate.

In a *Wall Street Journal* article discussing this vitally important retirement planning matter, other noted financial planners and published authors suggested the big picture was rosier than Bengen's pessimistic presentation. They were quick to point out this was a bleak worst-case scenario, and that fortunes could be improved through inclusion of small-cap and international stocks as part of prudent portfolio management.

Jonathan Clements, the article's author, put this whole issue in context by concluding:

> "Mr. Bengen's study carries with it a timely warning, which is that rotten markets can rip apart the best-laid retirement plans. Your best defense is to invest in stocks for the long haul, while staying flexible on your spending."
>
> —Jonathan Clements, *The Wall Street Journal,* December 3, 1996

FRED AND ETHEL

Fred and Ethel Golden, whom you met in Chapter 2, are now retired, a reasonably healthy, robust, family-centered couple looking to have some fun.

Ethel is a reserved 72-year-old. Fred recently celebrated his 70th year with a lively party. Fred took the occasion to echo famed astronaut Senator John Glenn, who in announcing his decision not to seek reelection quipped, "There is still no cure for the common birthday."

Fred's birthday celebration also served as his retirement send-off. He had opted to postpone this event for a variety of reasons, including financial concerns, psychological dependency on his work, and the fact that he really enjoyed what he did for a living.

Fred fancies himself a comic and is always the life of the party. When asked in a data gathering planning meeting the value of his and Ethel's investment stake, he repeated a joke from one of his idols, Milton Berle: "I don't know how much I have in the bank. I haven't shaken it lately."

On the serious side, the couple amassed an investment portfolio of

$750,000, a tidy sum garnered through long years of hard work and savings efforts. By continuing to work until age 70, Fred earned a higher pension, increased Social Security benefits, and gained more time in which to build and grow a retirement nest egg. The couple's attention is turned now to enjoying the fruits of their labors.

Ethel is the serious partner in this relationship. She has managed the home front and nurtured six children, five of whom are alive. They have six grandchildren, a number that includes two step-grandkids, whom they love and treat as their own. Like other large and close families, their saga has included pain and hardship as well as joy.

Their youngest daughter, Lucy, endured a difficult divorce the year before and moved back to the home of her parents, bringing two active teenagers. Ethel assures her friends that having young people around will keep her young.

Fred describes this boomerang occurrence by using the humor of another favorite comic, Bill Cosby: "Human beings are the only creatures on earth that allow their children to come back home."

It appears to the Goldens they might never be empty nesters; after their children were grown, Fred's mother lived with them the last few years of her life.

Ethel's deep concern is harbored by many seniors; namely, "What if something happens to him?" As in many marriages, Ethel realizes she doesn't know where anything is, including the assets, bills, tax papers—even the checkbook.

Fred's retirement and the loss of a steady paycheck has added to her sense of unease.

One area of concern has been health insurance coverage. Both Fred and Ethel are on Medicare, but they were used to having a supplemental policy that was a basis of Fred's employment package. Now they have to shop for a policy and pay the premiums.

Ever the joker, Fred ribbed the insurance agent: "At my age and condition, I don't know what I need more, major medical or a minor miracle."

The Goldens at this stage in life are looking to plan five years at a time. They want to continue traveling and visiting their far-flung friends and family throughout the United States and Canada.

Fred and Ethel have already taken their two eldest grandchildren to

Germany for a month-long trip to explore their roots and gain a sense of ancestry. This proved to be a great experience and built a bond between generations. They look forward to escorting their four other grand darlings once the youngest turns 16.

In working with their financial planner, the Goldens identify the following objectives from their portfolio. Fred jokes that they want ESP—not extrasensory perception, but Enjoyment, Security, and Preservation.

To fulfill this retirement picture will require the following from their $750,000 nest egg.

1. They plan to generate regular monthly income to the tune of 5% of their pot, or $3,125 monthly, $37,500 annually.
   This income source will act as the critical third leg to supplement Social Security and pension income. To facilitate their travel plans and structure their income, this money will also be automatically deposited into their personal checking account.
2. They plan to minimize taxable income taken in light of their high tax bracket, the result of Social Security income, pension taxation, and the loss of itemized deductions exceeding the standard level on Schedule A of their Form 1040.
3. They plan to balance their portfolio in a conservative, risk-averse, income-oriented fashion. To accomplish this they will allocate 67% of their money to conservative investments and 33% to moderate-risk stock funds.
4. They plan to maintain their current nest egg relatively intact, and, if possible, grow it slightly to keep pace with inflation pressures. To do this, they will aim to average a 7% annual return on investment.

TWO RULES OF SUCCESSFUL INVESTING

"The first rule is not to lose.
The second rule is not to forget the first rule.
Preservation of capital is a challenging yet bedrock objective of investment management."

—Warren Buffett

From an investment management standpoint, the Goldens further desire convenience, access, consolidation, and peace of mind. They will build their portfolio using mutual funds, whose flexibility, features, and choices provide the tools to meet their targeted objectives. All these investments will be held in one consolidated custody (safekeeping) account.

With regard to their estate plan, the Goldens will be setting up a joint revocable trust. Each of their mutual funds will be registered in the name of the trust. Fred likes the idea of the trust because it will avoid probate.

Ethel feels better because if Fred dies or becomes incapacitated, the trust company will step in as successor trustee and administer and manage the terms of this document. Lately, Fred seems preoccupied with death. When anyone asks how he is doing, he says at least he is still on the right side of the grass.

Here is how the plan would allocate their $750,000 nest egg to meet their goals.

Portfolio Makeup

$50,000   U.S. government money market fund

Rate-of-return estimate	5%
Annual income estimate	$2,500
Percent of portfolio	6.67%

Features:
- liquid, stable, safe, accessible, state tax-exempt
- this sum is automatically directed into their personal checking account at the beginning of each month
- this fund is the cash account, accepting dividend and interest flows and dispensing needed cash flow of $3,125, for a total of $37,500 per year
- cash flow drawn from principal is a tax-free return of their own money

$100,000   Insured jumbo CD

Rate of return estimate	6%
Annual income estimate	$6,000
Percent of portfolio	13.3%

Features:
- ultimate safety, FDIC-insured
- interest will flow into money fund
- the Goldens are members of their bank's Senior Travel Club and benefit from special free banking privileges

$350,000   **Intermediate-term tax-exempt bond fund**
          Rate of return estimate   4.6%
          Annual income estimate $16,100
          Percent of portfolio   46.67%

Features:
- federal tax-free income
- conservative, income-oriented
- dividend income flows into money fund

$200,000   **Equity income fund**
          Rate of return estimate   11%
          Annual return estimate $22,000
          Percent of portfolio   26.67%

Features:
- value-based, diversified stocks, professionally managed stock fund
- dividend income of 3.5%, or $7,000, flows into money fund
- capital gain distribution automatically purchases additional shares

$50,000   **International stock fund**
          Rate of return estimate   12%
          Annual return estimate $6,000
          Percent of portfolio   6.67%

Features:
- professionally managed foreign stocks from 30 largest markets outside U.S. provide balance
- dividends and capital gains are reinvested in additional shares

TOTAL $750,00

Asset Allocation Totals

Rate of return estimate   7%
Annual income estimate $52,600

2/3	Cash & bonds	$500,000	67%
1/3	Stocks	$250,000	33%
3/3	TOTAL	$750,000	100%

$750,000 principal @ 5% withdrawal = $37,500 per year

Chapter 12

EQUITY INCOME FUNDS: GIVING THE DIVIDEND ITS DUE

An equity income fund is a solid building block in constructing a postretirement portfolio. Funds with an equity income orientation are basically stock (equity) funds whose holdings yield above-average return (income) in the form of dividend payouts.

Such a makeup allows conservative investors the ability to play defense and offense simultaneously. In the inevitable down markets an equity income fund has proven capable of outperforming the stock market as measured by the S&P 500. This is due in large part to the return the dividend adds to total return. Additionally, higher yielding stocks typically tend to be low-volatility, value-characterized companies.

A well-managed equity income fund helps a retired investor become more defensively positioned and prepared to cope with a market decline. Yet the focus on yield and dividend income from these quality, well-known stocks is not at the expense of appreciation potential, which can be significant in bull markets.

Bruce Hutson is portfolio manager of the Marshall Equity Income Fund. Bruce believes this type of fund should appeal to conservative retired investors. By design, it affords the best of both worlds: upside potential with market appreciation of stocks coupled with downside protection buoyed by its attractive dividend income.

WINIFRED THE GOLFER

Winifred is a charming, fun-loving retired school teacher, avid golfer, and heartfelt supporter of the Children's Hospital in her home town.

She just turned 60, a major birthday in the planning scheme of things. As a healthy, active, single woman with good genes, she feels confident about the prospect of living to the century mark.

Winifred splits her time, along with many snowbirds, between southern climates during the winter months and her northern home when fair weather returns. This allows her to fulfill her passion for golf year-round. Just last month she was thrilled by acing a hole-in-one during a golf outing to benefit Children's Hospital. Her new goal is to break her personal best score with a round of 88 or better. Winifred is very goal-oriented.

She always prepared the best lesson plans among her teaching colleagues.

Winifred officially retired after devoting 30 years of her life to the classroom, patiently molding young minds. She now tells anyone who asks that she is busy working on her golf game, a pursuit she took up to recharge during the summer months of the school year.

Since Winifred has no dependents, her primary planning emphasis revolves around her own long-term security and generous support to Children's Hospital. She approaches her financial planning in the same diligent fashion she applies to her golf game and former classroom duties. She has clear objectives, knowing what she is trying to accomplish. She sets high standards and expectations and believes in the value of professional assistance and counsel.

Winifred is a clear winner when it comes to planning and following through, and she can expect to score in terms of her financial and retirement game plan.

She has identified six primary financial goals and possesses the intent to achieve all of them:

1. to secure her own long-term retirement
2. to lead a comfortable retirement lifestyle, with a plan in place in the event of incapacity
3. to minimize income taxes and eliminate completely estate taxation
4. to generate sufficient retirement income capable of comfortably supplementing her pension and Social Security
5. to manage her sizable portfolio using intelligent portfolio techniques
6. to provide generous support during her lifetime and at passing to Children's Hospital.

Winifred finds herself in a very fortunate financial condition. She receives a pension guaranteed for her life, earned from her 30 years in the teaching profession. This pension has a cost-of-living escalator, making it an ideal retirement income source. Her pension income almost covers her living expenses, and she can expect Social Security in two years when she turns 62.

As part of her retirement benefit package she carries solid health insurance, and 90% of the premium is picked up by the school district.

Winifred owns two homes, which she refers to as North and South. She carries absolutely no debt. Other than having more than one home and deriving exercise and a wider social circle from having two golf club memberships, Winifred has a fairly mainstream lifestyle.

Her investment portfolio is substantial, fueled largely by an inheritance of 10,000 shares of a blue chip stock from the estate of her Aunt Virginia nearly 10 years earlier. This stock holding has appreciated in value and split twice over this period, swept along by the current bull market. The dividend income alone throws off more than she can spend.

Winifred wisely participated in a tax-sheltered 403(b) annuity plan during her teaching career. This qualified money has now been rolled over into her IRA and is placed in treasury bonds to help balance her stock allocation. The plan calls for letting this retirement money continue to grow untouched, tax-deferred, for the next decade until she turns $70\frac{1}{2}$, when mandatory distributions will be required.

Much of her financial planning will revolve around the intelligent management of her portfolio. In meeting with her foursome of financial advisors (CPA, estate planning attorney, trust officer, portfolio manager), her objective is to design a course that neatly folds her planning goals with a common sense 21st century solution.

In analyzing her investment portfolio, her advisors discover a growing seven-figure value, heavily weighted in stocks, highly concentrated in one big-name, low-yielding growth stock, with a tax-cost basis of just 20 cents on the dollar of current market prices—and widening. This diagnosis, together with her six stated objectives, will form the basis for the recommended strategic plan. Any proposed solution must fit into her big picture plan.

Winifred is an ideal candidate to utilize a charitable remainder trust (CRT), whose multiple benefits meld perfectly with her objectives and intentions.

As a financial planner and someone active in planned giving, I can tell you from personal experience that solving a complex puzzle and creating an attractive picture is very exciting—the art of planning.

A CRT is a creative planned giving and retirement planning tool that brings the planning process full circle. This vehicle will offer Winifred income for her life, and upon termination of the agreement, the "remainder" of the trust is transferred to Children's Hospital as her designated charity.

In recommending a CRT, charitable intention is key. The other planning benefits such as tax savings will follow. Similar to the story of children's hospitals across the country, this caregiving institution was founded, inspired, supported, and energized by women. The women in Winifred's family have long been devoted to the hospital and are active society members. The Children's Cancer Treatment Center is named after her aunt in recognition of her lifetime support and a major gift. With no children of her own, Winifred has in a very real sense adopted these young patients as part of her family, keeping the legacy alive. Winifred sees the hospital as more than just an institution of bricks and mortar; she sees it as a critical resource and beacon of care, hope, and life that adds to the quality of life of the community at large.

She has seen many of her students cared for at the hospital through the years. She contends that if you can't open your heart to sick children, you don't have a heart. Her areas of special interest lie in the care and treatment of underprivileged children, which she regards as a tonic to heal society's ills, and she knows the value of such care in an outpatient screening, prevention, and counseling setting.

The gift of the highly appreciated blue chip stock offers enticing tax incentives favorable to her as the donor. Gifting alleviates the capital gain tax and provides a current income tax deduction based on the present value of the remainder interest that will pass to charity.

Tax law and charitable contributions have become interconnected. With proper estate planning, Winifred will be able to eliminate the estate tax completely by leaving her entire estate to the qualifying charity. This effectively nullifies the largest single tax that is ever assessed on an asset. She reasons that her wealth is better spent by the charity than by her allowing it to go into government tax coffers.

By making this gift in a CRT, our donor will realize a higher stream of income than is presently churned out from the low-yielding stock. She helps ensure her long-term financial security from receiving a 5% annual income payout from the trust agreement for the balance of her life. This amounts to $2\frac{1}{2}$ times her current income flow from the 2% dividend yield. She plans to take this excess income and funnel it into a tax-exempt bond fund as a reservoir for future needs.

With that mission accomplished, Winifred turns her attention to finalizing her plan. Without any surviving family, Winifred is acutely aware of the need to have her complicated financial affairs looked after in case of her incapacity.

Basically, what Winifred wants is a continuous, long-term financial services relationship with a trusted, value-added, professionally competent source.

She opts to have the trust company of the local bank serve as trustee of her trusts. The same bank administered and managed her aunt's affairs, and as a beneficiary she grew to have confidence in their professionalism. These services include administering the terms of her trusts by managing the investment portfolio, distributing income, completing tax filings, and providing quarterly accounting statements, all in a fiduciary manner.

Should she ever need it, the trustee will pay her bills, sell her property, and generally provide for her personal finance needs in her best interests.

Fully satisfied, Winifred finds it is time to whittle down her golf score.

EPILOGUE

> "You are financially secure when you can afford anything you want, and you don't want anything."
>
> —Art Buck

MEET MY UNCLE JOHN

John Monaghan, born in 1907 in County Galway in the west of Ireland, is now the oldest man in the parish.

In calling to arrange my 1997 visit, I reminded Uncle John of my first visit back in 1973. "Oh yes, John," he said, "that's when I was good."

Uncle John is my granduncle, the youngest of 10 children, born, raised, and still residing in the modest thatched roof cottage where he had first welcomed me. His oldest sister, Mary, my maternal grandmother, emigrated to Chicago prior to World War I. She had attempted and failed to book passage on the ill-fated maiden voyage of the *Titanic*.

Fortunately, she arrived safely the next year and lived a full life, reaching 100 years of age. Two sisters followed her to build a life in America. One of them, Sister Dell, is now age 99 and still living in her own home.

John and his brother Pat never married and stayed on in Galway to farm the small family plot. Grandma affectionately corresponded with her brothers for close to 75 years in their beloved village of Clooneen.

The proprietor at the local pub suggested Uncle John should have been a history professor, labeling him a genius. Still sharp, my uncle is the one to whom anyone in search of his or her roots is directed.

During my visit in 1997, he shared how at age 80 he "went on the pension" (retired) and at 88 had to give up riding his bicycle. "It was the knees." A cane now completes his standard attire, which includes his cap, a well-worn coat, and an ever-present pipe.

This is not to imply that he is not active, for he varnished the wooden door to his home in honor of my visit.

It was a beautiful Sunday afternoon in May when I prepared to say good-bye. He asked if I was up to the one-mile hike back alone to the center of town to catch my ride. I assured him I could manage.

Before departing, I asked if there was anything he needed or whether I could do something for him. "Tell my family that I am reasonably well and want for nothing," he replied.

At the door he mentioned that he does miss the atlas map and book on the U.S. presidents my father had given him, but which had been destroyed in a fire. His knowledge of American history and geography, amazing especially for someone who never set foot off the Emerald Isle, keeps his mind active and is an interest and passion he can share with others.

All in all, Uncle John considers the riches of mind and health as important as financial well-being. At the end of the day, it is what we do with our lives that makes the difference.

Success

> To laugh often and much;
> To win the respect of intelligent people and affection of children;
> To earn the appreciation of honest critics and endure the betrayal
>   of false friends;
> To appreciate beauty;
> To find the best in others;
> To leave the world a bit better, whether by a healthy child, a
>   garden patch or a redeemed social condition;
> To know even one life has breathed easier because you have
>   lived;
> This is to have succeeded.

―Ralph Waldo Emerson

RECOMMENDED READING

Bogle, John C., *Bogle on Mutual Funds: New Perspectives for the Intelligent Investor,* Irwin Professional Publishing

Chilton, David, *The Wealthy Barber: Everyone's Common-Sense Guide to Becoming Financially Independent,* Prima

Covey, Stephen R., *The Seven Habits of Highly Effective People: Powerful Lessons in Personal Change,* Simon & Schuster

Dreman, David, *The New Contrarian Investment Strategy,* Random House

Gibson, Roger C., *Asset Allocation: Balancing Financial Risk,* Irwin Professional Publishing

Graham, Benjamin, *The Intelligent Investor,* Harper & Row

Gross, William H., *Everything You've Heard About Investing Is Wrong! How to Profit in the Coming Post-Bull Markets,* Times Business

Hill, Napoleon, *Think & Grow Rich,* Fawcett Crest

Lynch, Peter, *One Up On Wall Street: How To Use What You Already Know To Make Money In The Market,* Penguin Books

McCarthy, John T., *Financial Planning For A Secure Retirement,* International Foundation of Employee Benefit Plans

Reinhardt, Carl, Alan Werba, and John Bowen, *The Prudent Investor's Guide To Beating The Market,* Irwin Professional Publishing

Stanley, Thomas J., and William D. Danko, *The Millionaire Next Door,* Longstreet Press

Train, John, *The Money Masters,* Harper & Row

_____, *The New Money Masters,* Harper & Row

_____, *The Midas Touch,* Harper & Row

Wanger, Ralph, *A Zebra in Lion Country: Ralph Wanger's Investment Survival Guide,* Simon & Schuster

INDEX

A

AAA (accumulate appreciating assets) 38
AGI (adjusted gross income) 109
adjustments to income 109
annuities, variable 105
Armstrong, Michael 207
ASD (automatic/systematic/disciplined) 45
asset allocation 138, 146, 233
automatic payroll contribution 229

B

balance sheet 33
basis 166
beneficiaries 161
Bengen, William 263
Bogle, John 49, 144, 185, 211, 212
bonds 61; *also see* junk bonds
   compared with bond funds 255
   high yield 62
   mutual funds 240, 249
book value 35
Brinson, Gary 140
Bryant, Jane Quinn 189
Buffett, Warren 9, 51, 64, 198, 211
Bultman, Tim 248, 250, 256
Burger, Warren 154

C

capital gain 103
   distributions 193
Capiello, Frank 73
Carret, Philip 53, 187
cash management tool 181
CDs 62, 249
charitable remainder trust 17, 271
Chilton, David 9
Clements, Jonathan 264
CMOs (collateralized mortgage obligations) 70
Cohen, Marilyn 250
commissions 180, 190
company stock 236
compound growth 11, 48, 222
contrarian investing 74, 232

Corneliuson, William 197
cost of living 226
Covey, Stephen 19
credit risk 62, 244
custody account 267

D

Danko, William D. 30, 47
debt 224
   analysis 37
deduction, itemized and standard 109
deferred assets 33
defined benefit plan 216
defined contribution plan 216, 231
derivatives 71
Dines, James 188
disability insurance 82
diversification 66–67, 179, 255
divorce 91
dollar-cost averaging 46, 236
Dorsett, Tony 30
downsizing 7
Dreman, David 142, 143
DRIP (dividend reinvestment plan) 47
durable power of attorney 162

E

Elves 70
employment
   benefits 237
   trends 6
   income 7
equities 198
equity income fund 269
estate planning 100, 151
estate taxes 167
exemption amount 169

F

federal deficit 5
FICA 40
financial advisors 271
financial planning
   lack of 9
   process 11, 20

financial services industry 7
Fisher, Kenneth 188
fixed income investing 243
fixed obligations 40
401(k) 216, 229
403(b) 230
fund supermarket 191

G

GARP 204
Gates, Bill 88
Getz, Jim 215
Gibson, Roger 141, 142
GIC (Guaranteed Investment Contracts) 231
gift taxes 167
gifting 272
Glaudiet, Henry 143
global bond funds 256
Goldman, David 249
government bonds 244
Gross, Bill 203, 211, 242, 248, 253, 256
growth stocks 205, 234
guardianships 162

H

Hand, Learned 155
Hardy, Dorcas 224
health care power of attorney 164
health insurance 83
Heckmann, Dick 43
Hill, Napoleon 10
home
   ownership 119
   tax on sale of 106
Hopewell, Lynn 142
Hughes, Howard 154
Hulbert, Mark 190
Hutson, Bruce 269

I

income 252
   flow 31
   protection 82
   replacement 82
   reportable 108
   shifting 105, 126

   statement 38, 39
   supplemental 227
indexing 208
inflation 3, 215, 218, 261
   indexed bonds 248
insurance 40, 80
   liability 84
   disability 82
   health 83, 238
   life 159
   property and casualty 84
interest 244
   compound 49
   rates 246
International Association for Financial Planning 12
international investing 149, 212
Internet 8
intestate, 153
investment strategy 225
IRAs 14, 121, 150, 235

J

Jaffe, Charles 189
Jefferson, Thomas 152
joint tenancy 160
junk bonds 62, 65, 150, 179, 254

K

Kee, LeeShaw 51
kiddie tax 126
Kilpatrick, Andrew 198
Knowles, Warren P. 77, 166

L

laddering 251
leverage 120
leveraged buyout (LBO) 66
liabilities 33
life-cycle
   financial planning 24
   funds 233
Lipper Analytical Services 194
liquidity 33, 58
living trusts 158, 162
loads 190, 253
long-term care insurance (LTC) 16, 83
Lynch, Peter 8, 69, 120, 186, 204

M

MacKinnon, Ian 254
marginal tax bracket 112
market timing 141
McCarty, Oseola 51
medical expenses 110
Medicare 7, 238
Merrill Lynch 11
mission statement 15
modern portfolio theory 138
money markets 62, 175
Morningstar ratings 189
MS Society 17
Munger, Charlie 51
municipal bonds 244, 256
mutual funds 174
   advantages 177
   problems 185
   tax efficiency 105

N

Nasgovitz, William 205
net worth 34, 82
   statement 33, 238
Neuberger, Roy 180
Newton, Wayne 30
Nicholas, Ab 77, 105, 200, 211

O

Onassis, Jacqueline Kennedy 155

P

P/E ratio 204
Paluch, Susan 232
pension plans 231
Phillips, Don 209
planned giving 17
portfolio analysis 238
portfolio investment management 134
preservation stage 36
principal 244, 261
probate 158, 160
PYF (pay yourself first) 44

R

retirement
   cost of living 226
   funds 235
   plan contributions 229
   planning 114, 213
return on investment (ROI) 260
revocable living trust 162
Rice, William Lummis 154
Richard, JamesRodney 29
risk 61–62, 234, 241
   return 247
   reward 199
risk management 80
Rogers, Jim 48
Rohn, Jim 43
Roth IRA 26, 123
rule of 72 50

S

S&P 500 54
Sauter, George 211
savings 41, 43, 220, 239
Schulz, David W. 252
sectors 179
self-employment 7, 91
Social Security 6, 7, 40, 215
special needs trust 82
spread 250
Stanley, ThomasJ. 30, 47
stocks 198, 234
Stowers, James 29, 167
Strong family 193
Strong, Richard 194
survivorship, right of 160

T

T. Rowe Price 6
tax
   code 4
   deductibility 115
   deferral 14, 116, 229
   exempt bonds 111
   minimization 102
   shelter 119, 229, 235
   strategy 106
taxes, state 40, 125
Tax Reform Act of 1986 102
taxable income 110
Taxpayer Relief Act of 1997 4, 102
Templeton, Sir John 8, 66
time value of money 22, 50

titling 153
total return 246
Train, John 203
treasury bonds 244–45
treasury notes 250
Trump, Donald 29
trustee 164, 273
12b(1) fees 190
Tyson, Laura 202

U

unified credit exclusion 157, 167–69
Uniform Gifts to Minors Act 183

V

value style 205
VanCaspel, Venita 10, 50, 103
variable investments 199

Vinik, Jeff 186
volatility 137, 199

W

Walton, Sam 28
Wanger, Ralph 203, 205, 211
wealth management 11
Welch, Jack 88
Williams, Bruce 84
wills 160
windfalls 11

Y

yield 246, 247, 252

Z

zero coupon bonds 245
Ziglar, Zig 9